THE LEGEND OF QUEEN CĀMA

Cetiya at Wat Phradhātu Haripuñjaya

THE LEGEND OF QUEEN CĀMA

Bodhiraṃsi's Cāmadevīvaṃsa, *a Translation and Commentary*

Donald K. Swearer and Sommai Premchit

State University of New York Press

SUNY Series in Buddhist Studies
Matthew Kapstein, editor

Published by

State University of New York Press

Printed in the United States of America

For information, address State University of New York Press
State University Plaza, Albany, NY 12246

Production by Dana Foote
Marketing by Nancy Farrell

Library of Congress Cataloging-in-Publication Data

Bodhiraṅsī.
[Cāmadevivaṃsa. English]
The legend of Queen Cāma: Bodhiraṃsi's Cāmadevīvaṃsa, translation and commentary / Donald K. Swearer and Sommai Premchit.
p. cm. — (SUNY series in Buddhist studies)
Includes bibliographical references and index.
ISBN 0–7914–3775–2 (hc. : alk. paper). — ISBN 0–7914–3776–0 (pbk. : alk. paper)
1. Cāma (Legendary character) 2. Legends, Buddhist—Thailand––History and criticism. 3. Buddhism—Thailand—Lamphun (Province)––Folklore. I. Swearer, Donald K., 1934– . II. Sommai Premchit. III. Title. IV. Series.
BQ5815.B6313 1998
398.2'09593'02—DC21 98–15911
CIP

10 9 8 7 6 5 4 3 2 1

IN MEMORY OF
SINGKHA WANNASAI

1920–1980

CONTENTS

PART I. INTERPRETATION

PART II. THE *CĀMADEVĪVAṂSA*

Illustrations

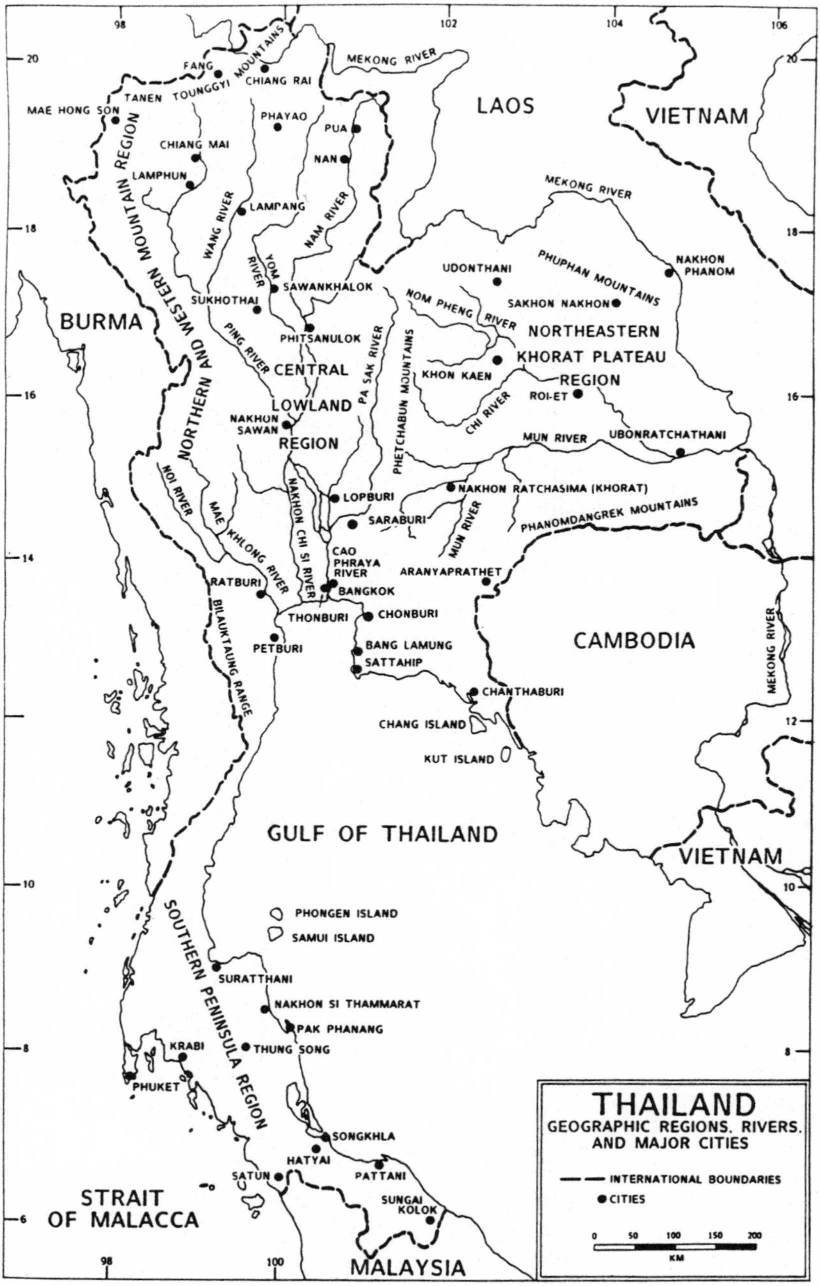

Thailand: Geographic Regions, Rivers, and Major Cities

จามเทวีวงษ์ ปริเฉท ๑

ปริเฉท ๑ ถึงปริเฉท ๘

พระยาปริยัติธรรมธาดา (แพ ตาละลักษมณ์) แปล

นมัต์ถุ สุคตัส์ส

อาทิจ์จวํโส ชิโน โย
มนุส์สชาโต ทิปทานมิน์โท
พ์ยามัป์ปภาโส อภิป์ปมาโร
มณิปโชโต ชินํ ตํ นมามิ.

สมเด็จพระชินสีห์เจ้า ผู้เปนวงษ์พระอาทิตย์ผู้ประเสริฐ พระองค์ใด ได้ถือเอากำเนิดในชาติมนุษย์แล้ว พระองค์ก็เปนเจ้าเปนใหญ่กว่าสัตวสองเท้าทั้งหลาย มีพระกายอันงามส่องรัศมีสว่างข้างละวา. ประดุจดังว่าดวงมณีโชตอันรุ่งโรจอยู่ฉนั้น ข้าพเจ้าขอนมัสการ ซึ่งสมเด็จพระชินสีห์เจ้าพระองค์นั้น (ด้วย)

คัม์ภีรมัต์ถํ นิปุณ์ณํ สุทุท์ทสํ
สาสัป์ปพีชีว สิเนรุเหฏ์ฐํ
นานานยานํ มุนิเสวิตัน์ตํ.
สุขุมธัม์มํ ปวรํ นมามิ.

ชุงนุงธรรมทั้งหลายมีนัยต่าง ๆ ธรรมชาติอันใดเล่า มีอรรถอันลึกล้ำคัมภีรภาพเต็มที่ ยากที่บุคคลจะเล็งเห็นได้ง่าย เพียงดังว่าเมล็ดพรรณผักกาดอันอยู่ภายใต้เขาพระ

Specimen page from the 1920 edition of the *Cāmadevīvaṃsa*

Dramatis Personae

Ādittarāja. The ruler of Haripuñjaya in the eleventh century C.E. who enshrined the bodily relic of the Buddha at the site known today as Wat Phradhātu Haripuñjaya.

Aṅgurisi. Born of Vāsudeva and a doe. Consecrated as ruler of Migasaṅghanagara, construed as a Lawa town at the base of Mount Suthēp.

Anantayasa. Cāmadevī's twin son. Ruler of Khelāṅga (modern Lampāng).

Brahma (Subrahma). One of the four mountain ascetics in the story. He is associated with Khelāṅga (modern Lampāng). Identified as Indravara in the JKM.

Cāmadevī. The first ruler of Haripuñjaya in the seventh century C.E.

Gavaya (Gaveyya). The messenger sent by the sage, Vāsudeva, to the King of Lavo requesting permission for his daughter, Cāma, to become the queen of Haripuñjaya.

Kunarikadhaṃsa. Son of Aṅgurisi and Migūpatī and ruler of Purinagara.

Kunarikanāsa. Son of Aṅgurisi and Migūpatī and ruler of Rammanagara, antecedent to Haripuñjaya.

Kunarikarosa. Son of Aṅgurisi and Migūpatī and ruler of Avidūranagara.

Mahantayasa. Cāmadevī's twin son. Ruler of Haripuñjaya (modern Lamphūn). Identified as Mahayāsa in the JKM.

Migūpatī. Wife of Aṅgurisi.

Putriya. Army commander of the King of Lavo who led a failed attack on King Ādittarāja.

Sajjanāleyya. One of the four mountain ascetics in the story. He is associated with Sīsatchanālāi near the early Thai capital of Sukhōthai. Identified as Anusissa in the JKM.

Sirigutta. The son of a Lavo military commander who led a second failed attack on Ādittarāja.

Sukkadanta. One of the four mountain ascetics in the chronicle. He is associated with Lavapura (modern Lopburī).

Ucchiṭṭhacakkavatti. King of Lavapura who gained suzerainty over Haripuñjaya in the early tenth century C.E. and who appears to have defeated the Khmer at Lavapura (Lopburī).

Vilaṅga. The chief of the Milakkha (i.e. the Lawa) in the Lamphūn valley.

Vāsudeva. The mountain ascetic instrumental in the construction of Haripuñjaya and arranging for Cāmadevī to rule the city.

ACKNOWLEDGMENTS

This work has been in process for several years. Many have made possible its eventual completion. It is a privilege to acknowledge my indebtedness to those who have contributed to the project.

For my knowledge of northern Thai Buddhism, I am especially beholden to my teacher, the late Singha Wannasai of Lamphūn, Thailand, to whom this book is dedicated. Ājān Singkha first introduced the *Cāmadevīvaṃsa* (CDV) to me in the 1970s. His unsurpassed cultural and literary wisdom has informed much of my work since that time.

The noted scholar-monk Phra Dhammapiṭaka (P. A. Payutto) with whom I first began reading the Pāli CDV in 1981 identified borrowings in the text from the *jātaka* commentary.

Ronald Renard of Payap University, Chiang Mai, Thailand, kindly provided me with a copy of the 1920 published text of the CDV.

My former Oberlin College student, Thanissaro Bhikkhu (Geoffrey DeGraff) currently abbot of Mettārāma Forest Monastery, Valley Center, California, translated into English Camille Notton's French translation of *The Lamphun Chronicle*. I am also grateful for his critical reading of this monograph in its penultimate form.

Nancy Chester Swearer's editorial suggestions on several drafts of the manuscript greatly improved the accuracy and style of the text.

I also wish to thank Mani Payǫmyong, Emeritus Professor, Chiang Mai University; Hans Penth, Social Research Institute, Chiang Mai University; Louis Gabaude, École Française d'Extrême-Orient, Chiang Mai; and Harald Hundius, University of Passau, Germany, and Chiang Mai, for advice related to my research on northern Thai culture and religion; Frank E. Reynolds, University of Chicago, and Anne Blackburn, University of South Carolina, for their suggestions regarding revision of the manuscript; John Butt, Director of the Institute for the Study of Religion and Culture, Payap University, Chiang Mai, for providing living and study space at the Institute in January, 1996; and Wattana Wattanaphun for his photographs of the murals of the Legend of Queen Cāma on the temple walls of Wat Kukut, Lamphūn, Thailand.

For financial support I am grateful to the John Simon Guggenheim Foundation, the Council for the International Exchange of Scholars

(Fulbright), and Swarthmore College during the academic year 1993-1994. My thanks also to Thailand-United States Educational Foundation, Dr. Pathamakha Sukontamarn, Director, for supporting Sommai Premchit as a Fulbright scholar at Swarthmore College for the academic year, 1992-1993, and my Fulbright appointment to the Social Research Institute, Chiang Mai University, in 1994. Finally, my appreciation to Nancy Ellegate of the State University of New York Press for supporting the project and to Dana Foote, the production editor.

A special acknowledgment must be given to Sommai Premchit for his collaboration on this project. Although I am responsible for Part I of this monograph and the explanatory annotations, the translation was a joint effort and relied heavily on his expertise in Pāli. Since the early 1970s Ājān Sommai has been both friend and colleague. In 1977 our collaboration resulted in the publication of a translation of the *Mūlasāsanā Wat Pā Daeng* and a study of the relationship between state and *saṅgha* in northern Thailand from the fourteenth to the sixteenth centuries.

The present collaboration honors one of northern Thailand's exemplary rulers and celebrates the 700th anniversary of the founding of the city of Chiang Mai.

Donald K. Swearer
Swarthmore College, 1997

Abbreviations

A	*Aṅguttara Nikāya*
BV	*Buddhavaṃsa*
CDV	*Cāmadevīvaṃsa*
Dh	*Dhammapada*
D	*Dīgha Nikāya*
J	*Jātaka*
JKM	*Jinakālamālīpakaraṇaṃ*
Mhvs	*Mahāvaṃsa*
MD	*Maṅgaladīpanī*
PvA	*Petavatthu Aṭṭhakathā*
PY	*Phongsāwadān Yōnok*
PT	*Phuttha tamnān*
PJLL	*Phrajao Liap Lōk*
Sn	*Sutta Nipāta*
TMC	*Tamnān Mu'ang Chiang Mai*
TML	*Tamnān Mu'ang Lamphūn*
TM	*Tamnān Mūlasāsanā*
TMSL	*Tamnān Mūlasāsanā Samnuan Lānnā*
TNJT	*Tamnān Nāng Jām Thewī*
TPPS	*Tamnān Phraphutthasihiṅg*
TWPD	*Tamnān Wat Pā Daeng*
VvA	*Vimānavatthu Aṭṭhakathā*
Vism	*Visuddhimagga*

INTRODUCTION

The *Cāmadevīvaṃsa*[1] [CDV] was composed by the Thai monk, Mahāthera Bodhiraṃsi in the early fifteenth century.[2] Little is known about his life and work apart from the two Pāli chronicles he authored: the story of Queen Cāma, the first ruler of Haripuñjaya, and the legend of the most famous northern Thai Buddha image, the Siṅhala image (*Tamnān Phraphutthasihiṅg*).[3] Taken together these two texts suggest that Bodhiraṃsi was more interested in the devotional side of Buddhism than either of the two noted Chiang Mai scholar-monks of the sixteenth century with whom he is compared, namely, Sirimaṅgalācariya, who wrote a commentary on the *Maṅgala Sutta* (*Maṅgaladīpanī*) [MD] and Ratanapañña Thera who compiled the more traditional Theravāda chronicle, the *Jinakālamālīpakaraṇaṃ* [JKM] (*The Sheaf of Garlands of the Epochs of the Conquerors*),[4] a text that follows more closely the form of the Theravāda *vaṃsa* or chronicle genre, such as the *Mahāvaṃsa*.

Bodhiraṃsi states in the first chapter of the CDV that he was working from an earlier non-Pāli story in composing the text: "Because the language of the scholar who wrote this story is inferior and unsuitable for Buddhist city dwellers, I shall translate it into Pāli, into lines and stanzas so delightful to hear that it will engage the mind and kindle the interest of [both] men and women." However, internal evidence in the text, combined with evidence from other northern Thai chronicles, indicates that the CDV was not a simple work of translation, but more likely a creative collation from several sources. As is typical of this tradition, the text is more a work of authorship—rather than simple transmission—than the author feels proper to claim or wise to admit.

That Bodhiraṃsi composed his work in Pāli, even though it was not a scholarly work, suggests his intention to promote the significance of the two major subjects of the chronicle, the founding of Haripuñjaya and the enshrinement of its central Buddha relic (*phradhātu*). Pāli scholars note that Bodhiraṃsi's style and grammar lack the erudition of Sirimaṅgalācariya and Ratanapañña. One may speculate that Bodhiraṃsi's Pāli composition might have been substantially influenced by the fact that he was translating from a northern Thai legend, a very different endeavor from Sirimaṅgala's commentary on a Pāli *sutta* text written primarily for scholarly study by monks.

In recent years, popular folk veneration of Cāmadevī has grown as part of a nationwide resurgence in magical religion and devotional cults of which the most prominent are the cults of King Rama V/ Chulalongkorn (r. 1868–1910) and of Guan Yin, the savior *bodhisattva* of Mahāyāna Buddhism.[5] A newly constructed memorial statue of Cāmadevī in the northern Thai town of Lamphūn (formerly Haripuñjaya) has become a devotional center, and a former television personality who claims to be possessed by the spirit of Cāmadevī has received wide media attention. At the same time, scholarly circles have focused increased interest on the study of northern Thai chronicles such as the the JKM, the *Tamnān Mūlasāsanā* [TM] (The Chronicle of the Founding of Buddhism), and the *Tamnān Mu'ang Chiang Mai* [TMC] (The Chiang Mai Chronicle). However logical it would seem, the folk interest in Cāmadevī and scholarly interest in northern Thai chronicles have not led to a thorough scholarly study of either the Cāmadevī or Haripuñjaya/Lamphūn chronicles.

A pragmatic reason for this omission, as David Wyatt has noted, may be that even though the northern Thai chronicles offer a broad and diverse field of research, most scholars have focused their attention on a limited number of texts as, for example, Wyatt's own recent study of the Chiang Mai Chronicle.[6] Another reason for this lack of interest is that since the 1920s the study of the northern Thai chronicles has been dominated by historical and factual concerns. Scholars have examined the texts for information about historical personages and places rather than attending to the religious, mythic, and legendary elements found in the CDV.

Some early studies sought to mine the CDV for historical nuggets, and then criticized it for its paucity of facts on this account. The best illustration of this approach may be George Coedès's "Documents sur l'Histoire Politique et Religieuse du Laos Occidental" in which he devotes most of his attention to the JKM because of its greater reliablity as a historical document. He translates only that portion of the CDV that holds the most historical interest, omitting entirely the frame story of the Buddha's prediction of the appearance of his relic at Haripuñjaya during the reign of Ādittarāja. Furthermore, he tends to dismiss the mythological, legendary, and Buddhological or religious aspects of the text. He considers the first chapter of the CDV to be the obligatory appearance the Buddha makes in *phuttha tamnān* (Buddha chronicles) and judges the specifically Buddhist teachings sprinkled throughout the story to be tired and formulaic.

Although Camille Notton translates the entire *Tamnān Mu'ang Lamphūn* [TML] (Lamphūn Chronicle), which is another version of the Cāmadevī story, his annotations indicate a similar bias toward the historical and factual. He pays particular attention to the present locations of the archaic place names in the text. More recent work on the northern Thai chronicles has also tended to focus on either northern Thai secular or religious *history*, for example, the *Tamnān Mu'ang Chiang Mai*/The Chiang Mai Chronicle, and the *Tamnān Mūlasāsanā*/Chronicle of the Buddhist Religion, rather than interpreting the chronicles through the lenses of myth, legend, and religion.

To balance the historical interests that have dominated work on the northern Thai chronicles, I have focused this annotated translation of the CDV on the text as it was intended to be read and heard, primarily as a document of religious instruction, presenting the founding of Cāmadevī's kingdom, Haripuñjaya, not just as a historical story but as a religious and cosmologically significant event.

This translation is based on the 1920 published edition of the CDV for two reasons: (i) it is the only published edition of the Pāli text, and (ii) this study examines the CDV as myth and legend and is not intended as a critical historical or linguistic analysis of the text. Although there are many interesting questions about the text that such a historical or linguistic study might address, and although I hope that this monograph will prompt further research in that direction, none of the unsettled questions in that area affect the religious and mythic dimensions of the CDV.[7] For my purposes, the 1920 published edition has proved to be adequate.[8]

The study incorporates two types of annotation. First, it glosses Pāli terms and phrases into the translation. While the translation can be read without attending to the glossed Pāli terms, for those readers with an interest in Pāli the glosses serve to illustrate the translation. The second type of annotation is substantive footnotes that accompany the text. In some cases they identify terms or place names; in others they offer interpretations of particular points in the narrative written from the point of view that the CDV is a narrative of a mythic-legendary genre in which etiology, cosmology, and Buddhist doctrine and practice take precedence over historical facts. *Part I, Interpretation*, provides a systematic analysis of the CDV but it is not intended to substitute for reading the story and the accompanying annotations.

THE SCHOLARLY STUDY OF NORTHERN THAI CHRONICLES AND THE CĀMADEVĪVAṂSA[9]

With few exceptions, the rich variety of northern Thai chronicles has received only modest scholarly attention. The earliest substantial study of these texts was done by Camille Notton and George Coedès during the early decades of this century.[10] Notton served as French Consul in Chiang Mai from 1925 to 1940; Coedès was appointed Curator of the National Library of Siam in 1918 and the Secretary General of the Royal Institute of Siam in 1927. In recent years both Western and Thai scholars have turned their attention to a more thorough study of northern Thai Pāli and vernacular manuscripts, of which chronicles (*tamnān*) constitute an important genre. The first major contribution was the publication of *Jinakālamālīpakaraṇaṃ* (JKM) in 1962 by the Pāli Text Society followed by an English translation. In northern Thailand significant momentum began in the early 1970s when the Siam Society commissioned Singkha Wannasai to conduct a survey of palm-leaf manuscript collections in northern Thai monasteries. Ājān Singkha generated the first collation of these manuscripts, subsequently systematized by his student, Harald Hundius who has become a major figure in the cataloguing, preservation, and study of palm-leaf manuscripts in northern Thailand and Laos.[11]

Later, in the mid-1970s, Chiang Mai University, with financial support from the Toyota Foundation, began its own northern Thai manuscript survey and microfilm project initially led by Sommai Premchit. This project has produced the largest collection of northern Thai manuscripts on microfilm and is an invaluable resource for scholars of northern Thai history, literature, culture, and religion.[12] The collection now constitutes the archival unit of the Social Research Institute (SRI) of Chiang Mai University.[13] Additionally, Oskar Von Hinüber (University of Freiburg) with the assistance of Balee Buddharaksa, Deputy Director of the Social Research Institute (SRI), is compiling a catalogue of northern Thai Pāli manuscripts of which the SRI collection is a primary resource. A major conference on northern Thai literature held in Chiang Mai in November, 1994, assessed the state of the field and proposed guidelines for further research.[14]

Included in the SRI collection are numerous *tamnān* that constitute one of the largest single body of texts in the collection. In addition to the archival work and encouraging on-site manuscript preservation, several northern Thai chronicles have been published. The first such publications were either Thai translations from the northern Thai vernacular (Tai Yüan) or transliterations into central Thai script from the northern Thai *tham* script in which the texts were written.[15] Subsequently, several important chronicles have been studied more closely, edited, and/or translated. These include the *Tamnān Wat Pā Daeng* (The Chronicle of the Red Forest Monastery) [TWPD],[16] the *Tamnān Mūlasāsanā Samnuan Lānnā* [TMSL] (The Northern Thai Version of the Founding of Buddhism),[17] *Prawat Phrathāt Doi Tung* (History of Phra Thāt Doi Tung),[18] and *The Chiang Mai Chronicle* (*Tamnān Mu'ang Chiang Mai* [TMC]) and

The Nān Chronicle.[19] Analyses of the Thai chronicle traditions have been done by David K. Wyatt, Charnvit Kasetsiri, and Hans Penth.[20]

The earliest study of chronicles that treat the related topics of Cāmadevī and the founding of Haripuñjaya/Lamphūn appeared in the 1920s and 1930s. Camille Notton's translation of the *Tamnān Mu'ang Lamphūn* (TML) into French (*Chronique de La:p'un*) with extensive annotation was published in 1930.[21] Seven years earlier in 1925, George Coedès brought out a transliteration and French translation of chapters 12–14a of the CDV together with a critical introduction to the entire text based on the 1920 edition printed in Thai script.[22] Coedès notes that the content of Bodhiraṃsi's CDV is identical to the story of Cāmadevī translated by Auguste Pavie in *Mission Pavie* (Paris, 1898) that was based on a Luang Prabang manuscript dated 1646; however, Coedès observes that it is impossible to determine the date of the original manuscript on which Pavie based his translation.[23] Following the work of Coedès and Notton, the Thai translation of the CDV was reprinted in 1967 by the Fine Arts Department, and in 1982 Sanong Waraurai translated the northern Thai vernacular story of Phra Nāng Cāmadevī into Thai.[24] While I am indebted to the work of Coedès and Notton, this study of the CDV is distinctive in two major ways: it is the first English translation of the complete Pāli text, and my hermeneutical perspective differs considerably from the historical interests of Coedès and Notton.

NOTES TO INTRODUCTION

1. My decisions regarding transliteration were governed by three different considerations: standard conventions for Pāli and Thai; current use for place names; and reader recognition. Transliteration of Pāli follows standard Pali Text Society conventions. Transliteration of Thai follows the Library of Congress system with a few exceptions. In particular "j" is substituted for "čh." I have retained "u' " instead of "ü," a change some scholars prefer. In most but not all cases I have chosen to transliterate proper names in their Pāli rather than their Thai form. A major exception to this rule is the title of texts other than the *Cāmadevīvaṃsa* and the *Jinakālamālīpakaraṇaṃ*. In such cases I follow the Thai pronunciation, e.g., *Tamnān Phraphutthasihiṅg*, rather than the Pāli, *Tamnān Phrabuddhasīha* or the Sanskrit, *siṅgha*. I have also chosen to use common spellings for some place names, Haripuñjaya, rather than the Pāli form, Haribhuñjaya, the river Ping rather than the Pāli, Biṅga. When Pāli terms appear frequently in the text I transliterate the word in its Pāli rather than its Thai form, e.g. *dhātu* or *cetiya* rather than *thāt* or *jedī*.

2. Bodhiraṃsi's *Chronicle of the Lion Buddha Image* (*Tamnān Phraphutthasihiṅg*) was probably written in 1417 C.E. George Coedès surmises that the *Cāmadevīvaṃsa* was written around the same time. (George Coedès, *Documents sur l'Histoire Politique et Religieuse du Laos Occidental*, vol. 25 of the *Bulletin École Française d'Extrême-Orient* [Paris: École Française d'Extrême-Orient, 1925], 13.) Hans Penth dates the composition of the CDV around 1410 C.E. Penth is an epigraphist and research scholar of Lān Nā (northern Thai) history at the Archive of Lān Nā Inscriptions of the Social Research Institute, Chiang Mai University.

3. Camille Notton, *P'ra Buddha Sihiṅg* (Bangkok: Bangkok Times Press, 1933). For a recent analysis of the Phra Siṅgha image see, Stanley J. Tambiah, *The Buddhist Saints of the Forest and the Cult of Amulets: A Study in Charisma, Hagiography, Sectarianism, and Millennial Buddhism* (Cambridge: Cambridge University Press, 1984).

4. Ratanapañña Thera, *Jinakālamālīpakaraṇaṃ,* ed., A. P. Buddhadatta Mahāthera. Pali Text Society (London: Luzac & Company, 1962). English translation, Ratanapañña Thera, *The Sheaf of Garlands of the Epochs of the Conqueror* (*Jinakālamālīpakaraṇaṃ*), trans. N. A. Jayawickrama, Pali Text Society Translation Series, no. 36 (Luzac & Company, 1968).

5. Nidhi Aeusrivongse, "Latthiphithī Sadet Phọ̄ Rāma 5" [Beliefs and rituals regarding the Royal Father Rāma 5], *Silapawattanatham (Arts and Culture)*, 14, no. 10 (August 1993): 78–102; Nidhi Aeusrivongse, "Latthiphithī Jao Mae Kwanim" [Beliefs and rituals regarding the Lord Mother Guan Yin], *Silapawattanatham (Arts and Culture)*, 15, no. 10 (August 1994): 79–106.

6. David K. Wyatt, "The Case for the Northern Thai Chronicles" (paper presented at the Fifth International Conference on Thai Studies, London, England, July 1993).

7. According to Hans Penth, the several chronicles (*tamnān*) related to Cāmadevī and the founding of Haripuñjaya/Lamphūn can be divided into two strands, an old northern Thai line that may have had Mon roots, e.g., the *History of Nāng Jām Thewī*, and a Pāli line, e.g., the *Cāmadevīvaṃsa* (Hans Penth, "Literature on the History of Local Buddhism," in *Wannakam Phutthasāsanā Nai Lānnā* [The literature of northern Thailand], ed. Panpen Khruathai (Chiang Mai, Thailand: Silkworm Books, 1996), 74–92. On the basis of evidence internal to the CDV but also in the light of the *Tamnān Mu'ang Lamphūn* (TML), and relevant materials in the JKM, the *Tamnān Mūlasāsanā* (TM), and the late-nineteenth-century chronicle, the *Phongsāwadān Yōnok* (PY), I suggest that what became the two story lines to which Penth refers may contain sev-

eral story strands that were incorporated into one or possibly two master stories with minor variations created in transmission.

8. A thorough literary-critical study of the CDV would entail the following: (i) a properly edited version of the Pāli CDV with variants based on selected palm-leaf manuscripts; (ii) a careful study of related texts, e.g., *Tamnān Nāng Jām Thewī* (NJT), *Tamnān Mu'ang Lamphūn* (TML); (iii) an analysis and evaluation of the structure and content of the CDV in the light of the foregoing research.

9. The discussion in this section is primarily for scholars with a special interest in Thai and Southeast Asian historical scholarship.

10. Camille Notton, *Chronique de La:p'un: Histoire de la Dynastie de Chamt'evi*, vol. 2 of *Annales du Siam*, 3 vols. (Paris: Charles Lavauzelle, 1930); George Coedès, *Documents sur l'Histoire Politique et Religieuse du Laos Occidental.*

11. Harald Hundius, *The Colophons of Thirty Pāli Manuscripts from Northern Thailand.* Journal of the Pali Text Society, vol. 14 (London: Pali Text Society, 1990).

12. *Lan Na Literature: Catalogue of 954 Secular Titles among the 3,700 palm-leaf manuscripts borrowed from wats throughout Northern Thailand and preserved on microfilm at the Social Research Institute of Chiang Mai University* (Chiang Mai, 1986). This catalogue is only modestly useful since the collection is more extensive. The most recent list of manuscripts in the collection is, *Raichu' Nangsu'boran Lan Na: Ekkasan Maikhrofim Khong Sathaban Wichai Sangkhom Mahawitthayalai Chiang Mai, 2521–2533* [Catalogue of Palm-Leaf Texts on Microfilm at the Social Research Institute, Chiang Mai University 1978–1990] Chiang Mai, 1990).

13. David K. Wyatt briefly discusses these and other efforts at manuscript cataloguing in "The Case for Northern Thai Chronicles."

14. Papers from the conference have been published: *Wannakam Phutthasāsanā Nai Lānnā* [The Buddhist literature of northern Thailand].

15. One of the most recently published chronicles is the *Tamnān Mu'ang Chiang Saen* [Chiang Saen Chronicle] (1995). Others included in the more than sixty titles printed are: *Tamnān Mūlasāsanā Chabap Pā Daeng* [The Chronicle of the Founding of Buddhism. Wat Pā Daeng Version], *Tamnān Mu'ang Chiang Mai* [The Chiang Mai Chronicle], *Tamnān Rawaek* [The Rawaek Chronicle], *Tamnān Mu'ang Fāng* [The City of Fāng Chronicle], *Tamnān Sibhārājawong* [The Chronicle of the Fifteen Dynasties] 3 vols.

16. Bumphen Rawin, ed. and trans. into Thai, *Tamnān Wat Pā Daeng* [The chronicle of the Red Forest Monastery] (Chiang Mai: Chiang Mai University, 1993). There are two English translations of the *Pā Daeng*

chronicle: Donald K. Swearer and Sommai Premchit, "The Red Forest Monastery Chronicle of the Founding of Buddhism," *Journal of the Siam Society* 65, no. 2, (July 1977): 73–110; Sao Sāimöng Mangrāi, *The Pādaeng Chronicle and the Jengtung State Chronicle Translated*, Michigan Papers on South and Southeast Asia, no. 19 (Ann Arbor: University of Michigan, 1981). Mangrāi's volume also includes plates of the palm-leaf manuscript on which he based his translation.

17. Bumphen Rawin, *Mūlasāsanā Samnuan Lānnā* [The northern Thai version of the Mūlasāsanā] (Chiang Mai: Chiang Mai University, 1996). An earlier printed edition is the *Tamnān Mūlasāsanā* (Bangkok: Department of Fine Arts, 1975) that first appeared in 1960 as a memorial volume on the occasion of the funeral of Mr. No Jutimā.

18. Hans Penth, ed. and trans., *Prawat Phrathāt Doi Tung* (*History of Phra Thāt Doi Tung*) (Bangkok and Chiang Rai, Thailand: Mae Fah Luang Foundation in collaboration with the Social Research Institute of Chiang Mai University, 1993).

19. David K. Wyatt and Aroonrut Wichienkeeo, ed. and trans., *The Chiang Mai Chronicle* (Chiang Mai: Silkworm Books, 1995). Two additional volumes are projected, a translation into Thai and the plates of the northern Thai palm-leaf manuscript on which the English and Thai translations were based. David K. Wyatt, *The Nān Chronicle*, rev. ed. (Ithaca: Cornell University Press, 1994).

20. For an overview of northern Thai historical literature see, Hans Penth, "Literature on the History of Local Buddhism."

21. See note 10.

22. *Ru'ang Cāmdevīvaṃsa Phongsāwadān Mu'ang Haribunchai* [Queen Cāma and the chronicle of the kingdom of Haripuñjaya] (Bangkok: Wachirayān Library, 1920). It is likely that the 1920 published edition of the CDV was based on a manuscript in the Wachirayān Library collection. The Pāli in the northern Thai *tham* script was transliterated into central Thai script with side-by-side translation into Thai. The relatively free Thai translation was done by Phrayā Pariyatithamthādā and Phrayā Yānawijit. Some of the grammatical and spelling errors in the Pāli are footnoted, although errors still remain in the text. It would be difficult to determine whether errors were introduced into the published text, whether they were copyist errors in the manuscript, or whether some may reflect Pāli conventions of northern Thailand in the early fifteenth century, or some combination of the three.

23. Coedès, *Documents sur l'Histoire Politique et Religieuse du Laos Occidental*, 12.

24. Sanong Waraurai, *Phrarāchachīwaprawat Phramaejaojāmadevī Boromarāchanārī Sīsuriyawong Ongpatinat Pindhānīharibunchai*

[The royal history of the lord mother queen Cāma, supreme royal woman, lineage of the sun, sovereign of the unsurpassed capital of Haripuñjaya] (Sanpātong: Dantanakorn Museum, 1982). Sanong Waraurai is an Associate Professor in the Department of Biology, Faculty of Science, Chiang Mai University.

Part I

INTERPRETATION

THE *CĀMADEVĪVAṂSA* AND THE CHRONICLE TRADITION IN NORTHERN THAILAND

Because northern Thai chronicles are so diverse, a singular or univocal characterization is impossible. Scholars have proposed different ways of classifying these texts. Hans Penth divides northern Thai or Lān Nā ("land of a million rice paddies") historical literature into two categories, factual history and fictional (i.e., mythical, legendary), although he notes that these categories are fluid and overlapping.[1] In addition to this broad distinction, he proposes five classifications for Lān Nā Buddhist literature that can be considered historical: chronicles that deal in general with the history of Buddhism, chronicles about Buddha images, chronicles of religious sites, inscriptions, and a miscellaneous category into which he places the CDV.[2]

Charnvit Kasetsiri explores the conceptualization of ancient Thai history in terms of the categories of *tamnān, phongsāwadān,* and *jotmāihaet.*[3] The first two terms are usually translated by the word, *chronicle* and the second as *annals* or *records.* He proposes that premodern Thai records or historical documents fall into two main categories: the history of Buddhism (*tamnān*) and the history of dynasties (*phongsāwadān*).[4] *Tamnān* history or the history of Buddhism, he contends, flourished from before the fifteenth century into the seventeenth century at which point it began to decline. Dynastic history or *phongsāwadān* history appears in the seventeenth century. It is a history that begins with the foundation of the kingdom and then lists accomplishments of successive kings.[5] *Tamnān* history, by contrast, highlights the Buddha and particular events in the development of the tradition (*sāsana*). In a manner reminiscent of the *Mahāvaṃsa,* the classic Pāli chronicle of the Sinhalese Mahāvihāra tradition, *tamnān* such as the sixteenth-century JKM begin with Gotama Buddha, his vow to reach enlightenment and a sketch of his life. The story continues through the major Buddhist councils, King Asoka, and an account of Buddhism in Sri Lanka before concluding with the establishment of Buddhism in northern Thailand. Kasetsiri summarizes the nature of *tamnān* history as follows:

> The main theme of *tamnān* history is clearly religion and it is Gotama Buddha who is the moving force in it. Its purpose is to describe the development of Buddhism. Kings and kingdoms come into the picture in so far as their actions contribute to the promoting of Buddhism. History in this sense is not concerned with the past. The past is continuous with the existence of the present and the present is also part of the future. Thus the past, the present, and the future are parts of one whole, the history of Buddhism.[6]

While the distinction between *tamnān* and *phongsāwadān* ways of understanding the past (and the present) refines a crude sense of "chronicle," it fails to address the variety of northern Thai *tamnān* suggested by Penth's categories and also fails to capture the intentionality of a chronicle like the CDV.

David K. Wyatt develops a more thorough and nuanced classification of northern Thai *tamnān*: the *tamnān* of the distant past; the "universal histories" in Pāli and Thai, the product of Buddhist efflorescence in Lān Nā in the fifteenth and sixteenth centuries; and "monumental *tamnān*" concerning Buddhist images, relics, and institutions.[7] He classifies the CDV with universal histories. Although the CDV begins with the Buddha's visit to Haripuñjaya and in this sense seems to connect with Buddhist history beyond the area, it differs significantly from the model of the *Mahāvaṃsa* more nearly reflected in the JKM and the TM. The nature of the CDV as presented in this monograph suggests that Wyatt's categories may be inadequate to fully appreciate the CDV. In many respects the chronicle exemplifies what he calls "monumental *tamnān*," although it also shares the dynastic characteristics he attributes to "universal *tamnān*."

Classifying northern Thai *tamnān* can be heuristically useful but in the end it may be best to follow Bodhiraṃsi's advice to deconstruct all classifications and simply listen carefully to the story:

> Upon her death she was born in the world of the gods (*devaloka*). The beauty and prosperity of the *deva*s in Tusita heaven is beyond description . . . Therefore, no one can describe the wonder of Cāmadevī's attainment. Listen well to her story.

The story of Queen Cāma is Bodhiraṃsi's rendering of a northern Thai folk legend about an extraordinary woman who founded the first northern Thai city-state, today known as Lamphūn. According to the JKM, the founding date would have been in 663 C.E.[8] But in the CDV, the Queen Cāma legend is linked to another story, the discovery and enshrinement of a Buddha relic at Haripuñjaya by King Ādittarāja (c. 1047 C.E. in the JKM).[9]

Although the chronicle has a *vaṃsa* or dynastic element, Bodhiraṃsi finds more interest in myth and legend than in history. Hence, the chronicle resembles two genre of Buddhist literature produced in great quantities in northern Thailand, the *jātaka* (previous lives of the Buddha) and *tamnān*. The association of the CDV with these forms of oral/aural or so called popular literature prompted George Coedès to characterize the text as follows: "C'est une sorte de poème épique entremèlé de réflexions morales, et les faits y sont noyés dans un intarissable verbiage."[10]

In terms of literary genre the two most distinctive types of Buddhist literature produced in northern Thailand are the *jātaka*[11] and *tamnān*. That the two are closely related is indicated by the fact that they are referred to as *nidāna-jātaka* and *tamnān-nidāna*. In short, both *jātaka* and *tamnān* are classified as *nidāna* or "legend." From a historical perspective it is reasonable to assume that many of these texts originated in Chiang Mai during the fifteenth and early sixteenth century considered to be the Golden Age of northern Thailand. From the perspective of popular Buddhist devotional practice such texts served several functions, in particular: (i) to legitimate the founding of a monastery-temple (Thai, *wat*; Pāli, *āvāsa*) and other sacred sites associated with a Buddha relic; (ii) as texts incorporated into particular rituals, e.g., the consecration of a Buddha image, (iii) as sermons preached on special occasions, e.g., the beginning of the rains retreat.

The CDV, like a *jātaka* tale, begins with a story of the past, in this case the Buddha's visit to Haripuñjaya and prediction of the discovery of a Buddha relic by King Ādittarāja. This discovery appears in the last chapter of the chronicle, thus providing a frame for the entire narrative in the same way that the final chapter of a *jātaka* tale connects past and present.

The second chapter, "Vāsudeva and the Founding of Migasaṅghanagara," provides another story of the past that focuses on the sage (Pāli, *isi;* Sanskrit, *ṛṣi*) Vāsudeva. Vāsudeva and other mountain-dwelling ascetics featured in the story have a special relationship with Queen Cāma. Thus, the first two chapters can be seen as representing two stories of the past. In effect, Haripuñjaya has two strands of mythic origin: one associated with the Buddha and the other with Vāsudeva. Haripuñjaya's history is grounded in a mythic time represented by the Buddha and the legendary sage, Vāsudeva. This mythic time is actualized in history by the ruling dynasty of Haripuñjaya, in particular, Cāmadevī and Ādittarāja. This dual thematic structure of the CDV will be examined in further detail in the following section.

While the CDV may resemble the form of a *jātaka*, one strand reflects the content of *phuttha tamnān* texts, which are legends of the Buddha's visit to northern Thailand. These texts vary greatly in scope. Some, such as the *Phrajao Liap Lōk* (PJLL) (The Buddha Travels the World), construct a northern Thai sacred geography created by the visit of the Buddha to the region.[12] Others focus primarily on a single site, for example, the Haripuñjaya Buddha relic.[13] *Phuttha tamnān* are characterized by two basic elements: (i) a visit by the Buddha to the region, (ii) the enshrinement of a Buddha relic or the prediction of the appearance of a relic. In short, PT focus on instantiating the presence of the Buddha—the creation of a "Buddha land" (*buddha-desa*). Within the context of the PT, this *buddha-desa* is actualized by the Buddha with the assistance of *devatā*, usually Indra, and King Asoka. When the narrative moves from myth toward history, the Buddha's presence in the form of a relic is actualized by rulers, as in the case of Ādittarāja of Haripuñjaya. All of these elements are present in the CDV.

THE STRUCTURE OF THE *CĀMADEVĪVAṂSA*

The *Cāmadevīvaṃsa* has much in common with the literary genre associated with preaching and other modes of popular instruction in the vernacular, e.g., *jātaka, nidāna, tamnān*. This is hardly surprising when one finds that Bodhiraṃsi wove into his story a *nidāna*, the legend of Queen Cāma, and a "Buddha history" (*phuttha tamnān*) associated with the central Buddha relic (*mahādhātu*) of Haripuñjaya. Bodhiraṃsi not only wove these two strands into his narrative, he also used them to ground the creation of the kingdom of Haripuñjaya in the dual powers associated with ascetical renunciation and fertility. In the first of these origin stories two powerful, liminal figures, sages (*isi*), among whom Vāsudeva and Brahma (Subrahma) are the most prominent, and a pregnant woman, Queen Cāma, create order/cosmos out of disorder/chaos. Together they build a walled, moated city out of the dark tangle of jungle and in so doing bring civilization to an indigenous people referred to in the text as the Milakkha, who are assumed by scholars to be the Lawa. The CDV's juxtaposition of the rational order of the royal city-state with the seeming irrational disorder of the jungle suggests a culture/nature duality; however, the CDV reverses the conventional woman-equals-nature equation by associating Cāmadevī with culture and the male ruler of the Milakkha with nature.[14]

The secondary origin story serves as the climax to the chronicle—the discovery and enshrinement of a Buddha relic by King Ādittarāja, an event predicted by the Buddha, himself, during his legendary visit to the area. In this narrative strand the world-renouncing power of the Buddha is conjoined with the sovereign power of the world-ruling king (*cakkavatti*). This part of the chronicle reflects one of the major features of popular Thai Buddhist practice, namely, the veneration of Buddha relics.[15] The association of Buddha relics with Buddhist kingship dates from the origins of the tradition, if the *Mahāparinibbāna Sutta* is to be believed, and certainly from the Mauryan period of Indian history (viz. Asoka). Buddha relics enshrined by rulers in *cetiya* (Thai, *jedī*) serve as the axial center of the kingdom. The fact that they may be homologized with the axial world mountain (Mount Sumeru) of Indian cosmology only adds to their grandeur and power.[16]

Both Cāmadevī and the Buddha bring "seeds" to Haripuñjaya. Queen Cāma's seed (*bīja*) bears the fruit of a dynastic lineage; the Buddha's seed (*dhātu*) bears the fruit of the *sāsana* or the Buddha's religion, his teaching (*dhamma*), and the monastic order (*saṅgha*). Bodhiraṃsi weaves the polarity of renunciation and production/fertility into his story: a pregnant Cāma leaves her husband (who becomes a monk) in order to rule Haripuñjaya, an act mediated by an ascetic, Vāsudeva; Prince Siddhattha renounces kingship for spiritual enlightenment and, as the Buddha, brings a bodily relic/seed to Haripuñjaya that becomes Wat Phradhātu, the center of the kingdom. Vāsudeva, an *isi,* actualizes the fertile power of Queen Cāma; Ādittarāja, a monarch, actualizes the ascetical power of the Buddha. The bodies of women and Buddhas are so potent and powerful that they must be channeled by the charisma of ascetics and kings. The overlapping polarities of male and female, asceticism and fertility are at the heart of the dual structure of the CDV.

Although from an historical-critical perspective the two major strands Bodhiraṃsi integrates into the CDV—the Cāmadevī-*isi* strand and the Ādittarāja-Buddha relic strand—can be seen as distinctive if not separate narrative traditions, in the CDV they are synthesized into one story. Was this Bodhiraṃsi's doing or did synthesis occur over time? On the basis of an examination of other northern Thai chronicles, such as the *Tamnān Mu'ang Lamphūn* and the Haripuñjaya section in other northern Thai chronicles, especially the *Tamnān Mūlasāsanā*, it appears probable that storytellers prior to Bodhiraṃsi had brought together various narrative strands. However, this does not necessarily mean that

Bodhiraṃsi was simply translating one composite vernacular story into Pāli. It appears likely that Bodhiraṃsi used several sources, not just northern Thai texts, but standard doctrinal teachings based on the Pāli canon and commentary as well. Bodhiraṃsi's references to *porāṇavacanaṃ* ("ancient words") throughout the text can be seen as an attempt to legitimate his unique story, something akin to the Theravāda use of *buddhavacanaṃ* ("Buddha's words") to lend authority to Pāli *suttas*.

Keeping in mind that the strands or components of the CDV are parts of a single story, the narrative can be divided into four distinct sections:

I. Stories of the Past: The Buddha's prediction of the appearance of his relic and the founding of the first town [Migasaṅghanagara] (chapters 1–2)

II. The Cāmadevī Era. From the founding of Haripuñjaya to the death of Queen Cāma (chapters 3–11)

III. The Interlinear *Vaṃsa* or Genealogy of the rulers of Haripuñjaya (chapter 12)

IV. King Ādittarāja's reign and the Discovery and Enshrinement of the Buddha Relic (chapters 13–15)

Within this structure, Part I establishes the dual perspective taken by the chronicle on the origin/creation of Haripuñjaya; Part II, as verified by Bodhiraṃsi's own statement at the end of chapter 11, is the story of Queen Cāma translated and interpreted by Bodhiraṃsi; Part III, the brief genealogy of the rulers of Haripuñjaya, formally links the CDV with the *vaṃsa* genre of Buddhist chronicles; and Part IV associates the story with the extensive tradition of northern Thai *phuttha tamnān* or Buddha-chronicles.[17]

THE *CĀMADEVĪVAṂSA* AS A NARRATIVE TAPESTRY OF MYTH, LEGEND, AND HISTORY

If one accepts Bodhiraṃsi at his word, the reason he wrote the CDV in Pāli was to enhance the prestige of a vernacular northern Thai legend. He offers no other rationale. A variant interpretation of Bodhiraṃsi's claim would be that he wanted to Buddhicize a centuries-old folktale about the founding of the first kingdom in the Chiang Mai valley. He accomplished this goal by writing his story in Pāli, synthesizing the Cāmadevī *nidāna* with what David Wyatt characterizes as a monumental *phuttha tamnān* or history of the central reliquary (*phradhātu*) of the kingdom of Haripuñjaya, and, finally, by incorporating into the text Buddhist teachings typical of the early fifteenth century. Bodhiraṃsi's story is not so much a history as a colorful narrative tapestry woven together on the warp and woof of two master stories. That Bodhiraṃsi puts into Pāli two widely known vernacular stories suggests that he is attempting to bridge what is simplistically characterized as "monastic" and "lay" Buddhism. In other terms, one could read Bodhiraṃsi's narrative as an effort to legitimate by means of the CDV, varied forms of Buddhist thought and practice that has constituted the Buddhist tradition of northern Thailand since its origin.

There is no specific evidence that indicates whether a particular historical occasion prompted Bodhiraṃsi to write the CDV; he might have written the text as a response to the religious situation of his day; perhaps he hoped to enhance his own reputation as a scholar-monk; or some combination of the above. Even though Bodhiraṃsi wrote the text in Pāli, it does not appear that the CDV was intended as a book for scholarly study or monastic edification as was the case with Sirimaṅgalācariya's commentary on the *Maṅgala Sutta.* It is more reasonable to assume that it was written to be preached. Even though the lay audience would not have understood the Pāli language, the stories of Cāmadevī and of Ādittarāja would have been well known and the doctrinal homilies inserted into the text so familiar that many in the audience would have recognized the Pāli terms. Perhaps the CDV was occasioned by a royal donation to Wat Haripuñjaya or Wat Cāmadevī in Lamphūn or was written to be preached during a rains retreat (*vassa*). Whatever the motivation, Bodhiraṃsi composed the CDV to elevate the status of Queen Cāma as the progenitor of a lineage that ruled Haripuñjaya (modern Lamphūn) and Khelāṅga (modern Lampāng), the two Mon city-states that predate the Tai kingdom of Chiang Mai; to promote veneration of Lamphūn's central relic at Wat Phradhātu Haripuñjaya both as an authentic Buddha relic and for its connection with the princely family of Lamphūn; and to propagate Buddhist ethical teachings within this narrative context.

The diverse and colorful strands of the Cāmadevī and Ādittarāja stories can be separated into four major thematic subjects. These include: (i) the prominence of polarities within the dual structure of the narrative; (ii) the liminal nature of the *dramatis personae*; (iii) the syncretic flavor of early fifteenth-century Buddhism in the Chiang Mai valley; and (iv) the ethical teachings and the doctrinal themes that dominated the popular preaching of Bodhiraṃsi's day. The subsequent analysis follows this outline. It is not meant to replace but to enhance and commend a reading of the text itself.

(i)

The CDV moves between the dual perspectives of Cāmadevī and Ādittarāja, a duality determined partially but not exclusively by the author's integration of two different narratives into a single story. From a structural point of view these two poles provide Bodhiraṃsi with a literary device through which he incorporates several other polarities into the narrative. Prominent among them is the creative opposition of procreation and renunciation. As previously suggested, this polarity does not divide strictly along female and male gender lines: Cāmadevī procreates a lineage biologically; the Buddha generates his religion (*sāsana*) primarily through the promise of a bodily relic (*sārīrikadhātu*); the power of Cāmadevī who comes to Haripuñjaya pregnant is mediated by an ascetic (*isi*); the power of the renunciant Buddha is actualized by the militarily victorious king, Ādittarāja, who enshrines the Buddha's bodily relic.

Within the context of the northern Thai *phuttha tamnān* tradition, the Buddha can be understood as sacralizing the entire region by impregnating it with his bodily relics following an itinerary that is at once an etiological justification for Buddhist pilgrimage sites and a symbolic guarantee of the order, prosperity, and productivity of the land. As Cāmadevī travels from the Mon city-state of Lavapura to Haripuñjaya, her retinue founds towns along the way with, as the TML notes, the thrust of a spear into the ground. The power of Cāmadevī's sexuality emerges even more prominently in other versions of the Cāmadevī story. In one, the king of the Lawa, Vilaṅga, pursues Cāmadevī's hand in marriage. The good queen foils the tribal chieftain's ardent intentions through an act symbolizing the power of female procreative sexuality and the taboos surrounding it (see, "Which Cāmadevī?").

Other types of polarities are woven into the narrative. Some are oppositional as in the polarity of urban culture versus wild nature, the city dweller versus the hunter and gatherer. Haripuñjaya in its civilized splendor stands over against the jungle and rustic villages that the CDV presents as being both culturally and morally deficient. Those who look to Buddhism for an apologia of wild nature will not find it in the CDV. This oppositional character also has an ethnic or racial dimension: the Mon versus the Lawa and the Khmer.

Other polarities are complimentary rather than oppositional. Twinning, for example, is an important literary device in the CDV. Shortly after Cāmadevī arrives at Haripuñjāya she gives birth to twin sons. One becomes the ruler of Haripuñjaya, and in time the second twin rules Khelāṅga. They marry the twin daughters of the King of Milakkha. Biological twins rule twin cities guarded by two sages, one of whom lives on

Twin Peak Mountain. That Cāmadevī's twin sons and the twin daughters of the king of the Milakkha are small children when they marry suggests several possible interpretations: (i) that youth is innocence, innocence is purity, and hence the lineage lines will be worthy; (ii) that marriage alliances were arranged by families through child betrothal; (iii) or that what appears as differences—political, ethnic, gender—are but two sides of the same interdependent reality. The CDV depicts the samsaric world of change in terms of polarities that reflect the fluid, ambiguous, sometimes complimentary, often oppositional world of nature, animals, humans, and divine beings.

(ii)

The major classes of *dramatis personae* who populate the CDV are royalty (*devī, rāja*), ascetics/sages (*isi*), gods (*devatā*), children, and animals, especially crows. Presiding over them all is the absent Buddha made present by his relic. All participate in and help to create a fluid, sometimes liminally defined social universe that lacks absolute distinctions. With the exception of the Buddha, no one—human, animal, or divine—as portrayed in the narrative, is either absolutely good or absolutely evil. Royalty can be deceitful and vengeful as well as brave and caring;[18] ascetics possess the foresight gained by intensive meditation, but they are also subject to anger; the *devatā* are both malevolent and benevolent, protective and violent; and crows, consistent with their trickster nature, protect the Buddha but also profane the king.

The ambiguity of the *devatā* stems, in part, from the very fluidity of the term, for the Theravāda tradition classifies 308 different varieties. Kings, also, are depicted in ambiguous terms. Their power may be used for good or ill. At the very point where Ādittarāja discovers the Buddha relic buried under his palace, Bodhiraṃsi decides to poke fun at the prerogatives of royaḷ privilege and power with ribald humor (see chapter 15). One wonders if the good monk was employing a culturally sanctioned technique to ridicule the rulers of Lamphūn or Chiang Mai for some real or imagined slight, or to humor or gently chide them to make large donations (*dāna*) to the monastic order (*saṅgha*).

Ambiguity and relativity find expression in paradox and reversal. Kings defeated in battle one day are victorious the next and vice versa. As mere babes the twin sons of queen Cāma defeat the powerful king of the Milakkha (see chapter 7). In defiance of logical rationality, the princes return from battle to suckle at their mother's breast, thereby further reinforcing the paradox of the child warrior. The paradox serves the author's intent of weaving various polarities into the tapestry of his narrative, in this case the contrast between the calm, peaceful scene of babies nursing and the violent chaos of war that can be interpreted as narrative representations of the polarity of destruction and creation. Cāmadevī's sons feed on mother's milk which, like menstrual blood, symbolizes the procreative power of Queen Cāma not only as the fertile progenitor of a new lineage but as co-cosmocrator of Haripuñjaya in tandem with the Buddha.

In the narrative, children have a special but seemingly contradictory relationship to animals. In the Cāmadevī-*isi* strand of the story children discovered by Vāsudeva in the footprints of animals represent instinctual behaviors incompatible with the rational and orderly form of town life; however, in the Ādittarāja-Buddha relic strand of the narrative a child learns crow language and reveals to the king the location of the Buddha relic. Similar to other major actors in the CDV, children embody contradictory qualities.

Central characters in the narrative are not only the *dramatis personae* in a morally ambiguous and relativistic social universe, they embody a sui generis liminality. Foremost among them is the pregnant Cāmadevī who arrives at Haripuñjaya without a husband. The pregnant queen is symbolically powerful, and her arduous journey from Lavapura to Haripuñjaya without a protective spouse defies conventional canons of social rank and status of the time.

The ascetic sages (*isi*) who bring Cāmadevī to northern Thailand are betwixt-and-between figures, neither laymen nor Buddhist monks, neither entirely human nor divine. The *isi*s play several mediatorial roles. In particular, they mediate Mon culture to the Milakkha, and they integrate Brahmanical and Buddhist traditions. Vāsudeva and the other ascetics live in the mountains on the margins of the city-states located in the river valleys of northern Thailand. But, while they lack political authority—just as Cāmadevī's five-year-old sons lack physical power—it is only through their agency that the towns of Haripuñjaya and Khelāṅga come into being.

In terms of spiritual ideals, life style, and role as teachers, the sages embody the norms of the Buddhist monkhood. Yet, as *isi*s rather than *bhikkhu*s they perform ritual functions, such as royal coronations, that monks do not perform. Within the narrative, their lives as monks prior to adopting the life of an *isi* qualifies them to play a *bhikkhu* role even though technically they are not monks. Within the context of contemporary northern Thai Buddhist practice, the role of the *isi* in the CDV is not unlike the role of the lay temple teacher (*ājān wat*) in northern Thai Buddhism who mediates between monk and laity. Customarily the *ājān wat* serves as a monk for several years. Upon leaving the monastic order he becomes the principal ritual leader for the lay community in the *wat*.

Within the life of the community, the *ājān wat* plays a role of equal or even greater importance than the monk.[19] In the CDV, no monk rivals the role of Vāsudeva and his cohorts.

In this fluid, ambiguous, relativistic social universe, populated by a pregnant queen without a husband, trickster crows, sometimes violent *devatā*, and betwixt-and-between sages, the Buddha stands alone as an absolute value both in the material form of his body-cum-relic and in the *dhamma* as embodied in the doctrinal and ethical homilies Bodhiraṃsi inserts into the narrative. Thus, even though the king of the Milakkha had a larger army than Haripuñjaya he was defeated because he lacked the dhammic qualities of "mindfulness and discrimination."

(iii)

It is not surprising that the living Buddhism of early fifteenth-century northern Thailand as depicted in the CDV is highly syncretic and apotropaic in nature. In fact, Buddhism as currently practiced in the Chiang Mai valley closely resembles Bodhiraṃsi's description of fifteenth-century northern Thai Buddhism.[20] The fluid ambivalencies that characterize the narrative world of the CDV naturally characterize the relationship between Buddhism and non-Buddhist systems of belief and practice. Vāsudeva and his hermit colleagues are ordained first as Buddhist monks but then surrender the monastic life to become *isis*. Within the narrative, their role as the spiritual progenitors of Haripuñjaya and Khelāṅga dictates that they leave the monkhood. Nevertheless, the ease with which monks become mountain hermits who then become euhemerized guardian deities, illustrates the problematic of univocal characterizations of Buddhism within a given cultural tradition. Still today, Vāsudeva is believed to reside on Mount Suthēp on the outskirts of Chiang Mai as a cohort of the Lawa guardian spirits of the city, Pu Sæ and Ya Sæ, and as a guardian of the Buddha relic enshrined on the mountain at Wat Phradhātu Doi Suthēp.

Guardian and protective spirits play as important a role in the CDV as they do in contemporary Thai Buddhism. In one of the story's most poignant moments an elderly tree deity pleads with the sages not to uproot his dwelling as they go about clearing the land to build Haripuñjaya. Yet, the CDV also depicts the *devatā* as agents of extraordinary violence. Above all, the *devatā* function as guardians of the major contending city-states, Haripuñjaya and Lavo. Battles are depicted not only as struggles between armies but also between guardian deities of warring kingdoms. More importantly for the purposes of this study, shrines dedicated to the *devatā* are venerated in much the same way that

Buddha relics are enshrined and venerated. Although guardian spirits in northern Thailand are more informally constructed than in Myanmar (Burma) and Sri Lanka, the scope of their dominion determines the extent and nature of their power.[21] Some are assigned specific locations—for example, a house compound, a rice paddy—while others protect a town or a kingdom, as in the case of Haripuñjaya and Lavo.

Paradoxically, in the CDV the Buddha and *devatā* share important characteristics: both are absent in the sense that they are unseen, but both are embodied in the narrative as actors in life and by their material presence in the form of relic or image after death. The king of Lavo not only venerates the cremated remains of the guardian deity of the city enshrined in a *cetiya* but he also worships a statue: "Since that time the Khmer have venerated the *devatā* thinking, 'This statue (*devatārūpaṃ*) is our city guardian deity.'" In like manner, the absent Buddha is made present in a material form as relic and image. In Lamphūn today devotees pay their respects to the *cetiya* reliquary and images of the Buddha at Wat Phradhātu Haripuñjaya and then across town venerate the statue of Cāmadevī as the guardian spirit of the city. Within the uncertain, ambiguous, samsaric world of the CDV, the principal function of religion-on-the-ground—be it Buddhism or animism, veneration of the Buddha or veneration of the *devatā*—seems to be apotropaic. Even Bodhiraṃsi prefaces his story with the expectation that "having paid homage to the Triple Gem, to the [Buddha's] relics in all places and to the noble *bodhi* tree, I am protected from danger everywhere I go."

Modern interpretations of Buddhism often emphasize its rational, ethical nature. From this perspective the Three Refuges or the Three Gems (Buddha, Dhamma, Saṅgha) to which Buddhists pay respect at the opening of all Buddhist ceremonies is rationalized as a ritual honoring the founder of the tradition, his teaching, and the monastic order that perpetuates it. Such an interpretation ignores the apotropaic intent of taking refuge in the Triple Gem as expressed by Bodhiraṃsi in the CDV and found in most popular devotional texts. Apotropaism constitutes a fundamental ingredient in northern Thai Buddhist belief and practice as much in Bodhiraṃsi's fifteenth century world as in the twentieth century world of modern Chiang Mai.[22]

(iv)

Buddha-dhamma, that is to say the specifically Buddhist teachings in the CDV, include the three traditional Theravāda divisions of the Buddhist path (*magga*), namely, ethics (*sīla*), mindfulness (*samādhi*), and wisdom (*paññā*); nevertheless, as befits a text intended for a broad audience, the *Buddha-dhamma* of the CDV is primarily ethical in nature. The two ethical concerns that dominate the story are social and political. In a manner similar to the *Sigālaka Sutta* and the social sanctions governing action and speech (e.g., the *pañcasīla*), social ethics in the CDV are predicated on the family or local community, the prime example in the narrative being the relationship between Queen Cāma and her sons. Behaviors based on social hierarchies of status, gender, and age such as respectful deference, are woven into the story. During his travels in northern Thailand, the Buddha teaches the Mon whom he encounters to "support [your] parents, respect your elders in the family; speak politely; do not steal; in the morning and the evening venerate the Buddha, the *dhamma,* and the *saṅgha*; do not speak in a demeaning manner." After receiving this teaching the Mon acknowledge the authority of the Buddha and accept membership in the Buddhist community by taking the Five Precepts—refrain from taking life, from stealing, from adultery, from lying, and from intoxicants—a ritual act that continues to define the Buddhist moral community in Thailand. All formal gatherings begin with the congregants taking refuge in the Buddha, his teaching, and the monastic order, and repeating the precepts.

More striking, however, are the virtues of caring and love underlying socially constructed external behaviors. A mutual care and concern characterizes the relationship between the queen and her two sons. In one episode, Cāmadevī faces the dilemma of whether to continue in her mothering-nurturing role in relationship to her son, Anantayasa, or force him to act independently once he came of age. It took great moral courage for the queen mother to make the right choice in the light of her immature son's plea, "Mother, when you stay here, I am happy. How can I be happy when you have gone? Therefore, I beg you not to leave me. If you leave, I'll soon die." The wise Bodhiraṃsi recognized that Queen Cāma's dilemma was common to all parents regardless of social status (see chapter 11 of the CDV).

Political ethics focus primarily on kingship. Consistent with the *jātaka* tradition, the CDV upholds the Ten Royal Virtues model of ideal Buddhist kingship—generosity, high moral character, self-sacrifice, honesty, kindness, self-control, nonanger, nonviolence, patience, and conformity to the law. The ideal king has "eliminated anger, is fully aware, cares for his soldiers under all conditions, has eliminated in himself and others discontent, greed, hatred, and delusion, and is indifferent to pride and conceit." In the narrative, royal behavior sometimes exemplifies this ideal but more often it incorporates two other modes of kingship—the mediocre (*majjhimarāja*) and the truly evil (*atipāpadhamma*): "When the righteous king rules, the city will be happy, prosperous, and pleasant; the

Buddha's religion will progress, and it will have a large, contented and satisfied population. When the unrighteous king rules, the city will experience famine and suffering as if it were consumed by fire. When the mediocre king rules, the people will decline and the Buddha's religion will vanish." The well-being of the people, the Buddha's religion, and the moral quality of the king are interdependent.

Structurally, the principle of causality or interdependent co-arising (*paṭicca samuppāda*) underlies the CDV. Rather than spelling out the twelvefold doctrinal formula, the narrative embodies various forms of the principle in its classical sense of cause and effect/arising and cessation. The behavior of kings, for example, leads to good or evil results. Certain inevitable consequences arise from the actions of an immoral king, and conversely as well. Although good and evil are not constructed as moral absolutes in the story, there is no doubt that the defeat of the Khmer by King Ādittarāja is a moral as well as a military victory. After defeating the Khmer, the good king provides his former enemies with food, shelter, and clothing and when he hears stories of rampant disease among them he is "so overwhelmed with sorrow" that he constructs a village for their benefit.

The principle of causal interdependence also finds expression in the classic terms of *kamma, saṃsāra,* and *puñña* (merit). The sages teach Cāmadevī and her two sons to: "Maintain mindfulness, be firmly established in the Buddha's religion, be well disciplined, observe the tenfold virtues of the king, care for the people, and do no harm to others and you will gain all that you desire both in this world and the world hereafter." Bodhiraṃsi often extols generosity (*dāna*) to the monks and the consequences of merit-making not only for one's own benefit "in this world and the next," but also for one's relatives, a notion of a shared field of merit that remains one of the core meanings of current northern Thai Buddhist ritual practice. Of particular importance is the dedication of merit to one's parents. Upon Queen Cāma's death her son, Mahantayasa, teaches the people assembled for her funeral, "Those who love their relatives should perform meritorious deeds—give *dāna*, observe the precepts, build *cetiya,* construct Buddha images—and dedicate the merit to your relatives, especially your parents. In so doing you will be returning your obligation and will become even more beloved by them."

Merit is also linked to the doctrine of impermanence. At one point the sage, Subrahma, instructs Queen Cāma: "all compounded things are impermanent, changing, and transient. Therefore, accumulate more and more merit [so that] you may travel safely by the power of your meritorious deeds (*puññakammena*)." After Queen Cāma's death and cremation, her son, Mahantayasa, advises the people not to grieve or lament "for the

Blessed One taught that death is common to all living beings." At the same time he acknowledges the natural feelings of attachment that one has for loved ones and sees merit-making on behalf of relatives as a natural expression of those feelings.

In contemporary northern Thailand, funeral sermons continue to stress the teaching of impermanence and acknowledge the inevitability of death in this uncertain, morally ambiguous, samsaric world. Consequently, one must not be attached to the things of this world—even one's beloved parents and children; nonetheless, it is equally true, that meritorious deeds bear good consequences not only for oneself but for others.

In this life and the next, we are not mere pawns in the hands of an impersonal fate nor are we merely at the mercy of whimsy or the uncertainty of day-to-day life. There is, after all, the enduring truth of the Buddha's *dhamma* and the hope against life's adversity gained through the protection of the gods and the Buddha, the rule of a just and righteous king, the love of family and friends, and the reward from generous support of the *saṅgha*.

Scholars of Thai Buddhism have long observed that the transfer of merit is at the very core of popular religious practice even though it seems to contradict a strict construction of *kamma* doctrine. From a logical point of view, furthermore, it seems contradictory to link the doctrine of impermanence and not-self (*anattā*) with merit-making practices on behalf of parents. It must be kept in mind, however, that devotional religious belief and practice are not determined by the logical constructions of either Buddhist or Western philosophy, but rather grow out of experience. In the case of the above passage, the experience of love and affection between children and parents extends beyond the boundaries of death. An atomized construction of *kamma* and *puñña* as doctrinal concepts is not reflected in the living Buddhist tradition of northern Thailand. The ritual acts of merit transference are rightly associated with the ethical concepts of sympathy (*anukampā*), loving-kindness and compassion (*mettā-karuṇā*).

AND HISTORY

The CDV is not without historical value. To interpret the text solely through a religio-mythic lens de-emphasizes or omits entirely important aspects of the story, in particular, the battles between Haripuñjaya and the Milakkha, presumed to be Lawa, and between Haripuñjaya and Lavo, presumed to be Khmer, the forebearers of modern Cambodians. This is the historical dimension of the chronicle that addresses the timing and extent of Mon influence in the Lamphūn area of northern Thailand and the relationship among the Mon, Lawa, and Khmer between the seventh and thirteenth centuries. An important historical feature of the CDV is the connection made between Lamphūn and the Mon towns of Thaton and Pegu in Burma, a claim that supports Mon suzerainty at Haripuñjaya at various times during the five-hundred-year period in question. The CDV makes clear, however, that the fortunes of the Mon rose and fell at Haripuñjaya and that at times the city was ruled by the Lawa and perhaps the Khmer. It is important to keep in mind that rigid distinctions made in the CDV between the uncivilized or barbaric Lawa and the civilized Mon probably have a more legendary meaning than a historical basis. If one assumes that the Cāmadevī story was originally created by the Mon of Lavapura to legitimate their domination of Haripuñjaya, it then logically follows that the legend makers would denigrate the local Lawa population. Neither the CDV nor any historical evidence of which I am aware supports the claim made by Kraisri Nimmanahaeminda that the Lawa were aborigines residing in the basin of the Ping River long before the Mon people founded their kingdom of Lamphūn and who were by nature savage headhunters practicing cannibalism, being "no different from the Wa of northern Burma or the Naga in northwestern Burma near Assam, where headhunting is practiced to this day."[23]

George Coedès was one of the first Western scholars to recognize the crucial place of the Mon in the cultural and religious history of Thailand: "One of the most striking, as well as the newest, facts resulting from the study of our Pāli texts, is the importance of the role played by the Mon in the history of Western Laos."[24] When Coedès made this claim in 1925 he was reacting to currently held Western views of Khmer cultural dominance as advanced by M. P. Lefevre-Pontalis, who maintained that Cāmadevī brought Khmer civilization into the area. Lefevre-Pontalis was of the opinion that the Khmer then dominated the region until the Thai challenged Khmer hegemony in the Menam basin after the thirteenth century. Prior to that time, he contended, the northern region was torn asunder by a series of fratricidal wars among the Khmer states, in particular, the parent state, Lopburī (Lavapura in the CDV) and its colonies, Lamphūn and Lampāng.[25]

Although Coedès agrees with Lefevre-Pontalis's identification of the CDV term *milakkha* (= uncivilized, primitive) with the Lawa, he argues that the Cāmadevī of the CDV was Mon, not Khmer. He accepts as historically true the claim that Cāmadevī was the daughter of the king of Lavo and the wife (or widow) of the ruler of a Mon state, Ramaññanagara, situated between Lopburī and Ayutthayā.[26] He also accepts the historical veracity of the cholera epidemic reported in the twelfth chapter of the CDV in which the population of Haripuñjaya decides to migrate to Sudhammapura (Thaton) and Haṃsavati (Pegu) because they spoke a common language. Coedès believes that such a seemingly factual claim validates the view that Haripuñjaya was Mon at the time: "If this were a matter of some miraculous or edifying incident, of which the text contains so many examples, one might have reason to suspect its authenticity. But it is a detail given in passing, dispensable to the narrative, and its simplicity is enough to inspire confidence."[27]

Coedès finds additional support for his interpretation of the CDV in inscriptional evidence from both Lopburī and Lamphūn. Several eighth-century Mon pillar inscriptions discovered at Lopburī confirm the Mon cultural identity of Lopburī at that time; hence, he concludes, "the emigrants who accompanied Cāmadevī and founded Haripuñjaya were therefore, if not of the pure Mon race, at least carriers of the Mon language and civilization, and of the Buddhist religion."[28] Mon stele inscriptions discovered at Lamphūn similar to Mon inscriptions at Pagan date from the early thirteenth century:

> Their appearance in locations relatively distant from one another proves that the Mon language imported from Lavo by Cāmadevī and spoken in the eleventh century by the fugitives to Pegu, had become by the beginning of the thirteenth century the official language of Haripuñjaya. Thus, it is quite understandable that in the retelling of the battles between Lavo and Haripuñjaya under the reign of Ādittarāja (twelfth century), the CDV regularly calls the inhabitants of Haripuñjaya, Ramañña.[29]

That the text identifies the inhabitants of Lavo (Lopburī) at that time as Kamboja (Khmer) is also corroborated by epigraphic evidence. While the inscriptions of the Cāmadevī period at Lopburī are Mon, by the eleventh century Khmer inscriptions were found in Lopburī and twelfth-century bas-reliefs at Angkor Wat depict the Lavo army dressed in Cambodian style under the direction of a Cambodian chief.[30] Even though Ucchiṭṭhacakkavatti, the tenth-century Lavo king recorded in the CDV, may have been Mon, Coedès contends that Ādittarāja fought against the Khmers of Lavo in the twelfth century and that these battles constitute a chapter in the history of the expansion of Khmer power into the lower Menam basin.

Coedès makes a strong case for the historical value of the CDV in interpreting the pre-Thai history of the region bounded by Lopburī in the south and Lamphūn in the north. His major contribution is twofold: convincingly establishing the political and cultural importance of the Mon in this region over against prevailing views of Khmer dominance; and, arguing for the historical value of northern Thai chronicles such as the CDV. While Coedès was essentially correct on both points, I offer two qualifications:

(i) Given Coedès' historical orientation to the CDV, he tends to accept as factual those parts of the story that support his strongly held convictions about the Mon. The episode of the cholera epidemic and the resultant emigration to Thaton and Pegu are interpreted by Coedès as confirmation that the population of Haripuñjaya is Mon. He contends that this view is supported by the fact that the narrative at this point is neither miraculous nor didactic in nature. Just because an episode in a narrative *appears* to be historical does not necessarily *make* the episode factual. Although it is reasonable to posit the facticity of the event, one can argue that the purpose of the episode is *etiological*, that is to provide an explanation for the festival of Loi Krathong (the festival of the floating boats) featured prominently in this episode. Such an interpretation does not depend on external evidence but on evidence within the text when it is seen through the lens of folklore, myth, and legend, a literary genre that features etiologies and etymologies. Therefore, if one sees the intentionality underlying the CDV as primarily mythic, legendary, and religious, then it seems prudent to withhold judgment on the historicity of the cholera epidemic episode on the grounds that an etiological explanation is more consistent with the nature of the text. Without dismissing historical explanation, viewing the CDV from the perspective of myth and legend opens up a wider range of hermeneutical possibilities that may well be more consistent with the text's genre and also to the oral/aural context in which it was probably used. The CDV was not written as a history book to be read in monastic schools. Rather, it was composed to enhance the prestige of Haripuñjaya and its central relic, and to inspire, instruct, and entertain an audience.

(ii) Perhaps the most important historical question asked of the text is whether Cāmadevī, herself, was fact or fiction. Coedès acknowledges that Cāmadevī might have been created as a historical fiction meant to represent Mon cultural and political influence in the Haripuñjaya area. He treats her as factual only in specific instances that support his theory, in particular, that she was the daughter of the king of Lavo and the wife or widow from the Mon town, Ramaññanagara. Coedès, therefore, begs the question of Cāmadevī's historicity and is inconsistent regarding her possible facticity.

In the last analysis there is insufficient evidence to determine whether or not the CDV's portrait of Cāmadevī can be taken as factual. We do know that, in the middle of the sixteenth century, residents of

Lamphūn probably believed she was historical. In a 1554 inscription found at the *cetiya* on Doi Noi in Chomthong District, where it is believed that Cāmadevī had enshrined relics and to whose service she had assigned descendents of the four sages who figure in the founding of Haripuñjaya, we learn that "Phayā Mekuti now gathers the descendants of the sages and assigns them again to the relics and the *cetiya* and donates rice fields and villages to the *wat*."[31] Yet, other evidence calls into question the historicity of Cāmadevī. A legend similar to the Cāmadevī story and celebrated ritually at the New Year in Champasak, Laos, indicates a wider provenance for the story than the specific historical circumstances regarding the founding of Haripuñjaya. Studies by Charles Archaimbault suggest that within the Lao context the legend of a pregnant queen was associated with New Year rites of purification and renewal. This perspective reinforces the mythic, cosmogonic significance of the story.[32]

The approach of this monograph to the CDV does not resolve fully or definitively the question of Cāmadevī's facticity, and considers this question to be of secondary importance to the religio-mythic nature of the text. As a figure who participates in the creation of Haripuñjaya, Cāmadevī is as necessary to the sages as Ādittarāja is to the Buddha. In the CDV, Cāmadevī enables the work of the sages to become a historical reality in the same way that Ādittarāja actualizes the presence of the Buddha at Haripuñjaya in the form of his relic. From this perspective, the logic of the text does not make Cāmadevī a factual personage but it does make her historical. By this I mean that *it is through Cāmadevī and Ādittarāja that the cosmological and ontological reality represented by myth becomes history.* In literary-critical terms Cāmadevī may be assessed as either a legendary fiction or a euhermerized heroine, but that judgment is as peripheral to the basic intent of the story as the debate over whether or not Cāmadevī was a living, flesh-and-blood person.

Historical events must certainly have prompted Bodhiraṃsi to write the *Cāmadevīvaṃsa*. Was this sermon-*tamnān* an effort on the part of a monk from Lamphūn to restore the former luster of the *cetiya* at Wat Phradhātu Haripuñjaya that was being eclipsed by the growing importance of Chiang Mai as the dominant Buddhist center in northern Thailand? Or could the CDV together with the chronicle of the Sihiṅg Buddha image [TPPS] authored by Bodhiraṃsi be seen as the monk's reaction to reformist aniconic piety of the Wat Pā Daeng tradition of forest monks?

Bodhiraṃsi lived at a time of religious and political transition at the beginning of the Golden Age of Lān Nā/Northern Thailand. Presumably he was alive during the reigns of Saen Mu'ang Mā (1385–1401) and Sam Fang Kaen (1401–1441). The revered monk, Sumana Mahāthera, arrived from Sukhōthai during Ku' Nā's reign (1355–1385) bringing with him the Siṅhalese Udumbaragiri order that had been established first at Martaban and subsequently at Sukhōthai. If we accept 1410 as the probable date of the *Cāmadevīvaṃsa,* the new Siṅhalese reformist tradition established at Wat Pā Daeng probably antedated Bodhiraṃsi because its founder, Ñāṇagambhīra, did not arrive in Chiang Mai until 1430.[33] While it is interesting to speculate what historical circumstances, especially in regard to possible controversy over religious practice, might have prompted Bodhiraṃsi's work, it is indisputable that the CDV celebrates Lamphūn at a time when Chiang Mai was emerging as the region's dominant political power and cultural center.

In terms of Bodhiraṃi's historical context, it is possible that the CDV did have a covert sectarian, political agenda. Perhaps the Mahāthera wanted to elevate Wat Phradhātu Haripuñjaya over Wat Suan Dọk in Chiang Mai where Ku' Nā had enshrined the Buddha relic Sumana Mahāthera brought from Sukhōthai. Or, perhaps Bodhiraṃsi wanted to legitimate a traditional devotional piety under threat from a fledgling reform movement that culminated a century later in the work of Sirimaṅgalācariya and Ratanapañña Mahāthera, members of the Wat Pā Daeng scholarly fraternity. Such speculation aside, however, it is certain that Bodhiraṃsi wrote a treatise to revitalize devotion to the oldest, most sacred site in the Chiang Mai valley, the Haripuñjaya reliquary in Lamphūn.

In this study I propose that the value of the CDV for an understanding of the traditional northern Thai Buddhist worldview is unique, and that an analysis of the text must go beyond a quest for historical facts to reveal the extraordinary nature of Bodhiraṃsi's story as a bridge between myth and history, the secular and the religious, a synthesis of Buddhism, Brahmanism and animism, and the integration of the devotional piety of ordinary lay practioners with Buddhist ethical ideals.

WHICH CĀMADEVĪ?

(i)

Other northern Thai chronicles, in particular the TML, TNJT, and the TM enlarge the CDV's portrait of Cāmadevī, especially her relationship with Vilaṅga, the ruler of the Milakkha. The humorous, ribald story of Cāmadevī and the Milakkha [Lawa] chieftain, Vilaṅga, is omitted from the CDV but appears in the TML, the TM, and the *Phongsāwadān Yōnok* [PY].[34] It is, furthermore, a well-known tale in popular folklore about

Cāmadevī. The following account is found in the *Lamphūn Chronicle* [TML]:

> There was a great chief of the Lua [Lawa], named Vilaṅga who, having heard of Nāng Cāmadevī's great beauty, desired her for his wife. Therefore, he sent a high-ranking official accompanied by five hundred men to pay respects to her. "Your majesty," the envoy said, "Vilaṅga, my master, who lives in the heights of the Lawa mountains and who is the chief of all the Lawa, has sent me with my men to tell you that he would like to have you as his major wife." "O messenger," she replied, "I have never seen your chief. What does he look like?" "Like us," was the answer. "Like you!" she cried. "Don't talk of making him my husband. He is not fit to even touch my hand! Leave my house immediately! You disgust me!" The envoy, expecting to hear only compliments, received nothing but insults. He returned to inform his chief. The latter, expecting a favorable response, received nothing but offensive news. Furious, he assembled approximately 80,000 men, descended from his capital, and camped on the plain. His army took up three rice fields which to this day are called Thong Nā Tem [Fields of Gold]. He then sent a messenger to Nāng Cāmadevī who spoke to her in Lawa, "Answer me! Do you want to be my wife or not?" "Mr. messenger," she responded, "to be the wife of your chief is beneath my dignity."[35]

Aside from the obvious sarcastic humor in the dialogue, which adds to listener interest, in the narrative the episode serves as the occasion for the battle between the Milakkha forces and the forces of Haripuñjaya led by Mahantayasa and Anantayasa, or Indavara as he is known in the TML, TM, and PY. The brief account of the battle is very similar in all versions of the story so it appears likely that Bodhiraṃsi knew the episode of Vilaṅga and Queen Cāma but decided to omit it from his account.

If we assume that the Vilaṅga-Cāmadevī episode was not at some later point excised from the *Cāmadevīvaṃsa*,[36] Bodhiraṃsi's omission may have been prompted by other popular versions of the story, such as the alternative account included in the TML and retold by Kraisri Nimmanahaeminda in a variant form.[37] In response to Vilaṅga's ardent pursuit of her hand in marriage, Cāmadevī sets an impossible task for him. She tells the Lawa chieftain she will marry him if on three attempts he can throw his spear from Mount Ṣuthēp to land inside the Lamphūn city walls. Vilaṅga accepts the challenge and with the first mighty throw nearly manages to reach the city wall. Cāmadevī, now fearful that her

Fig. 1 Vilaṅga throws a spear from Mount Suthēp toward Haripuñjaya

persistent suitor will succeed, plots Vilaṅga's downfall. With her undergarments she fashions a hat for the Lawa chieftain and presents it as a gift, feigning admiration for Vilaṅga's great strength. He puts it on his head and launches his second throw only to find that it lands far short of the mark. His third attempt is so feeble that the spear is caught in the wind and like a boomerang reverses its direction and pierces Vilaṅga's heart.[38] Unwittingly, by wearing the defiled hat Vilaṅga has broken the taboo of touching cloth profaned by menstrual blood.[39] Indeed, to make matters worse, he places it on his head, the most sacred and vulnerable part of the body.

In another oral version of the Vilaṅga story, Cāmadevī makes a gift of betel to Vilaṅga following his herculean spear throw from Mount Suthēp but the queen secretly smears menstrual blood on the betel leaves. When Vilaṅga chews the betel it has the same affect as wearing the hat made from Cāmadevī's undergarment. From this episode she acquired the name Jao Mae Bai Phlū (Mother Betel Leaf) and is venerated as the guardian spirit of betel.[40]

In the CDV the dealings of the Milakkha chieftain with Haripuñjaya are mediated through Cāmadevī's two sons; an alliance between Haripuñjaya and the Milakkha is created by intermarriage. The marriage between the twin Milakkha princesses and Cāmadevī's twin sons mirrors the symmetry of the twin cities, Haripuñjaya and Khelāṅga, and the residence of the sage, Subrahma, who lives on Twin Peak Mountain near Khelāṅga. Perhaps Bodhiraṃsi thought that to incorporate the lore of the Cāmadevī-Vilaṅga relationship into his retelling of the story of Queen Cāma would undermine the homologic symmetry he was trying to construct. Or, perhaps, as a pious monk he found the ribald humor of the folk legend with its overt sexuality problematical. In his recounting of King Ādittarāja's discovery of the Buddha relic buried beneath the king's toilet, Bodhiraṃsi may have felt that he had already stretched the limits of Buddhist monastic propriety. He may even have been unaware of this episode, although that seems highly unlikely. It is more probable that he thought its inclusion would diminish Cāmadevī's queenly stature.

Basic to the CDV's symmetry is the parallelism between the Cāmadevī-*isi* and the Ādittarāja-Buddha relic strands of the story. This parallelism may have resulted from the way in which Bodhiraṃsi integrated the two stories, an integration that may have occurred in earlier sources. But Bodhiraṃsi's brilliance lies precisely in the mimetic manner in which he overlaps the two motifs as two sides of the same story. In his account, the journeys of both the Buddha and Cāmadevī to Haripuñjaya have a similar purpose—to plant seeds in the form of *dhātu* (relic) and *bīja* (lineage). Both the Buddha and Cāmadevī bring seeds with them, in Cāmadevī's case the two fetuses in her womb; in the case of the Buddha a part of his bodily person. In the beginning, their respective seeds are latent. Cāmadevī's seed matures or becomes manifest seven days after her arrival in the birth of two sons who represent the beginning of the Cāmadevī lineage; the appearance of Buddha's seed, his relic and the enhanced symbiosis between Buddha and king that the royal *cetiya* represents, awaits the auspicious arrival of Ādittarāja. This mimetic parallelism between the Buddha and Cāmadevī in relationship to the origin of Haripuñjaya (literally, the "golden mound/mountain") reflects two very early constructions of the *cetiya*: (i) as a *dhātu-gabbha* (Sinhalese, *dagäba*) or relic-womb, and (ii) the body of the Buddha, which is at the same time the body of the cosmos.

How does such an analysis relate to Bodhiraṃsi's decision to omit the Cāmadevī-Vilaṅga episode from his narrative? In my view he did so not because the Mahāthera was too prudish, but rather because Cāmadevī's sexuality would have been profaned. For Bodhiraṃsi the bodies of both Queen Cāma and the Buddha reflect parallel sacralities; both Cāmadevī and the Buddha bequeath their bodies or portions of them to Haripuñjaya and in so doing ensure that this Golden Mount City (Hari-puñja) will be prosperous and endure.

(ii)

Cāmadevī emerges from the pages of the CDV in two quite different ways when seen in terms of modern-day Lamphūn, on the one hand, and contemporary constructions of Buddhist women and feminine gender, on the other. A thriving cult has developed in Lamphūn around the statue of Cāmadevī. Day and night dozens of devotees—Lamphūn citizenry, visitors, and tourists—present offerings of flowers, candles, and incense and respectfully kneel before Cāmadevī's heroic, standing image much as devotees venerate the image of the Buddha. Queen Cāma has become, in effect, the guardian deity of Lamphūn in a manner similar to that of Rama V (King Chulalongkorn), who since 1990 has emerged as the guardian deity of the nation. Just as the statue of Cāmadevī in Lamphūn serves as the focus of a new northern Thai cult, so the equestrian statue of Rama V located near the parliament building in Bangkok has become the center of a national cult. Royal cults are not new to Thai culture but their resurgent vigor suggests both the loss and the transformation of traditional religio-cultural values associated with Buddhism and Brahmanical cults of the city guardian spirit (Thai: *lak mu'ang*). This transformation comes at a time of rapid social change occurring in tandem with Thailand's dramatic economic transformation from an agricultural nation of small farmers to its place among the Asian NICs (Newly Industrialized Country) together with Singapore, Taiwan, and South Korea.

Veneration of Cāmadevī's statue goes beyond merely honoring the memory of an important ruler. As Buddha images are believed to re-present the person of the Buddha as well as his teaching (*dhamma*), so the Cāmadevī statue embodies her spirit.[41] Miraculous powers attributed to her statue were manifested even during its construction. The Sukhōthai sculptor who made the statue claims that the complete picture of the image appeared to him while he was meditating; that during the construction of the statue, the sculptor, his wife, and friends heard ancient northern Thai music; that his business increased dramatically from the time he began building the statue; that the unprotected hands of the monk who performed the ceremonial first bronze pouring were neither burned nor blistered; and that prior to transporting the statue to be installed, Cāmadevī appeared to him in a dream and said that she was returning to the place she had previously ruled.[42] The expectations of the devotees who make offerings at the Cāmadevī statue correspond to the miraculous signs that accompanied its construction—in particular, material success and protection from danger.

Another feature of the Cāmadevī cult borrows from Thailand's rich shamanistic traditions of spirit possession. Most shamans are women, although men are not excluded. In 1994 a former television star, Duangchīwan Komonsen, became the *rāng song* (the vessel, recipient, form) for the spirit of Cāmadevī. As a nationally known celebrity who developed a cultic practice as a *rāng song* for Cāmadevī, she has garnered substantial media attention in numerous magazine articles and interviews. Duangchīwan was observed and interviewed while possessed by the spirit Cāmadevī, and photographed in the Cāmadevī attire she

Fig. 2 Statue of Cāmadevī at Lamphūn

wears when she performs the *pūja* ritual prior to being entered by the spirit of Queen Cāma. Duangchīwan Komonsen and her devotees accept without question the historicity of Cāmadevī and fervently believe that her protective spirit continues to be present in Lamphūn.

(iii)

Within the emerging field of Buddhist feminist writing and studies of Buddhist women, Cāmadevī deserves to be counted among the noted exemplars in the Buddhist tradition. A substantial literature in this field has emerged, although the focus has been primarily women renunciants.[43] Alan Sponberg surveys a wide range of Indian Buddhist texts to determine attitudes toward women and the feminine in early Buddhism.[44] He sees four different constructions that he believes represent a rough chronological development ranging from soteriological inclusiveness found in the *Therīgāthā* to institutional androcentrism (for example, the story of the founding of the nun's order), and ascetic misogyny illustrated by selections from the Pāli *suttas*, to the soteriologic androgyny in Indian Tantrism. In general terms Sponberg contends that the early Indian Buddhist tradition acknowledged gender differences but rendered them as soteriologically insignificant (i.e., soteriological inclusiveness). As the Buddhist movement grew and cenobitic monastic traditions became the norm, women's renunciant lives became more regulated and subordinated to men (i.e., institutional androcentrism). As class and caste differences came to be determined by constructions of purity and pollution, women were defined by men as a threat to the purity of the male monastic vocation (i.e., ascetic misogyny). Finally, in the Vajrayāna tradition Sponberg finds that gender differences become insignificant relative to the salvific goal, and that ultimately they are perceived as unreal or mutually complimentary (i.e., soteriological androgyny). As valuable as it is, by focusing exclusively on women renunciants and the pursuit of Buddhism's ultimate, salvific goal, Sponberg's typological construction omits other women's roles.

New studies by historians, feminists, and anthropologists have expanded the range of consideration. Nancy Auer Falk has done a comparative study of the exemplary lay supporters of the early Buddhist *saṅgha,* Visākhā and Anāthapiṇḍika;[45] Rita M. Gross has written a wide-ranging Buddhist-feminist interpretation of the tradition;[46] and the increasing number of books and articles by Buddhist women or about women and Buddhism has prompted Karma Lekshe Tsomo to edit a forthcoming volume with the title, *The Feminization of Buddhism.*[47] Several studies of Thai Buddhism and women have appeared including descriptions of women renunciants, lay women meditation teachers, and the role of lay women in village Buddhism.[48]

Thomas A. Kirsch and Charles F. Keyes explore the relationship between Buddhism and women from a different perspective, namely, the cultural construction of women in Thailand.[49] In general terms Kirsch argues that the Thai Buddhist worldview constrains women to be more worldly and more attached than men to the realm of desire that impedes the attainment of salvation. Within the Thai context Buddhism, according to Kirsch, has not only failed to elevate women but has diminished them. Keyes takes the opposite view. Based on his analysis of three different texts—an ordination sermon, Lao courting poetry, and the *Vessantara Jātaka*—Keyes contends that women are seen as having a greater sensitivity to suffering and, hence, a greater natural propensity to overcome suffering and attachment, that is, to realize *nibbāna*.

Within the context of the contemporary discussion of women and Buddhism Queen Cāma represents an exemplary model of social responsibility and bold political leadership.[50] As seen within the narrative, she accepts the risk of political leadership in a new place rather than remain within the secure comfort of the familiar. Of all the several journeys recounted in the story, hers is the greatest adventure, an arduous trip of seven months from the cultured setting of Lopburī to the relative unknown of Haripuñjaya. In the social sphere she is an exemplary mother encouraging her sons to be as independent as herself and to assume the responsibilities of political authority. She is, furthermore, an appreciative friend, open in her gratitude for the guidance and help of Vāsudeva. In all spheres she is an exemplar of lay Buddhist practice by supporting the *saṅgha*, giving generously of her material wealth to build monasteries, studying the *Buddhadhamma* and striving to put these teachings, especially the Ten Royal Virtues (*dasarājadhamma*), into practice. To be sure, the CDV paints an idealized portrait of Cāmadevī as one who exemplifies the paradigmatic Buddhist ruler and layperson, but it is precisely this ideal that Bodhiraṃsi wishes to uplift as a model for both royalty and Buddhist laity of all classes.

In a more subtle way, the CDV celebrates Queen Cāma's gender. Here is not an ascetic denial of the body but an acknowledgment of the body as the very medium through which the ruling lineage will be established. Even more remarkable, the CDV superimposes the templates of the Cāmadevī and Buddha stories: both make long journeys to an unknown destination to create a civilized and peaceful place where all could live, prosper, and achieve both material and spiritual well-being; furthermore, both of them do so by means of their actual, living bodies. This is not an abstract or theoretical vision of Buddhism. Rather, the CDV offers a Buddhism-in-place brought by both the Buddha and Nāng Cāmadevī, one of the most remarkable women in the history of northern Thai Buddhism. As Bodhiraṃsi admonished his audience, "listen well to her story."

NOTES TO PART I

1. Sanong Waraurai, *Phrarāchachīwaprawat Phramaejaojāmadevī Boromarāchanārī Sīsuriyawong Ongpatinat Pindhānībaribunchai* [The royal history of the lord mother queen Cāma, supreme royal woman, lineage of the sun, sovereign of the unsurpassed capital of Haripuñjaya] (Sanpātong: Dantanakorn Museum, 1982). Sanong Waraurai is an Associate Professor in the Department of Biology, Faculty of Science, Chiang Mai University, 74.

2. Ibid., 74–78.

3. Charnvit Kasetsiri, *The Rise of Ayudhya: A History of Siam in the Fourteenth and Fifteenth Centuries* (Oxford and Kuala Lumpur: Oxford University Press, 1976), 1.

4. Ibid.

5. Ibid., 9.

6. Ibid., 3.

7. David K. Wyatt, "Chronicle Traditions in Thai Historiography," in *Southeast Asian History and Historiography: Essays Presented to D. G. E. Hall,* ed. C. D. Cowan and O. W. Wolters (Ithaca, N.Y.: Cornell University Press, 1976), 107–22.

8. 657 C.E. in the PY.

9. 1043 C.E. in the PY.

10. George Coedès, *Documents sur l'Histoire Politique et Religieuse du Laos Occidental,* 13. "It is a kind of epic poem intermixed with moral reflections, and the facts are drowned in interminable verbiage." Despite Coedès's prodigious knowledge he fails to recognize the significance of the mythic and legendary elements of the chronicle.

11. *Paññāsajātaka,* [Fifty jātaka stories] 2 vols. (Bangkok: National Library, 1945 [2488 B.E.]). I. B. Horner and Padmanabh S. Jaini, *Apocryphal Birth-Stories (Paññāsa-Jātaka),* 2 vols., Sacred Books of the Buddhists, vol. 38 and 39 (London: Pali Text Society, 1985–1986).

12. These more comprehensive legends are also known by two other titles, *Tamnān Phrabat Phrathāt* [The chronicle of the Buddha's footprints and relics] and simply *Phuttha Tamnān* [Buddha chronicle]. Although no one to date has done a close, critical reading of these texts, Hans Penth considers them to be essentially the same basic text. Colo-

phons in palm-leaf manuscripts of both the *Phrajao Liap Lōk* and *Phuttha Tamnān* record the earliest transcriptions in northern Thailand in the late fifteenth century (Katanyoo Chucheun, *Phrajao Liap Lōk Lān Nā: Botwikhrǫ* [An analysis of the northern Thai phrajao liap lōk] (Bangkok: Silapakorn University, 1982).

13. Singkha Wannasai, *Tamnān Phrathāt Jao Haripuñjaya* [The chronicle of the Haripuñjaya relic] (Chiang Mai: Thailand, 1973).

14. See Sherry B. Ortner, "So *Is* Female to Male as Nature Is to Culture?," in *Making Gender: The Politics and Erotics of Culture* (Boston: Beacon, 1996).

15. Although the narrative focuses on a bodily relic of the Buddha, the story provides a window to popular beliefs regarding the widespread veneration of the three categories of relics in Theravāda Buddhism: bodily relics; relics of use, such as, alms bowl; relics of association, such as a Buddha image.

16. For an introduction to various interpretations on this subject, see Donald K. Swearer, *The Buddhist World of Southeast Asia* (Albany: State University of New York Press, 1995). See also, Stanley J. Tambiah, *World Conqueror and World Renouncer: A Study of Buddhism and Polity in Thailand against a Historical Background* (Cambridge: Cambridge University Press, 1976).

17. In general terms there are two types of *phuttha tamnān*: an inclusive type and a localized type. Both center on the visit of the Buddha to northern Thailand but the first type includes a comprehensive itinerary of sites whereas the second focuses on the founding of a particular site. The purpose of the Buddha's visit is to connnect the actual person of the Buddha with the emplacement of relics and images.

18. For a discussion of the ambivalent attitudes toward kingship in Buddhist *avadāna* literature, see John S. Strong, *The Legend of King Aśoka: A Study and Translation of the Aśoka Avadāna* (Princeton, N.J.: Princeton University Press, 1983).

19. For a fuller analysis of the role of the *ājān wat* see, Donald K. Swearer, "The Layman *Extraordinaire* in Northern Thai Buddhism," *Journal of the Siam Society* 64, no. 1 (January 1976): 151–68.

20. For a similar observation about Buddhism in Sri Lanka, see Richard Gombrich, *Precept and Practice: Traditional Buddhism in the Rural Highlands of Ceylon* (Oxford: Clarendon, 1971).

21. For a discussion of the hierarchial authority of deities in Sri Lanka, see Gananath Obeyesekere, "The Buddhist Pantheon in Ceylon and Its Extensions," in *Anthropological Studies in Theravada Buddhism*, Cultural Report Series no. 13 (Yale University: Southeast Asia Studies, 1966), 1–26. For Burmese spirit cults, see Melford E. Spiro, *Burmese*

Supernaturalism: A Study in the Explanation and Reduction of Suffering (Englewood Cliffs, N.J.: Prentice-Hall, 1967), chap. 3.

22. See Nicola Tannenbaum, *Who Can Compete Against the World? Power-Protection and Buddhism in Shan Worldview,* Monograph and Occasional Paper Series, no. 51 (Ann Arbor: Association for Asian Studies, 1995) for a study of the apotropaic nature of Buddhism among the Shans of northern Thailand. On apotropaism in Burmese Buddhism, see Melford E. Spiro, *Buddhism and Society: A Great Tradition and Its Burmese Vicissitudes,* 2d ed. (Berkeley: University of California Press, 1982).

23. Kraisri Nimmanahaeminda, "The Lawa Guardian Spirits of Chiengmai," *Journal of the Siam Society,* 55, part 2 (July 1967): 185–95.

24. Coedès, *Documents sur l'Histoire Politique et Religieuse du Laos Occidental,* 15.

25. Ibid., 15–16. (Coedès refers to M. P. Lefevre-Pontalis, "l'invasion thaïe en Indochine," *T'oung Pao,* 1909: 495–507.)

26. Ibid., 16.

27. Ibid., 17. [See also George Coedès, *Prachum Silājārœk Phak Thī 2 (Recueil des Inscriptions du Siam Deuxième Partie)* (Bangkok: Siam Society, 1961].

28. Ibid.

29. Ibid.

30. Ibid., 18.

31. Hans Penth, "Kānsamruat Lae Wichai Chāru'k 1.2.1.1 Chulagirī B.S. 2097, C.E. 1554" [An investigation of inscription 1.2.1.1 on Doi Noi Hill Dated 1544 C.E.], *Silapākorn* 28, no. 6 (January 1985/2528 B.E.): 20–26.

32. See the following works by Charles Archaimbault: "L'histoire de Champasak," *Journal Asiatique* 249, no. 4 (1961): 519–95; "La naissance du monde selon les traditions lao," in *Structures Religieuses Lao: (Rites et Mythes),* vol. 2 of Documents Pour Le Laos (Vientiane, Laos: Editions Vithagna, 1973); "Le cycle de Nang Oua-Nang Malong et son substrat sociologique," *France-Asie,* no. 170 (novembre–decembre 1961): 187–200; *The New Year Ceremony at Basak (South Laos),* trans. Simone B. Boas, Southeast Asia Data Paper, no. 78 (Ithaca: Cornell University Southeast Asia Program, 1971).

33. See François Bizot, *Les traditions de la pabbajjā en Asie du Sud-Est: Recherches sur le bouddhisme khmer, iv,* Philogisch-Historische Klasse Dritte Folge, no. 169 (Göttingen: Vandenhoeck & Ruprecht, 1988), chap. 5.

34. Phrayā Prachākitkorajak, *Phongsāwadān Yōnok* [The Yōnok chronicle] (first printing 1898–99; Bangkok: Rungwattanā, 1972/2515 B.E.).

35. Camille Notton, *Chronique de La:p'un,* 29. The episode in the TM is virtually identical, which suggests a common source.

36. Because there appears to be a missing chapter in all known palm-leaf manuscripts of the *Cāmadevīvaṃsa* precisely at that point in the narrative where Vilaṅga's pursuit of Queen Cāma's hand in marriage would have occurred, it is possible that at a later time the ebb and flow of sectarian sentiment led to censorship.

37. Notton, *Chronique de La:p'un*, 59. Kraisri Nimmanahaeminda, "The Romance of Khun Luang Viranga" (private copy presented to the author, n.p., n.d.). My account follows Nimmanahaeminda.

38. This account follows Nimmanahaeminda. In the TML alternative account Vilaṅga is not killed and continues to wage guerrilla warfare. The author says that he took the story from the *Dhamma Desanā Sāsanā* whose title suggests that it was a book of sermons.

39. Donald K. Swearer, *Wat Haripuñjaya: A Study of the Royal Temple of the Buddha's Relic, Lamphun, Thailand,* American Academy of Religion Studies in Religion, no. 10 (Missoula, Mont.: Scholars Press, 1976). For a comprehensive analysis of taboos surrounding menstruation see, Mary Douglas, *Purity and Danger: An Analysis of the Concepts of Pollution and Taboo* (1966; reprint, London and Henley: Routledge & Kegan Paul, 1979).

40. Mani Phayọmyong, interview by author, Chiang Mai, Thailand, 5 January 1996.

41. For a discussion of the Buddha image consecration ritual in northern Thailand that empowers or brings the image to life in the eye-opening ritual see, Donald K. Swearer, "Hypostasizing the Buddha: Buddha Image Consecration in Northern Thailand," *History of Religions*, 34, no. 3 (February 1995): 263–80.

42. "Chāng Pan-Lo Phra Rūp Phra Māe Cāmadevī" [The sculptor who made Phra Mae Cāmadevī] *Silālaksana* (popular magazine published in Thailand) vol. 20:169 (April 1995): 76–77.

43. For example see, Susan Murcott, *The First Buddhist Women* (Berkeley, Calif.: Parallax, 1991).

44. Alan Sponberg, "Attitudes Toward Women and the Feminine in Early Buddhism," in *Buddhism, Sexuality, and Gender*, ed. José Cabezón (Albany: State University of New York Press, 1992): 3–36.

45. Nancy Auer Falk, "Exemplary Donors of the Pāli Tradition," in *Ethics, Wealth, and Salvation: A Study in Buddhist Social Ethics*, ed. Russell F. Sizemore and Donald K. Swearer (Columbia: University of South Carolina Press, 1990): 124–43.

46. Rita M. Gross, *Buddhism After Patriarchy* (Albany: State University of New York Press, 1992).

47. For other books on Buddhism, women, and the feminine, see Tessa Bartholomeusz, *Women Under the Bo Tree: Buddhist Nuns in Sri*

Lanka (Cambridge: Cambridge University Press, 1994); Anne Klein, *Meeting the Great Bliss Queen: Buddhists, Feminists, and the Art of the Self* (Boston: Beacon, 1994); Miranda Shaw, *Passionate Enlightenment* (Princeton, N.J.: Princeton University Press, 1994); Karma Lekshe Tsomo, *Sisters in Solitude: Two Traditions of Buddhist Monastic Ethics for Women* (Albany: State University of New York Press, 1996); Janice W. Willis, *Enlightened Beings: Life Stories from the Ganden Oral Tradition* (Boston: Wisdom Publications, 1995).

48. See Chatsumarn Kabilsingh, *Thai Women and Buddhism* (Berkeley: Parallax, 1991) and Penny Van Esterik, ed., *Women of Southeast Asia,* Monograph Series on Southeast Asia, Occasional Paper no. 17 (DeKalb: Northern Illinois University Center for Southeast Asian Studies, 1996).

49. Thomas A. Kirsch, "Buddhism, Sex Roles and the Thai Economy," in *Women of Southeast Asia,* ed. Penny Van Esterick, 16–41; Thomas A. Kirsch, "Text and Context: Buddhist Sex Roles/Culture of Gender Revisited," *American Enthnologist,* 12, no. 2 (May 1985): 302–20; Charles F. Keyes, "Mother, Mistress, But Never a Monk: Buddhist Notions of Female Gender in Rural Thailand," *American Ethnologist* 11, no. 2 (May 1984): 223–41. Other voices in the cultural debate regarding Buddhism and women in Thailand include Khin Thitsa, *Providence and Prostitution: Image and Reality for Women in Buddhist Thailand* (London: Change International Reports, 1980); Marjorie Muecke, "Mother Sold Food, Daughter Sells Her Body: The Cultural Continuity of Prostitution," *Social Science Medicine* 35, no. 7 (1992): 891–901.

50. For other Buddhist royal feminine exemplars, see Alex Wayman and Hideiko Wayman, *The Lion's Roar of Queen Srimala* (New York: Columbia University Press, 1974), and the selection on the Empress Wu in Diana Y. Paul, *Women in Buddhism: Images of the Feminine in Mahayana Buddhism* (Berkeley, Calif.: Asian Humanities Press, 1979).

PART II

THE *CĀMADEVĪVAṂSA*

CHAPTER 1

THE BUDDHA'S PROPHECY

I pay homage to the Conqueror who is in the lineage of the sun, the greatest of all human beings, whose body is like a gemstone emitting glittering rays for two meters in all directions.[1]

I pay homage to the Dhamma which is profound, subtle, as difficult to perceive as seeds of lettuce under Mount Sineru.[2] [I pay homage] to that noble Dhamma which is complex in meaning and practiced by the sages.

I pay homage to the Saṅgha, the disciples of the Buddha who are virtuous, well trained, with guarded senses, nonattached, worthy of offerings and hospitality.

Having paid homage to the Triple Gem, to the [Buddha's] relics in all places and to the noble *bodhi* tree, I am protected from danger everywhere I go.[3]

By the power of the Triple Gem may all danger be dispelled. Having eliminated [these] dangers, I shall now translate [this] story (*cāritaṃ*).[4]

Among all the kingdoms, Haripuñjaya, the kingdom (*nagaraṃ*) where the Buddha's relics appeared, is the most glorious. In this kingdom can be found all kinds of precious gemstones,[5] many races,[6] and all the necessities and luxuries of life. It is as splendid as the abode of the gods.

Because the [vernacular] language of the scholar who wrote this story is inferior and unsuitable for Buddhist city dwellers, I shall translate it into Pāli, into lines and stanzas so delightful to hear that it will engage the mind, and kindle the interest of [both] men and women.[7] Therefore, let all people listen respectfully to me as I relate this tale.

Once upon a time our Blessed One resided in the Isipatana Deer Park near Vārāṇasī observing the four postures. What are the four postures?[8] The four postures are: standing, walking, sitting, and lying down.[9] Furthermore, while the Buddha resided [there], he engaged in other activities.

The writer of the text explained these activities of the Buddha as follows: "going forth for morning alms (*piṇḍapātaṃ*), preaching (*dhammadesanaṃ*) in the late afternoon, instructing the *bhikkhus* in the evening, solving the problems of the gods (*devapañhakaṃ*) at midnight, and near sunrise cogitating on whether or not human beings are capable of being trained [in the Dhamma]."[10] Such is the work of the Noble Sage (*munipuṅgavo*).

Once upon a time, while the Conqueror (*jina*) was surveying the world with his divine eye, he observed the residents of a Mon village (*meṅgaputta*) called Jarohagāma[11] wandering about in a great forest. They appeared in the net of the Buddha's divine eye (*ñāṇajāla-paviṭṭhāna*) as worthy to receive his teaching.

When the Conqueror awoke he performed his morning ablutions, took his alms bowl and yellow robes, flew through the air, and descended into the forest. There he sat down in the shade of a *davāla* tree located between the two villages of Kontagāma and Jarohagāma. Therefore, the inhabitants called that place Mānadavāna. Approaching the base of a tree, the Buddha hung his alms bowl on a branch and put on his yellow robes. Taking his alms bowl in one hand and his walking stick in the other, the Enlightened One embarked on a journey to the village to receive alms.

When the Mon, who were hunters and gatherers,[12] saw the Buddha approach—resplendent in form, handsome, with a radiant visage, unlike anyone they had ever seen before—they were overcome with joy and happiness. They gathered around him at that place and asked the Blessed One, "Who are you? Are you a divine being (*devo*), a heavenly musician (*gandhabbo*), the god Sakka [Indra], a serpent (*nāgo*), or a demon (*rakkhaso*)? Who are you? Whose son are you? Will you tell us who you are?[13]

Upon hearing the Mons' questions, the Blessed One (*bhagavā*), supreme among human and divine beings, opened his mouth from which pleasing fragrances issued forth,[14] and spoke to the Mon in the Brahma voice of eight characteristics:[15] "I am not a *deva*, nor a *gandhabba*, nor Sakka, nor a *nāga*, nor a *rakkhasa*. I am the Omniscient One, the Enlightened One (*sabbaññūbuddho*), the son of King Suddhodana, worshipped by all *devas*. O Mon, know that this is who I am."

All the Mon, both men and women, having been instructed by the Buddha, expressed their faith in the Blessed One saying, "*Buddho, Buddho*," and gave alms to him. After that they respectfully paid homage to the Buddha and said to the Blessed One, "O Enlightened Lord Buddha, from where did you come?"

The World Savior (*lokanātha*),[16] supreme among all beings in the world, opened his sweet smelling mouth and spoke in a Brahma-like voice, "O Mon [friends] who wander in the forest,[17] I traveled from the city of Vārāṇasī, a great distance from here."

The Mon asked, "O Blessed One, [if] your journey was so very long, then why did you come here?"[18]

The Buddha replied, "The *tathāgata* came here for your welfare. The way from this place[19] to the north is not that far. A Mon [village] is [already] there and in the future will be the site of a large city. When I reach my *parinibbāna*, [I predict] that the Mon will divide my bodily relics among all their towns. One relic will appear in that city [Haripuñjaya]. I came here to see if this place is [also] suitable [for a relic]."[20]

The Mon said to the Buddha, "O Blessed One (*sādhu bhante*) your words are most excellent. We are as ignorant[21] as deer in the forest. By your compassion (*anukampituṃ*) may the Blessed One preach the Dhamma to us for our welfare."

The Blessed One, perceiving their confused state of mind, preached his *dhamma* (*dhammaṃ sapurisagatiṃ*) in a manner appropriate (*yathānurūpaṃ*) [to their level of understanding]: "Support [your] parents; respect the elders in the family; speak politely; do not steal; in the morning and the evening venerate the Buddha, the *dhamma*, and the *saṅgha*; do not speak in a demeaning manner.[22] If you follow my teachings you will be reborn in the realm of the divine beings (*devaloke*)."

After the Blessed One preached his *dhamma* to the Mon, he then gave them the five precepts, saying, "Refrain from taking life, from stealing, from adultery, from lying, and from intoxicants. Accept these meritorious precepts [as the basis of your life]." "*Sādhu,*" acknowledging their assent, the Mon took the precepts, and having bowed before the Blessed One, they stood up.[23]

Then, while the Mon were standing attentively, the *tathāgata* ascended into the air and flew to the north side of the Ping River. At the same time, a white crow who ruled the crow kingdom flew behind the Blessed One.[24] The sons of the forest dwelling Mon (*vanameṅgputtā*) led by the village headman followed the Blessed One along the bank of the river.

The Blessed One, descending to the splendid, densely forested site of the future Haripuñjaya[25] on the west bank of the [Kwang] river, stood at the place where the relics would appear and looked for a place to set down his alms bowl.

At that moment, a square stone slab smooth as a drum about twelve *sǫk*[26] wide arose from the earth near the *tathāgata*'s feet. The Blessed One then placed his alms bowl on the stone, put his robe (*mahāpaṃsukulacīvaraṃ*) over one shoulder, and looked around carefully. As a governor inspects a city in order to protect it, so also the Buddha inspected the site so that the sons of the Mon would remember [the place]. While the Blessed One was so engaged, he spoke to the Mon, "O forest Mon, in the future a great city will appear here and a king named Ādiccarāja [Ādittarāja] will govern it.[27] He will be of your lineage. When I have reached my *parinibbāna* my relics (*sārīrikadhātu*) will appear at this place, and the king will protect them."

Having spoken, the Blessed One took his alms bowl and after putting it in the palm of his hand, it immediately rose into the air and proceeded ahead of the Buddha.[28] The Blessed One then ascended into the air following the alms bowl until he arrived at the Isipatana forest near Vārāṇasī.

As the sons of the forest Mon witnessed this miracle, they marveled at the power (*guṇa*)[29] of the Blessed One, and then returned to their village. The white crow, hearing the words of the Buddha and telling another crow of his intention, appointed [the second crow] to guard the place and then he flew to the Himavanta forest.

The compiler,[30] in order to explain the meaning [of this event] said, "The Enlightened One, endowed with great compassion (*mahākaruṇā*), knows how to tame (*vinayo*) human nature. He discerns the way in which humans can attain happiness and practice the *dhamma*. The Buddha enlightened the sons of the Mon and instructed them in the supermundane and mundane truths (*lokuttara-dhammaṃ, lokiya-dhammaṃ*). Having established them in this noble state, the Conqueror returned to his residence to resume his former activities.

All of the forest-dwelling Mon were overjoyed. Paying homage to the Buddha and being inspired by his teaching, they took leave and returned to their village.

Having overheard the words of the Buddha, the white crow appointed another crow of noble birth to guard the place [where the relic would be found] and flew to the Himavanta mountains.

This is the description of Haripuñjaya composed by the Mahāthera Bodhiraṃsi[31] from his recollection of an important [northern Thai] story (*mahācārikānusārena*).[32]

[The End of the First Chapter of the Buddha's Prophecy]

Chapter 2

VĀSUDEVA AND THE FOUNDING OF MIGASAṄGHANAGARA

Wherever our Blessed One resided, he performed all the activities of a Buddha. After his *parinibbāna*, the *arahanta* monks and ordinary monks who were his disciples also engaged in intense religious practice. They recited the entire *tipiṭaka*, instructed each other, and encouraged everyone to follow the Buddha's teachings.[33]

Once upon a time there were four young men who, in the course of their wanderings, took delight in the Buddha's religion (*Buddhasāsana*). They entered the Order and diligently studied the entire *tipiṭaka*. Knowing the path and its fruit (*magga-phala*),[34] they said to each other: "We have dutifully followed the teachings and observed all the disciplinary rules but these are very difficult tasks. Let us leave the monkhood and become householders for it is a far easier life. We will continue to observe and earnestly uphold (*rakkhāma appamādakaṃ*) the five and the eight precepts. Because of our dedication we will be at peace [with ourselves] and will surely go to heaven (*saggaṃ*)."

The four young men agreed, left the monkhood, and took up the life of laymen. Before long, however, they perceived the [negative] consequences of sensual pleasure (*kāmādīnava*) and grew discontented [with lay life]. They left their homes and went forth to the Himavanta forest as ascetics (*isipabbajjaṃ*). By diligent meditation (*kasiṇaparikammaṃ*), they soon achieved the five higher knowledges (*abhiññā*) and the eight meditative attainments (*samāpatti*).[35]

"What then are the five higher knowledges?" In order to explain their meaning, the [writer of the text] says:[36] "The five higher knowledges which were proclaimed by the Buddha, he who is supreme among sages, are: psychic power (*iddhividhi*), divine ear (*dibbasotaṃ*), telepathy (*paracittavijānanaṃ*), recollection of previous lives (*pubbenivāsānussati*), and divine eye (*dibbacakkhu*)."[37]

"What are the eight meditative attainments?" "The eight meditative attainments proclaimed by the [supreme] sage are: the first absorption (*paṭhama-jhānaṃ*), the second absorption, the third absorption, the fourth absorption, the sphere of infinite space, the sphere of infinite consciousness, the sphere of nothingness, [the sphere of neither perception nor non-perception (*nevasaññānāsaññāyatana*)]."[38]

Then the four sages returned to the world (*patilabbhanti nu loke*) where they engaged in meditation (*jhānakīla*) and ate only tree roots and fruit. Before long, they began to crave foods with salty and sour flavors[39] so they came down from the Himavanta mountains.

4 sages 4 mts One [of them] resided on the top of Sugar Cane Mountain (*ucchupabbatamuddhani*). He was known as Vāsudeva. Another sage named Brahma dwelt on Twin Peak (*dvidhagga*) Mountain. A third, Sajjanāleyya by name, dwelt on Creeper Vine (*latāṅga*) Mountain. A fourth, the wise and able Sukkadanta, lived on Righteous (*dhammika*) Mountain and ruled the city of Lavo.[40]

Those sages were endowed with supernatural powers and enjoyed the bliss of higher states of consciousness (*jhāna*).[41] The sage Vāsudeva descended to the foot of the mountain and looking in all directions saw many animals such as elephants, rhinoceros, wild cattle, and antelope deer fighting and playing with one another. They frolicked about from the bottom of the hill to the river. The sage followed the footprints of the animals as they appeared in various places. He saw four pairs of boys and girls in the footprints, born spontaneously by the power of their previous deeds (*kammaja upapātikaṃ*).[42] The sage took the children to his residence where he raised them. After they had grown up, he united the couple born in the elephant's footprint as husband and wife as well as those born in the footprints of the rhinoceros, cow, and buffalo. Later they became the sage's attendants.[43]

Once upon a time a doe chanced to drink the sperm-infused urine of the hermit and consequently became pregnant. Having reached term (*paripuṇṇe*), she gave birth to twins, a boy and a girl. Upon seeing the pair, Vāsudeva took them [to his hermitage] where he raised them. They soon developed into a handsome couple. The sage named them Aṅgurisi and Migūpatī and arranged for them to become husband and wife. They are regarded as of the lineage of Vāsudeva.

Those who have never heard the *dhamma* will find it difficult to believe this story.[44] Only the wise can make sense of such a tale. It is similar to the Isisiṅga Jātaka wherein a hermit is born in the womb of a deer, [or the story of] Saṅka, the queen of Vārāṇasī, who was born in a lotus bud.[45] These stories were told by the Enlightened One.

Having built a city near the foot of the mountain for their residence, the hermit consecrated Aṅgurisi and Migūpatī as king and queen. Their retinue consisted of those [other twins] who were born in the animal footprints.[46] He also arranged for the Mon to live with them. Hence, that region was called Migasaṅghanagara (City of the Deer Herd) because deer lived there.[47]

The pair lived together with their four children, three boys and a girl. The eldest among them was named Kunarikanāsa (Prince Overwhelming). Why was he called Kunarikanāsa? The king, it is said, conquered many people on the day the prince was born; therefore, at the naming ceremony the people gave him the name Kunarikanāsa [Kumārakanāsa?].[48]

His younger brother was called Kunarikadhaṃsa (Prince Destroying). Why was he so named? On the day this prince was born, the king destroyed all evildoers; therefore, on the day of his naming ceremony the people gave him the name, Kunarikadhaṃsa [Kumārakadhaṃsa?].

The third was called Kunarikarosa (Prince Anger). Why was he given this name? On the day the prince was born the king became angry and threatened scoundrels; therefore, on the day of the naming ceremony the people gave him the name, Kunarikarosa [Kumārakakodha?].

The youngest child was known as Padumadevī (Princess Lotus Flower). Why was she given this name? On the day the princess was born, people brought a large bouquet of lotus flowers (*paduma*). Therefore, on the day of the naming ceremony, the people gave her the name, Padumadevī. When Padumadevī came of age (*vayappattā*) she was married to the eldest prince, Kunarikanāsa.[49]

King Aṅgurisi ruled for thirty years before he passed away. Vāsudeva presided over the funeral ceremony for him and then consecrated Kunarikanāsa, his grandson, as the king of Migasaṅghanagara with Padumadevī as queen.

At that time Vāsudeva thought, "The appellation, Herd of Animals, (*migasaṅgha*) is an inauspicious name for a city." For this reason, the hermit built another city to the east of Migasaṅghanagara and consecrated Kunarikadhaṃsa to rule there. That city was known as Purinagara [Īsinagara?] because it was built by the sage (*isi*).[50]

In addition, the hermit built a third city not far from Migasaṅghanagara in the northeast and consecrated Kunarikarosa to rule it. It was known as Avidūranagara because it was located nearby (*avidūra*).

Afterward, the hermit thought, "The city of Migasaṅgha is neither level nor beautiful. I will look for a level region and if I am successful I shall build a city there." While contemplating this matter, he envisioned a flat area to the south where the relics of the Blessed One (*bhagavato dhātussa*) would emerge. There he built a city and consecrated Kunarikanāsa to be its ruler. The city was called Rammanagara (City of Delight) because the place where it was built was so delightful.

In time many people migrated there to live. They succeeded in acquiring wealth and abundant food and were exceedingly happy. In the city there lived a man who was coarse, aggressive, and vicious. He even scolded and rebuked his own mother. Unable to tolerate her son's offensive behavior any longer, the mother went to see Kunarikanāsa. After paying respects to the king, she wept as she told him of her situation.

Then the king said to the woman, "Oh, wretched woman! It is wholly justifiable for a son to strike his mother. A mother, when struck by her son, resonates like a bronze bell (*kaṃsatāla*).[51] What does it matter if a son beats his mother in secret? Why are you crying? Leave at once." All of the officials and ministers agreed with the king.

The woman was bewildered (*appaṭibhāṇā*) and left the palace. Kneeling on the ground, she beat the earth with her fists and said, "O Mother Earth (*ayye basundari*), all living beings reside in you.[52] May you, the celestial beings (*devatā*), and the world guardians (*lokapāla*) know of my plight." Standing up and paying homage to the *devatās*, she returned to her house.

All the *devatās* were united in their anger at the officials. That night a *devatā* appeared to the woman and said, "Tomorrow take all those you love and leave the city. We will destroy this city, along with its king and all the unrighteous people (*adhammikamanussa*), by plunging it under the ground." Saying this, the deity disappeared.

The woman was overjoyed at this [revelation]. That morning she took her loved ones out of the city to live far away. At that very moment the *devatā* caused the whole city to be innundated. Water flooded all of the houses rising to the level of the roof line. All the unrighteous people including King Kunarikanāsa immediately drowned.[53]

The people who lived in the city heard the story and gathered around to witness this event. At this time, Vāsudeva, the great sage, looking with his divine eye saw a large crowd of people. In order to warn them, he traveled by using his supernatural power to where they were. Sitting on a throne in the air, he preached to them the *dhamma* he had learned from the teachings (*vacanānukulaṃ*) of the Blessed One.[54]

This is the truth taught by the Buddha who strove for the welfare of the entire world (*lokahitesinā*), "A person should neither associate with evil friends (*pāpake mitte*) nor unrighteous people (*purisādhamme*) but instead should associate with good friends (*mitte kalyāṇe*) and righteous persons (*purisuttame*). One who associates with evil friends will always suffer; one who associates with good friends will always attain happiness."[55]

"A lazy layperson who enjoys sensual pleasure (*kāmabhogī*) is without virtue as is a monk who is unrestrained (*asaññato*), or a king who does not deliberate carefully prior to performing his duties (*anisammakārī*), or a *pandit* who is subject to anger. Rank and honor (*yaso kittiñca*) will accrue to the king who considers carefully before performing his duties. The *pandit* who is virtuous (*sīlasampanno*) and free from anger will be highly regarded."[56]

The sage taught in this manner in order to convey the Buddha's words to all of the people. After listening to Vāsudeva's teaching, the large assembly gratefully folded their hands in supplication and paid homage to the sage.

Then Vāsudeva made a dire prediction in order to persuade all of them (*sabbesaṃ gaṇhanatthāya*) according to his purpose (*attanādhippāya*): "Disasters will strike a country which is ruled by an evil, obstructive king (*viruddho*[57] *kurājā*), as happened to Nalika Island, the city of Indapattha, and other countries that met with disaster (*vināsaṃ pāpunaṇti*).[58] When an unrighteous, thoughtless king who adheres to the wrong view rules the country, the people who live there will suffer continually."[59]

After the people had heard this prediction, Vāsudeva returned to his residence [by flying] through the air. [As he had predicted], the region was flooded, forming a great lake. From that time forth, it was known as Aṇṇavasīdoramma (Without the Pleasure of Food and Dwelling).

The following day another evil, brutal, aggressive, coarse man in the city of Avidūranagara rebuked and berated his mother. Unable to tolerate this abuse any longer, his mother went to King Kunarikarosa and, weeping, related the incident [to the king]. Because he was unaware that the same thing had happened to his brother, the king replied, "Wretched woman! Why are you crying? Of course, a son beats his mother. Like a bronze bell hanging around the neck of a water buffalo, a mother's [reputation] resounds only when beaten by a son. If a son does not strike [her], how can the sound [i.e., reputation] be heard? This is a universally held view (*sabbalokavinicchеyyaṃ*). Why are you complaining?"

That woman was also bewildered (*appaṭibhāṇā*) and left the palace. Kneeling on the ground, she struck the earth with her fist and paid homage to the deities in all directions saying, "*Bhonto, bhonto*! May all celestial beings, world guardians, the powerful Indra, the *devas*, the Lord of Beings (*bhūpati*), and the great hermit with the divine eye [Vāsudeva] look upon me, one who is suffering, helpless, and desperate. I came here seeking help from the king. But the king and his unrighteous ministers (*rājā adhammamaccā ca*) opposed me saying, 'Of course, it is a son's right to beat his mother.' I am utterly speechless. You alone know what is just and unjust." Having spoken in this manner, she returned to her home.

At that time a certain man heard and recalled the behavior of the king's brother. He went to see the king and said, "Your majesty, your brother met with a great misfortune because of his bad judgment. You should not make the same mistake."

Upon hearing this admonition, the king was afraid and asked, "What shall I do?" The clever minister replied, "Your majesty, in this situation we should beseech forgiveness from the great sage, Vāsudeva, our grandfather, with offerings of perfume and flowers and ask him to remove [the consequences of] this offensive act (*viruddhakammaṃ*)."

The king agreed (*sādhu*) [with this advice] and ordered his men to arrange seats outside the verandah of his palace and to prepare offerings of candles, incense, perfume, and flowers. Turning his face toward Sugar Cane Mountain[60] and bowing repeatedly, he uttered the following request, "O Venerable Sir, please forgive me; do not bring misfortune on me (*dosaṃ khamāpetu mā maṃ vināsaṃ pāpetu*).[61] Vāsudeva heard the words of the king by means of his divine ear and thought, "Yesterday I cursed them. As long as they remain blind and unjust, I will not forgive [the people of Avidūranagara]."

All of the deities perceived what was in Vāsudeva's mind. In order to save those who had performed meritorious deeds, they removed the people from the city who had accumulated wealth for the purpose of making merit (*puññakaraṇa-dhanasanniccayaṃ*), together with their belongings.[62] All of the evil people and unrighteous people including the king were swallowed up by [the earth] in a great cataclysm. In this city the king's palace and courtyard became a great lake. The place became known as Yācitarahado [Forgiveness Lake] because the king asked for [Vāsudeva's forgiveness].

Remorseful over the consequences of his action, Vāsudeva taught the Buddha's *dhamma* known as *vilāsadesanā* ("Beautiful Teaching"): "Those who do good will receive good; those who do evil will receive evil. As one sows, so also one reaps.[63] A good man is hard to find; a man who liberates the world is even harder to find. Such a person is not born of a common family. The wise bring happiness to the family in which they are born; the foolish bring only suffering into the family in which they are born."[64]

"There are two kinds of people, evil and righteous (*pāpakādhammā*). The former is violent, harsh, and cruel (*caṇḍā pharusakakkhalā*). They fail to recognize their mother's goodness and beat her. They are like Mittabhindu who, while he was still in his mother's womb, brought disaster on the country, the king, and the people.[65] Previous *kamma* results in bad deeds, which leads to suffering. As a consequence of evil *kamma*, a village is plundered by robbers and a family suffers destruction by fire a thousand times. Wherever an evil man lives, in a village or in a forest, one should avoid him."[66]

This is the description of Haripuñjaya composed by the Mahāthera Bodhiraṃsi from his recollecton of an important [Northern Thai] story (*mahācārikānusārena*).

The End of Chapter Two

CHAPTER 3

THE PLAN FOR BUILDING HARIPUÑJAYA

The *devas, asuras,* and Brahma always came to worship the stone pedestal (*silāpatta*) which arose at the place where the Conqueror put down his alms bowl. Likewise, a group of renowned sages flew repeatedly from the Himālaya[67] mountains to worship the stone pedestal. That site was [later] designated as a repository for the Conqueror's relics.[68]

In addition, Vāsudeva, the renowned *isi* with matted hair (*jaṭāsudharo*), adept in trance meditation (*jhānadhāro*), also flew there to pay respects to the stone pedestal with precious flowers. The sage thought (*vitakkisino*) [to himself], "The noble Buddha prophesized, 'In the future this place will become a large, densely populated, prosperous city. Later, after the *tathāgata* passes away, a portion of my bodily relics will appear in this place.' I resolve to be a disciple of the Sage [the Buddha]. I cannot ignore the prediction of the Conqueror. Where should I build the city? And what friend will assist me in this work?"

While deep in thought, Vāsudeva saw his friend, the sage (*isi*) Sukkadanta, who was endowed with supernatural power and strength (*iddhividhijuti-vikkammabala-samannāgataṃ*), living in the city of Lavo located on the top of Dhammika Mountain. [Thinking to himself] "Sukkadanta, my devoted friend, is endowed with supernatural power, energy, and wisdom (*iddhibala-parakkama-byattipaṭibalaṃ*). He is skilled in all things and will help me complete my work. Who should I send to his residence?"

As Vāsudeva contemplated [this thought], a tree *devatā*[69] who resided in a clump of bamboo located to the northeast perceived Vāsudeva's thoughts and said, "Venerable Sir, I will act as your emissary. Write a letter and send me there."

"Excellent (*sādhu*)," said Vāsudeva. He wrote a letter expressing his wishes and sent it with the *devatā*. The *devatā* went down the Ping River on a clump of bamboo (*saveḷugacchena*) and after one day arrived at the landing of the city of Lavo.[70]

Just at that moment the wise sage, Sukkadanta, descended from the top of the mountain to go down to the river to bathe. When he saw the clump of bamboo he pushed it away with a stick. Even though he did this a second and a third time, still it returned to the same spot.

Then Sukkadanta thought [to himself], "There must be some [meaning] in this."[71] Walking up to the clump of bamboo, he spied the letter and asked, "What is this?" The *devatā* replied, "Venerable Sir, your friend Mahāvāsudeva told me to bring this letter to invite you [to help him build the city of Haripuñjaya predicted by the Buddha]."

Having heard the words of the *devatā* and after reading the letter, Sukkadanta was apprised of Vāsudeva's purpose and said, "*Ambho* (Look here), seven days from now I shall go. You proceed ahead and inform my friend." After saying this, he sent him back. The *devatā* agreed and paying homage to Sukkadanta returned upstream and informed [Vāsudeva]: "Seven days from now your friend, the wise sage (*paṇḍito*) will arrive."

Upon hearing this report, Vāsudeva was as overjoyed as though his wish would come true the very next day. On the seventh day Sukkadanta flew [to Haripuñjaya] by means of his supernatural power (*iddhibalena*) and dwelt in the midst of a pleasant bamboo grove (*veḷugumbassa*) in the Māluva forest.

At the same time the sage [Vāsudeva] used his own supernatural power to create (*nimmitvā*) a divine mansion (*devālayaṃ*). There he established the royal couple (*devañca devitthirūpañca abhinimmitvā*) and paid his respects (*pūjesi*) to them.[72]

We might ask why the sage, Sukkadanta, [decided to help Vāsudeva].[73] In truth (*kira*), on the day the hermit arrived, a *devatā* came that night and granted him a boon (*varaṃ adāsi*). Therefore, Sukkadanta was returning the favor (*guṇa-paccupakārakaṃ*) to the *devatā*. Later that place became known as Udakamañjusara or Mango Lake.

Staying there for one night, the sage arose early in the morning and after performing his ablutions (*sarīrapaṭijagganaṃ katvā*) thought, "At sunrise I will go to the residence of my friend, Vāsudeva." Then he went to Ucchupabbata Mountain [Doi Suthēp]. Likewise, Vāsudeva thought, "At sunrise I will go to the residence of my friend, Sukkadanta," and then he came down from the mountain. They met each other at the midpoint.

At that time Vāsudeva asked Sukkadanta, "O Friend, when did you leave?" Sukkadanta said, "Friend, I started just after sunrise." To this Vāsudeva replied, "So did I."

Thence, Sukkadanta said to Vāsudeva, "My friend, because our supernatural power, distance, and speed is the same (*sama-iddhividhi-sama-vithī-sama-vegasā*), we arrived at the same time at this place halfway from our starting points." Vāsudeva agreed. Both sages spoke to each other as they hovered in mid-air.[74] Since that time, the people have called that place "the midpoint of the ascetics' path (*maggaṃ pabbajitavemajjhaṃ*)."[75]

Vāsudeva invited Sukkadanta to accompany him to the Māluva forest where they stayed one day. The following morning, after finishing their ablutions, they left the forest and went to the stone pedestal where the Buddha put down his alms bowl. After offering flowers, they stood [respectfully beside it]. Then Vāsudeva said to Sukkadanta, "My friend, in the past it is said, our teacher stood at this very spot and prophesized, 'In the future this place will become a great city. When I enter my *parinibbāna*, one of my relics will appear here.' That is why I called you here, my friend, to determine whether or not this site is suitable for the construction of the city."

Sukkadanta said to Vāsudeva, "My friend, first we should dig [in the ground] here to see if a favorable sign (*bhūtanimittaṃ*) appears." After he spoke, Sukkadanta, the great sage, skilled in all the arts (*sabbasippa-kusalatā*), poked the ground with his walking stick. He picked up a clod of earth and, after investigating it, he saw [in it] seven kinds of precious minerals; in another clod he found green charcoal, and in [a third] he discovered both husked and unhusked rice.[76]

Then Vāsudeva said to the wise Sukkadanta, "Friend, we have seen three signs in the clods of earth. What does this mean? Should we build the city [here]?"

Sukkadanta replied, "My friend, this is indeed a suitable place. Our city, moreover, will be ruled by three kinds of kings: one will be endowed with the ten royal virtues (*dasavidharājadhamma-sampanno*);[77] another will be thoroughly evil (*atipāpadhammo*); and the third will be mediocre and unproductive (*majjhimo nipphalo*).[78] When the righteous king rules, the city will be happy (*khemaṃ*), prosperous (*subhikkhaṃ*), and more delightful (*abhirammaṇiyataraṃ*); the Buddha's religion will prosper and grow, and it will have a large, contented, and satisfied population. When the unrighteous king rules, the city will experience famine and more suffering (*dukkhataraṃ*), as if it were consumed by fire. When the mediocre king (*majjhimarājā*) rules, the people will go into decline and the Buddha's religion will vanish (*suññā bhavissanti*)."[79]

Vāsudeva responded saying, "My friend, if this is the case that in happy times the people will be happy and in times of suffering they will suffer, then we should act according to the instructions of our Teacher." Having said this, he spoke the following verses (*gāthā*):

> "Friend, this place is better than any other place because the word of the Buddha is unchangeable (*Buddhassa vacanaṃ viparitaṃ na hoti*).[80] We should build the city because the Buddha intended

(*sambuddhassā adhippāyena*) that his relics [be enshrined] here. Happiness and peace will flourish (*sukhō khemō bhavissati*) in [the city]. If the king is of bad lineage (*kubījo rājā*), we will prevent him from becoming king; we will allow only the king of good lineage to rule. By this means there will be stability and prosperity." The sage, Sukkadanta, agreed, "*Sādhu*."

Both sages entered the forest in order to investigate several other [possible] places. They announced to the tree *devatās*, "*Bhonto rukkhadevatā*, please leave this place because here we intend to build a city." When the tree *devatās* heard Sukkadanta ['s request] they uprooted their tree palace (*rukkhavimānaṃ*) and flew away to live in another region. The site [in the forest] was cleared immediately and leveled as smooth as the surface of a drum.[81]

One decrepit *devatā* trembling from old age (*jarājinnā*), who lived in an old tree called Kākapattakaraṇa, was left behind. This *devatā* went to the residence of the sages and after paying homage to them, said: "Venerable Sirs, endowed with great power and compassion for the world (*mahiddhisampannā lokakaruṇādhikā*), please be kind to me for I am very old and have not long to live. Because my tree is old and without pith and cannot stand for long, I am unable to leave this place. Please allow me to live here for the rest of my life." When the hermits heard the *devatā*'s desperate plea (*anāthavacanaṃ*) they agreed to his request. Having received permission from the sages, the *devatā* returned to his residence. That place became known as *labbhunā* because it was given as a place to live to the *devatā* who was left behind.[82]

Vāsudeva then said to Sukkadanta, the wise and great sage, "Friend, shall we plan the city (*nagarasaṇṭhāna*) in a square or a circle (*maṇḍala*)?"[83] Sukkadanta replied, "Friend, we will make it in the shape of a conch shell (*samuddasaṅkhapattasaṇṭhāna*)."[84] Vāsudeva said, "Where will we get a conch shell?" Sukkadanta said, "Please call your attendant. We will send him to the residence of the great sage, Sajjanāleyya."[85]

Vāsudeva agreed, "*Sādhu*," and called for Gavaya, his attendant. When he came, Sukkadanta said to him, "Gavaya, take this letter and go to the city of Sajjanāleyya and deliver it to the sage, Sajjanāleyya, and relate our message to him." Having spoken, Sukkadanta wrote the following letter: "Friend, we wish to build a new city in the shape of an ocean conch shell. Please find such a shell and bring it to us." Having finished and sealed the letter, he put it in Gavaya's hand and sent him on his way.

Gavaya replied, "*Sādhu*," took the letter and paid homage to the two sages. Then, by their power, he flew to the top of Laṅka Mountain.[86] Paying homage to Sajjanāleyya and giving him the letter, Gavaya related their request to the sage.

Upon hearing this request, Sajjanāleyya was delighted and sent a *hatthīliṅga* bird to remove a large conch shell from the ocean.[87] Soon after sending the bird, the hermit said to Gavaya, the messenger, "Gavaya, first return to my friend and say, 'I have sent a *hatthīliṅga* bird to bring back a conch shell. [When it returns with the shell] I will send it to my friend.'" Agreeing to Sajjanāleyya's request, Gavaya paid homage to him and then returned to inform the two hermits.

The *hatthīliṅga* bird departed and upon reaching the ocean divided the waters into two parts by rapidly beating its wings. Taking an ancient conch shell in its beak, the bird flew back and offered it to Sajjanāleyya, the hermit. Sajjanāleyya said to the elephant-like bird, "Hatthīliṅga, take this conch shell and offer it to my friends, the two sages, Sukkadanta and Vāsudeva, who live on Ucchuka Mountain.

The *hatthīliṅga* bird flew with the conch shell [in its beak] and through the supernatural power of the sages arrived instantly. Giving the shell to them, the bird returned to its home. [In the verses of the compiler:]

> Thereupon, Sajjanāleyya, the hermit, powerful and famous, resided on the top of a mountain near the city of Sajjanāleyya. Having seen his friend's letter, he sent the *hatthīliṅga* bird to fetch a conch shell from the middle of the ocean. The *hatthīliṅga* bird, born from an egg, having two births (*dvijātika*),[88] was very powerful (*iddhibala*). Dividing the waters into two parts by the *jhān*ic power of the hermits, the bird swooped down and picked up a conch shell[89] with its beak. It flew by the hermit's supernatural power and upon arrival gave [the shell] to him. The hermit praised the bird and sent it as an emissary to his friend. Upon the noble bird's arrival, it presented the conch shell to the sages and then returned to its home.

The two hermits placed the conch shell on the ground and pressed it into [the earth]. The impression left retained the shape of the shell with a circumference of 1,550 *byāma* (fathoms).[90] The two hermits then traced around the shell on the ground thereby marking the outline of the city wall (*nagarapākāra*).

All of the elements of the city such as walls, gates, and columns, as well as beautifully designed decorations of flags and long banners flown from portals suddenly appeared as a consequence of the supernatural

Fig. 3 The sages create Haripuñjaya

power of the two sages. Then the two drew a line [in the ground] around the city wall. Suddenly, the ground between the line and the city wall sank and became a deep moat around the city. It was beautiful, filled with water and fragrant lotus flowers of five different colors. Next, other parts of the city [appeared] such as a courtyard, the king's residence (*rājanivesanaṃ*), and palace. [In the words of the compiler of the text:]

> In this way, the two sages, Vāsudeva and Sukkadanta, built a pleasant city with their supernatural power (*nimmitaṃ nagaraṃ rammaṃ*). It consisted of many magnificent elements such as gates, walls, and precious, decorated gateways (*toraṇagghikabhūsita*). The king's high-pinnacled dwelling (*kūṭāgāranivesana*) was as beautiful as a celestial paradise; hence, it was known as Biṅga City. It was most pleasing and impressive.

This description of Haripuñjaya was composed by the Mahāthera Bodhiraṃsi from his recollection of an important [northern Thai] story.

The End of Chapter Three

Chapter 4

CĀMADEVĪ CONSECRATED AS QUEEN OF HARIPUÑJAYA

When the construction of the city was completed, Vāsudeva said to Sukkadanta, "My friend, our city is incomparably beautiful (*ativiya sobhamānaṃ*). Who will rule over it?" Sukkadanta replied, "Venerable Sir, your attendants (*paricārikā*) abound in great number. Among them we shall choose and consecrate (*rājābhisekaṃ*) one to rule the city."

Vāsudeva, the great hermit, then said to Sukkadanta, "My friend, those born of animals (*migajātikā*) are blind, ignorant, unkind, harsh, and obstinate. Because they are predisposed to behave according to their [animal] nature (*sakajātikānuvattigatā*), how can they govern the country?"[91]

"Why do I say this?" Among the animals, some are arrogant and proud (*mānahadayamānathaddhā*) because they were born in the footprint of the elephant;[92] others are crude and rough (*pharusahadayā kakkhalahadayā*) like a rhinoceros because they were born in the footprint of the rhinoceros; some are stupid and brutish (*dandhahadayā garuhadayā*) like a bull because they were born in the footprint of the bull; others are foolish and greedy (*bālahadayā lobhahadayā*) like a cow because they were born in the footprint of the cow; some are deceitful and dishonest (*bahumāyāyahadayā anujuhadayā*) like a deer because they were born in the footprint of the deer; some born as human beings are barbaric (*milakhhkamanussā*) forest people (*vanamanussā*). They do not know the difference between right (*suṭṭhaṃ*) and wrong (*duṭṭhaṃ*), good (*kusalaṃ*) and evil (*akusalaṃ*) because they were born of [primitive] human parents.[93] Therefore, I said to my friend, "These people lack the ability to rule." If there is one of your lineage, please present him to me and we will make him ruler of the city."

Hearing the words of Vāsudeva, the wise hermit, Sukkadanta, laughed and said: "O matted-hair ascetic (*jaṭādhāra*), listen to my words. Please forgive me. I have not actually seen the most excellent offspring [lit. seed] in the world (*bījaṃ uttamaṃ loke*). But if you will pardon my presumption, I shall tell you about such a person."

Having heard Sukkadanta's remarks, Vāsudeva replied, "O friend, you have nothing to fear by speaking candidly. I would never become angry with you even if you were to harm me."[94]

Then Sukkadanta said, "There is a princess of the king of Lavo. She is of good birth, perfect in body, a serious observer of the precepts, and intelligent (*rūpasampannā sīlavantā ca paññavā*). Her name is Cāmadevī. She is known far and wide as a young woman who is endowed with the five feminine charms (*pañcakalyāṇā*).[95] She is beautiful in all respects (*sobhaṇā itthiviggahā*). Her devout husband has become a monk (*saddho pabbajito*). We will ask the king for Cāmadevī and bring her to this city. This virtuous lady will produce a good lineage."[96]

After Sukkadanta had spoken in this manner, Vāsudeva said, "Friend, so be it, but we have no emissary well versed in fine language (*dūto vacanakusalo*). How can we accomplish this?" The wise Sukkadanta said, "Friend, send the young man Gaveyya to go with me to the King of Lavo." Vāsudeva agreed and making Gaveyya [his] emissary directed him to write a letter (*nidānaṃ likhapetvā*). He prepared many gifts for the king of Lavo to be sent with Gaveyya. The young man, accompanied by many boats, traveled downstream along the Ping River. The great sage Sukkadanta flew through air and arrived at the city of Lavo before Gaveyya. Gaveyya, moving by the supernatural power (*iddhibalena*) of the sage, soon reached [the city of Lavo]. Then the great and wise sage, Sukkadanta, instructed Gaveyya to prepare many gifts and, with the young man following behind, entered the palace. Standing respectfully, the sage greeted the king as follows: "Rāja, [I trust that] you [remain] virtuous (*kusalaṃ*)? That you are in good health (*anāmayaṃ*)? That you uphold the ten royal virtues (*cakkavattidhammaṃ*) and protect your kingdom (*raṭṭhaṃ pālesi*)? Are the rural people happy? Is the state united?"[97]

In response to Sukkadanta's questions, the Lavo king replied, "O sage, I am in good health; I uphold the ten royal virtues and protect my kingdom; the rural people are happy and the state is united."

Having replied [to Sukkadanta's questions], the king then asked him, "Venerable Sir, how long did your journey take? Are you in good health? Are you tired? Did you travel a long distance (*dūrepi gacchatha*)?"[98]

The sage replied, "O great king, it took me a long time to travel here but no illness or danger occurred along the way. My friend, Vāsudeva, who resides on the top of Mount Ucchupabbata beyond the river Ping, desiring the well-being of the people, summoned me. Then we built a beautiful and altogether delightful city (*nagaraṃ abhirammataraṃ sobhaṃ*) where the Buddha's relics are to appear. Upon its completion, I came directly here."

The king said, "Venerable Sir, did an emissary accompany you? Did he come with you or with someone else?" Sukkadanta replied, "O *mahārāja,* an emissary was sent by Vāsudeva in order to learn about you. He came with me."

Upon hearing the words of the sage, the king was delighted and invited him to sit down. After the sage had taken a seat, the emissary, Gavaya [Gaveyya], bowed his head and touching his folded hands to his forehead (*añjaliṃ katvā*) spoke to the king in the following verse (*diyaḍḍhagāthamāha*). "O king (*deva*), I pay homage to you.[99] May you prosper. May whatever gems found within Vāsudeva's region be yours. O sovereign, please give your daughter to us."[100]

Gavaya's request surprised the king. Smiling, he looked at Sukkadanta, the great sage, and said, "O sage, did I hear your ambassador correctly? He asked for my daughter? *Pandita*, I do not understand what you're talking about."[101] After the king had spoken, Sukkadanta, the great sage, said, "O, king of kings (*rājinda*), the emissary who came to ask for your daughter said, 'This place [Haripuñjaya] and its surroundings, foretold by the Buddha, are splendid and most pleasant (*ṭhānañca vatthuñca varaṃ surammaṃ*).'" Sukkadanta continued, "Let me tell you about his prophecy. When the Buddha was alive, he flew from Vārāṇasī [to Haripuñjaya]. When he got there, the Blessed One descended and, after inspecting the area, said, 'In the future this exceedingly beautiful place will become a large city (*idaṃ saṇṭhānaṃ abhirammarūpaṃ mahantapuraṃ*). After I have passed away my relics will emerge here.' Having spoken, the world teacher (*satthā*) returned [to Vārāṇasī]. From that time forward the place has been venerated by all human and divine beings. A group of matted-hair ascetics came to worship the relics. Both of us, Vāsudeva and myself, went there and built a new city. It is beautiful, possesses all necessities, satisfies all desires, and gives pleasure as if it were a divine city (*devanagarasadisaṃ*). Yet, alas, among all of the people no one was found worthy to rule, therefore, the emissary [came to ask for your daughter to rule the city]." [the end of fascicle one; fascicle two is missing and has been replaced by fascicle four of the *Jinakālamālīpakaraṇaṃ*].[102]

[FROM THE *JINAKĀLAMĀLĪPAKARAṆAṂ*]

At that time the two sages sent an emissary named Gavaya along with five hundred men. Gavaya went, paid his respects to the king of Lavo city, and related the story as told by Vāsudeva. Gavaya stayed there for one rains retreat. At the end of the rainy season he asked the king

Fig. 4 Gavaya delivering Vāsudeva's message to the king of Lavapura

Fig. 5 Cāmadevī travels to Haripuñjaya

(*cakkavattirājānaṃ*) for permission to leave. Cāmadevī, the princess daughter of the king, was the queen of a vassal state in the Mon kingdom, and she was three months pregnant. The *cakkavatti* sent his daughter, Cāmadevī, to rule Haripuñjaya. Cāmadevī boarded a boat with a retinue of five hundred men and five hundred venerable monks who knew the *tipiṭaka* by heart (*tipiṭakadharamahāthere*).[103] She sailed up the Ping River, arriving at the city of Haripuñjaya seven months later.

Vāsudeva and Sukkadanta together with all citizens [of Haripuñjaya] invited Cāmadevī to sit on a golden mound (*haripuñje*) where she was consecrated.[104] Thus, since that time the city has been called Haripuñjaya because Cāmadevī was consecrated as queen on a golden platform.

Seven days after reaching the city, Cāmadevī gave birth to twin sons during the full moon of the month of Māgha. The elder was called Mahāyasa [Mahantayasa in the CDV] and the younger who was named Indavara,[105] also known as Anantayasa. When her sons were seven years old, the queen consecrated Mahāyasa to rule the country of Haripuñjaya.

Cāmadevī accumulated great merit in the Buddha's religion (*buddhasāsane anekakusalasambhāre*). She dedicated this merit and paid appropriate respects to the guardian deities of the city. Because of the meritorious power (*puññānubhāvena*) of Cāmadevī, a host of

Fig. 6 Cāmadevī reaches Haripuñjaya

devatās brought a powerful elephant (*tejavantaṃ hatthiṃ*) to be an auspicious protector (*maṅgalavāraṇatthāya*) [for the city]. At that time, Tilaṅga,[106] the king of the Milakkha [the Lawa][107] surrounded by eighty thousand soldiers came to lay siege to the city of Haripuñjaya.

Mahāyasa sat on the auspicious elephant's neck, Indavara sat in the middle, and the mahout sat at the rear. They were followed by a large army of soldiers and proceeded out of the city's western gate to engage in battle. When King Milakkharāja saw a red ray emanating from the tip of the white elephant's tusks, he feared for his life.[108] Rooted to the spot and unable to fight, he fled [in fear]. The soldiers also ran pell-mell in all directions leaving the city of Haripuñjaya peaceful and free from danger. The account of the founding of Haripuñjaya is now completed.

Indavara, the second son of Cāmadevī, told his mother that he too wanted to rule a city. She told her son to so inform the sage, Vāsudeva. Vāsudeva said to Indavara, "An *isi* named Buddhajaṭila resides at Mount Juhapabbata [Sacrifice Hill] near the bank of the Sāra River[109] to the east of Haripuñjaya. From there a hunter named Khelāṅga resides near Mount Luddapabbata [Hunter's Hill]. Beyond that, a sage named Subrahma resides at Mount Subhapabbata [Pleasant Hill] near the bank of the Vaṅga River.[110] If he wants to rule the country, Indavara should go to pay homage to Buddhajaṭila. With the hunter, Khelāṅga, as a guide he should

***Fig.* 7** Cāmadevī gives birth to twin sons

continue on to the hermit, Subrahma, and after paying respects to him, ask him for the city."[111]

Upon hearing the words of Vāsudeva, Indavara bowed to his mother, took his retinue, and went by the way indicated by Vāsudeva. Paying homage to Subrahma, he asked for the city. Afterward, Subrahma, along with Khelāṅga, the hunter, built a secure city (*khemanagaraṃ māpetvā*)[112] and gave it to Indavara. For that reason, the name of city was called Khelāṅga.

[His wish fulfilled] Indavara wanted to honor his mother. He ordered one of his officials to invite her to come to the city of Khelāṅga. The official went to Haripuñjaya and told Cāmadevī. She was delighted for she wanted to see Indavara. She left Haripuñjaya with a large retinue and travelled until she reached Khelāṅga. There, with great splendor she consecrated Indavara as king of Khelāṅga (*indavaraṃ mahantena issariyena abhisiñci*).

Then Indavara honored his delighted mother with a munificent offering (*mahantaṃ sakkāraṃ vanditvā*). After staying at Khelāṅga for six months, Cāmadevī asked the sage, Subrahma, for permission to leave and return to Haripuñjaya. Upon her arrival, Cāmadevī performed numerous meritorious deeds (*anekakusalasambhāre*) and after two months passed away.

King Mahāyasa who had a strong faith in the Triple Gem ruled Haripuñjaya for eighty years.

Two years after Vāsudeva built the city, Cāmadevī was consecrated and crowned queen. She herself ruled Haripuñjaya for seven years. Subsequently, Mahāyasa ruled for eighty years. The reign of Cāmadevī is now complete (*uppattikālo paripuṇṇo*).

Chapter 4 (Continued), Chapter 5 and Chapter 6

SYNOPSIS FROM THE *JINAKĀLAMĀLĪPAKARAṆAṂ*[113]

Thereupon, 1,204 years after the death of the Buddha, about twenty-two in the Cūḷasakarāja calendar (C.S.),[114] on the full moon of the month of Phaguṇa [Phagguṇa],[115] the sage, Vāsudeva, built Haripuñjaya. Two years later Cāmadevī came from Lavo City to rule Haripuñjaya. About 409 C.S. (1047 C.E.) King Ādiccarāja [Ādittarāja] was consecrated to rule Haripuñjaya. Until about 425 C.S. (1063) the story of Haripuñjaya focused on the recollection of both the appearance of the relics in Haripuñjaya and its dynastic lineage (*rājavaṃsānusārena*). The story of the relics begins with their appearance at the founding of Haripuñjaya.

Previously, the five friends—Vāsudeva, Sukkadanta, Anusissa, Buddhajaṭila, and Subrahma[116]—ordained as Buddhist monks and studied the *tipiṭaka*. Because they found the disciplinary rules too difficult to observe, four left the monkhood and became ascetics. Sukkadanta became a layman and lived in the city of Lavo.

The other four hermits led by Vāsudeva achieved the power of the higher knowledges (*abhiññābala*)[117] and continued to live in the country of Syām. Vāsudeva resided at Ucchupabbata [Mount Suthēp] on the banks of the Rohinī River [the Māe Ping River at Chiang Mai];[118] Buddhajaṭila at Juhapabbata on the banks of the Sāra River [the Māe Sān River at Lamphūn]; Anusissa at the city of Haḷiddavalli;[119] Subrahma resided at Subhapabbata on the banks of the Vaṅga River [the Wang River at Lampāng].

One day Vāsudeva came down from Mount Ucchupabbata and found six children: two [one male and one female] in the footprint of an elephant, two in a rhinoceros footprint, and another two in the footprint of a water buffalo.[120] Taking them [home], he raised them. After they had matured, they married each other and all became Vāsudeva's attendants.

One female deer, it is said, came to the place where Vāsudeva urinated and drank his urine, which contained sperm. She became pregnant and gave birth to two human babies.[121] Vāsudeva, filled with pity, raised them, feeding them with milk that came from his finger. After they matured, they lived together. The male was named Kunarisi[122] and the female was called Migupatī.

Vāsudeva built a city called Migasaṅgha[123] and consecrated Kunarisi as king. He then had the three couples live in the city. Kunarisirāja followed Vāsudeva's instructions and ruled the city of Migasaṅgha for seventy-seven years. His three sons were named Kunarirāja, Kunarilola, and Kunarisitanāsa.[124] Vāsudeva built cities for each of them.

Among the three young men, Kunarisitanāsa ruled Migasaṅgha after his father's death and later moved to rule the city of Rammapura [a Mon city][125] that was built by the sage. The king destroyed the city because he had unjustly decided the case of the son beating his mother when he likened [the mother's complaint] to the sound of bell when it is struck by a clapper.[126]

As Vāsudeva was wandering about looking for a peaceful site (*khemaṭṭānaṃ*), he saw the place where the Buddha's religion was once established. Thinking that this site was exceptionally secure (*paramakhemantaṃ*), he built a city there on the banks of the Ping River.

Having built the city, Vāsudeva thought, "Sukkadanta, our friend, is endowed with moral virtue beyond comparison (*sīlādiguṇasamupeto*). I shall invite him to come here." He wrote a letter, attached it to a bamboo raft and floated the raft down the Ping River to the city of Lavo.

Sukkadanta read the letter and boarded the bamboo raft, which went up the Ping River against the current.[127] [Upon his arrival] Vāsudeva told Sukkadanta all that had happened, and Sukkadanta replied, "Venerable Sir, [the city] will be secure if its ruler is an offspring (*bījaṃ*) of the king of the city of Lavo."

Thereupon the two sages sent an emissary named Gavaya [to Lavapura] together with five hundred men. Gavaya went there, paid his respects to the king of Lavapura, and conveyed the entire message related [to him] by Vāsudeva. Gavaya stayed [at Lavapura] for one rainy season and after the rains retreat asked permission from the king (*cakkavattirājā*) to depart. At that time Cāmadevī, daughter of the king (*cakkavattissa rañño*), was the chief queen consort of the provincial ruler of the city of Ramañña.[128] She was three months pregnant.

The king (*cakkavattirāja*) sent his daughter, Cāmadevī, to rule the city [of Haripuñjaya]. She boarded a boat together with a large retinue of five hundred men and five hundred learned venerable monks who knew the *tipiṭaka*. Her journey up the river Ping [to Haripuñjaya] took seven months.

Fig. 8 Coronation of Cāmadevī

Vāsudeva and Sukkadanta together with the people of Haripuñjaya invited Cāmadevī to sit on a golden mound (*haripuñjaye*) where they consecrated her as ruler. For that reason the city has been successively known as Haripuñjaya up until now. Seven days after her arrival in the city, Cāmadevī gave birth to twin sons on the full moon of the month of Māgha.[129] The elder son was named Mahāyasa and the younger was called Indavara, also known as Anantayasa. When they were seven years old, Mahāyasa was consecrated and crowned king.

Cāmadevī accumulated incomparable meritorious deeds in the Buddha's religion (*buddhasāsane*) and dedicated merit and righteous offerings (*puññañca dhammikasakkāraṃ*) to the guardian deities of the city.[130] Because of Cāmadevī's meritorious splendor (*puññānubhāvena*), a host of *devatās* brought a powerful elephant to be an auspicious protector (*maṅgalavāraṇatthāya*).

Then the Milakkha king, Tilaṅga, with eighty thousand soldiers laid siege to Haripuñjaya. With Mahāyasa seated on the auspicious elephant's neck, Indavara in the middle and the mahout at the rear, and surrounded by a large retinue of soldiers, they set forth for battle through the western gate of the city. [The narrative now continues with the CDV].

Fig. 9 Cāmadevī's twin sons battle Vilaṅga

CHAPTER 7

VICTORY OVER MILAKKHARĀJA

Brave and courageous soldiers [attired] in green coats of mail with sharp swords, bows, shields, and a banner emblazoned with an image of a sword brought up the rear. Thereupon, the deities who safeguarded the city and the sacred tree (*tadā cārakkhakā devā nagaraṃ rukkha-mūlakaṃ*) announced that they would go to protect the soldiers.

The two courageous princes of good birth (*subījā dhitisatimā*) went [with their army to the battlefield]. Like a lion approaching a herd of deer, they bravely approached, Anekabalabāhana, the elephant of King Milakkharāja.

Upon arriving at a plateau, not too far or too near [to the city], they beat a drum to signal a rest for the army. They then sent an emissary to negotiate with Milakkharāja: "We, your nephews (*mayaṃ bāgiṇeyyā*) came here to warn you.[131] Alert your sons and prepare your forces right away. We are advancing now."

The emissary delivered the message from the two princes to Milakkharāja. Upon hearing the message, Milakkharāja said, "O, emissary, how old are the two princes? How many elephants, horses, and soldiers do they have?

After hearing Milakkharāja, the emissary told the king, "O, king, both princes are five years old. They are seated on the back of an elephant with the elder brother on the neck and the younger in the middle. They are followed by three thousand soldiers, each on an elephant."

When he heard the emissary's words, the king laughed, clapped his hands and exclaimed to his officials, "Oh, how extraordinary (*acchariyo*) is the speech of the two princes! They are so young that milk still drips out of their mouths. Their soldiers are also few in number. Each of their elephants is incapable of attacking even my younger daughter. How can they fight us?" He added, "Is it possible to compare frost on the tip of grass (*tiṇaggalaggikahimaṃ*)[132] to water in the ocean or the glow of a firefly to the full moon?"

Afterward, the king stood up but before his departure he said, "Prepare your army. We will capture the two princes and lay siege to the city." The king then gave an appropriate sum of money (*dhanatuṭṭhidāyaṃ*) to the princes' emissary and said, "I will do as my nephews wish. If they come here, there will be trouble (*idāgamissati dukkhapādā bhavissati*). Let them stay there. I will go to them." Then he ordered the emissary to return.

The emissary said, "I will relate this [news] to the two princes," and departed to inform them. Upon hearing the message, both princes were pleased. They showed the emissary the army and then assured the forces: "Oh, I say (*ambho ajja*), all of you should think (*cintayittha*), 'Today we will capture Milakkharāja, our enemy.'" The army replied, "Yes, your majesty, we think [we can do] so."

Meanwhile, Milakkharāja prepared his forces (*balaṃ sajjetvā*). At noon he approached with an army of eighty thousand men to the place where the two princes were encamped. The soldiers together with all of their forces advanced as quickly as the wind because they were afraid both princes would escape before they arrived.

About 200 or 300 *byāma* [500 to 750 meters][133] from the place where the princes had stationed their army, the forces of Milakkharāja became tired and thirsty. Sitting on their elephants' necks they sighed loudly, "Ah-h, ah-h." Overwhelmed by the radiance of the spears, arrows, spikes, swords, wheels (*satti-sara-tomara-khagga-cakka*) and the coats of mail, shields, and armor (*kacavara-vālāphaṇa-kavaca*) that reflected the afternoon sunlight, dispelling darkness and irritating the eye, they were momentarily blinded and unable to advance.

At that time the sun passed high noon, and flamelike rays struck the faces of King Milakkharāja and his soldiers. They began to sweat profusely and were greatly troubled. The deities who safeguarded (*ārakkhakā devatā*) the two princes caused intense heat to burn Milakkharāja and his soldiers. From their vantage point, the princes laughed at Milakkharāja.

Then Anantayasa asked the court astrologer (*horādhipatiṃ*), "Teacher (*ācariya*), will we be victorious or not?" The astrologer said, "Princes, rest assured, you will be [victorious]." Then the great diamond elephant (*mahāvajirahatthī*) and the gem elephant (*ratanahatthī*) raised their trunks and trumpeted loudly three times.

Thereupon, the princes had the drum beaten and commanded all the troops to stand up and shout loudly three times while advancing toward Milakkharāja. Upon seeing [the advancing troops], all the soldiers led by Milakkharāja were so frightened that the spears, spikes, swords, and other weapons fell from their hands.

Observing the powerful Mahāvajira elephant charging [toward them] from afar and imagining (*maññamānā*) their foreheads being pierced by the elephant's two tusks, all the elephants including the auspicious elephant of Milakkharāja ran in all directions (*vaggavaggā*). Unable to resist [the forces of Haripuñjaya] all the soldiers[134] and elephants fled.

Then the two brothers shouted loudly at their victory. They had a great victory drum, a tabor, a small drum, a conch shell, and a trumpet (*mahājayabheri-mudinga-paṇḍava-saṅkha-makhara-sarasa-saddavantaṃ*) sounded [to celebrate the victory], and gave chase to the scattered forces [of Milakkharāja].

The Lawa (*milakkhajanatā*) abandoned everything they carried and fled with empty hands. The two princes told their men to report their victory to Cāmadevī. Overjoyed at this news, she had the victory drum beaten throughout the city [and proclaimed], "The Milakkha troops headed by Milakkharāja have abandoned their weapons and fled. All citizens, men and women, who want these abandoned weapons may help themselves."

Thereupon, the delighted inhabitants of the city went to the Milakkha camp and took whatever they wanted. The two princes knowing the Milakkha would not come back, returned to Haripuñjaya with their retinue and entered the palace. After bathing, they paid their respects to the princess mother and each suckled at her breast (*mātaraṃ vanditvā ekekaṃ mātuthaññaṃ pivanti*).[135]

Cāmadevī held her two sons in her arms[136] and with boundless joy repeatedly kissed their heads. Calling to her chief of staff and attendants (*āyuttakañca kattārañca*) she told them to prepare a victory toast and wine (*jayapānasurāpānañca*) to entertain the soldiers. Everyone was then given gifts of clothing and adornments according to their status. The victory celebration continued for seven days. In addition, a great offering was presented to the court astrologers, Brahmans, and to the auspicious gem elephant.[137]

/ Overcome with joy and happiness, the citizens of Haripuñjaya brought various gifts of perfume and flowers to pay homage to the princess mother and the two princes. Expressing their gratitude they exclaimed, "Because of you we have gained happiness."[138] Afterward they went to the stable of the auspicious elephant. There they worshipped (*pūjitvā*) and paid homage to it by repeating the words, "Because of you we have gained happiness." Then they departed.

In referring to this event, the compiler (*saṅgahiko*) cited the ancient verse (*gāthā*) of the Buddha known as *Rājovādagāthā* (The Verses of Royal Instruction) and put them into this account:

> Any king who is a world conqueror (*pathavivijito*) but who is defiled by anger; who is oblivious to time and place, to the suffering or well-being of his soldiers; who is unaware of his own and others' defilement from discontent (*maṅku*), greed, hatred, desire, delusion due to ignorance (*lobha-dosa-mohamulhaṃ*); and who is indifferent as a result of pride and conceit, will be defeated on the battlefield. As his reputation and honor decline, he will be brought to shame.
>
> Any king who is undefeated in battle, who has eliminated anger, is fully aware of time and place, who cares for his soldiers under all conditions (*sukhadukkha*), has eliminated in himself and others discontent, greed, hatred, delusion and foolishness, and is indifferent to pride and conceit, such a king will be always victorious in battle. As his fame spreads, prosperity will accrue to him.

The ancient authorities have kept this saying since olden times.[139]

In fact, even though the king of the Milakkha had a large number of soldiers, he was easily defeated because he lacked mindfulness and discrimination. By contrast, King Mahantayasa with only a small retinue of soldiers cleverly organized his army with an effective strategy and was tactically astute in regard to timing and place. As a result, he defeated the larger Milakkha army.

This description of the Haripuñjaya Kingdom was composed by the Mahāthera Bodhiraṃsi from his recollection of an ancient story (*porāṇacārikānusārena*).

Here Ends Chapter Seven
The Victory in Battle

CHAPTER 8

THE CORONATION AND MARRIAGE OF MAHANTAYASA

After seven or eight days had elapsed the two brothers, Prince Mahantayasa and Anantayasa, consulted with Cāmadevī saying, "Mother, when we entered into combat with the king of the Milakkha, he challenged us.[140] Should we now respond to him (*vacanaṃ patipesetuṃ*)? Upon hearing her sons, she said, "Beloved sons, by all means do so."

Then the two princes prepared a tribute, called for the emissary and instructed him, "Go and tell the king of the Milakkha, O Lord (*deva*), your nephews (*nattāro*)[141] sent me to inquire after your health." In addition, the two princes instructed [him to say], "Earlier, our uncle [i.e., Milakkharāja] urged us to wage war (*sabbakaṇiṭṭhāya yujjhāpessati*) against your younger daughter. Soon we shall attack the city. You should fortify it with pillars of hard wood or iron bars." After instructing the emissary they ordered him to depart.

The emissary agreed to take the princes' request and after paying homage to them he went with his retinue to the king of the Milakkha. Upon his arrival, he presented the princes' tributes, and gave the king the message sent by the two princes.

Upon hearing this news, the Milakkha king was overcome with fear (*bhītatasitā*) and said, "O emissary, do not speak to me so. Until now I had not seen the young princes but, having witnessed my handsome nephews sitting on the neck of their richly caparisoned elephant, I see that their beauty is beyond comparison (*ativiyasobhaggā*). They are like a heavenly being (*khandhaputto*) who sits upon the back of Erāvaṇa, the great elephant.[142] The two princes [furthermore, wisely] placed their army strategically in front and behind, on the right, and on the left. The army was resplendent, like celestial warriors (*devayodhin*). On this continent of Jambudīpa no one dares attack them. My two daughters are as beautiful as angels. I propose to match them with the two princes, and from their union will result a lineage for many generations to come (*kulabandha saṇṭhavabhāvaṃ karissāmi*).[143]

"But now the princes have sent me a message calling for war. We must not enter into an unrighteous conflict (*adhammayuddhanā*); instead we should engage in a righteous battle (*dhammena yuddhaṃ*)."

Then the king of the Milakkha called for his two daughters and presented them to the delegation saying, "Emissary, please observe my daughters. They are beautiful in figure, complexion, age, and grace (*rūpavaṇṇaṃ ca vayaṃ vā sirivilāsaṃ*). Sitting, standing, or walking, they are admired by everyone. Both are of pure descent (*jātikā suddhā*) born of my queen (*devī*) on the same day from the same womb. My beloved daughters are beyond comparison, served by male and female servants, and adorned with golden jewelry. It is my intention to give my elder daughter to the elder prince and my younger daughter to the younger prince. Tell your master what I propose."

Saying this, the king arranged a feast for the delegation and gave them gold, silver, cloth, jewelry, elephants, horses, and so on. In addition, other gifts were also sent to the two brothers through the emissary from the king of the Milakkha.

When the delegations from the two kingdoms arrived, they paid their respects to Queen Cāmadevī, Mahantayasa, and Anantayasa. Having presented the tributes to the royalty, they gave them the king's message.

Upon receiving the message, the queen mother and the two princes were overjoyed and arranged a feast (*sakkāraṃ katvā*) for the Milakkha delegation. The queen, seated comfortably with her sons, asked her emissary, "Emissary, what do the two princesses look like? How old are they (*rājadhītaro kativassā*)? Are they mature? What color is their complexion and are they well spoken?"

In describing the attributes of the princesses, the emissary said to the three royal family members, "Please indulge me while I tell you about the two princesses. O, ruler of the continent (*bhūmipāla*), I hope you will be pleased with my report.[144] The twin daughters of the king of the Milakkha are five years old, in the prime of their youth,[145] as pretty as a picture (*vayena taruṇavayā rūpena abhirūpāti varabimbāva sobhaṇā*), neither thin nor fat, neither tall nor short. Their complexion shines as gold and their skin is beautiful without any dark blemishes. They are equally attractive whether sitting, walking, or standing.[146] While laughing and talking, their voices are as sweet as a swan's. Their long hair has not lost its luster and shines like the gossamer wings of a bee.[147] When they let down their hair, it reaches their ankles. They are endowed with all the feminine traits. The daughters of the king of the Milakkha are truly beyond comparison."

And so in this manner did the emissary describe the surpassing beauty (*itthilakkhaṇaparipuṇṇasundarībhāvaṃ*) of the two princesses of the king of the Milakkha. Cāmadevī and her two sons, after hearing the virtues of the princess daughters, agreed [to the marriages] and sent gifts and a message to the royal parents as well as their future daughters-in-law.

In this way the people of the two kingdoms became acquainted with one another and were exceedingly pleased. The king and queen of the Milakkha then sent their daughters to Haripuñjaya for the two princes. The princesses were beautifully adorned and accompanied by a large retinue of male and female servants.

In like manner, Queen Cāmadevī prepared various gifts and sent her subjects to welcome the [Milakkha] emissaries and bring them into the city. Each of the princesses was given a new house. The elder prince lived as a friend (*vissāsikagharavāsaṃ*) with the elder princess as did the younger prince with the younger princess. The wedding ceremony and the coronation were postponed because they were too young.

In this way the two states of Milakkha and Haripuñjaya lived together in harmony (*raṭṭhā ekato*)[148] and cooperation. The king of the Milakkha sent emissaries bearing gifts four times a month to bring back news of his two daughters. Queen Cāmadevī gave the gifts along with the message [from the king of the Milakkha] to her sons and daughters-in-law. Consequently, the two kingdoms became allies and joined family lines through the intermarriage of their sons and daughters.

Fig. 10 The marriage of Cāmadevī's twin sons to Vilaṅga's twin daughters

It is truly said, according to ancient authorities (*porāṇā*), "Children are beloved by human beings (*puttā piyā manussānaṃ*). They are born to bind their parents closer together. Anger and quarrels are short-lived [among children]. By the time their parents arrive to intervene, the squabble is forgotten and they are reconciled.[149] Even those who formerly were on bad terms with one another, whether or not they are relatives or of the same race, will be fondly reconciled (*aññamaññaṃ piyaṃ*) when their sons and daughters marry. Thus the people of Milakkha led by their king and the Khmer headed by Queen Cāmadevī (*cāmadevādikambujā*) came to love one another after their sons and daughters married.[150]

By the time they had lived together for two years, Mahantayasa and the Milakkha princess were seven years old. Queen Cāmadevī wanted to perform the royal consecration ceremony (*rājābhisekaṃ*) for Prince Mahantayasa, her beloved son. She asked for the two daughters of Gavaya, a village headman, and presented them to Mahantayasa and his wife, the daughter of the king of the Milakkha [as attendants]. By order of the queen a drum was sounded to inform all the townspeople to prepare for the royal coronation. In addition, she ordered that the city of Haripuñjaya be decorated and sent an invitation to the two sages, Vāsudeva and Sukkadanta.[151]

For this event everyone in the city, led by Brahmans and wealthy householders, assembled to perform the auspicious coronation and wedding ceremonies, and the palace blessing (*rājābhisekamaṅgalañca āvāhamaṅgalañca pāsādamaṅgala*) for [Mahantayasa].[152] Anantayasa was appointed [his] viceroy. The two sages, Vāsudeva and Sukkadanta, participated in the ceremony carrying a golden pitcher filled with perfumed lustral water that they poured over the head of the prince. As a blessing they chanted the following verses:

> Mahāyasa, hear us as we speak. We have brought you to perpetuate our lineage for generations to come and to protect the city. From this time forth may you be the progenitor of virtuous offspring. May you prosper in the four *dhammas*, namely, long life, good complexion, happiness, and power according to the virtue of the Buddha, the *dhamma*, and the *saṅgha*. May you always be victorious by the power generated by us in these ceremonies. If the daughter of king of the Milakkha gives birth to a son, he must succeed you as king in order to perpetuate your lineage. If the daughter of the headman of the Gavaya village gives birth to a son, you must designate him to be the next viceroy. May you be consecrated king in your mother's line. If the daughter of the king of the Milakkha (*milakkha*

Fig. 11 The coronation of Mahantayasa as the king of Haripuñjaya

> *rājadevī*) does not bear a son, and Anantayasa has a son by [his wife] the daughter of the king of the Milakkha, you must designate him king in order to perpetuate your lineage. By so doing, your offspring will prosper. This day we consecrate Anantayasa as viceroy.
>
> Together, we built the city of Haripuñjaya for the purpose of enshrining the Buddha's relics for the benefit of all humankind. May the king who takes refuge in the Buddha, the *dhamma,* and the *saṅgha,* and who observes the precepts, may he do no harm to his citizens and live a long life free from illness and accident. May Indra, Brahma, and all the *devatās* protect such a king forever.[153]
>
> A king who is unrighteous (*adhammika*), heretical, and brutal, who neglects the Buddha, the *dhamma,* and the *saṅgha,* who is disrespectful, greedy, hateful, and a teller of lies, who brings only suffering to the citizens—may such a king go to hell and meet with illness and calamity. May Indra, Brahma, and all the *devas* torment such a king for all eternity.[154]

The two great sages performed the coronation ceremony for Mahantayasa and bestowed their blessing (*varamaṅgala*) upon him. Then they offered instruction for the development of the kingdom. Finally, after uttering a curse (*abhisappiṃ*) [against an unrighteous king] they returned to their homes.

[The question arises,] Why did the sages do this? [The answer,] Because they were endowed with supernatural powers: the power of divine ear and eye, the power to know the minds of others and the previous lives of all living beings, and the power to predict the future.[155]

First it is appropriate to instruct, then to admonish, and finally to utter a curse in order to reinforce the instruction.[156] But is it appropriate to first utter a curse and then deliver an auspicious speech (*maṅgalagāthā*)? No, it is not suitable. Why is it unsuitable?

[The answer,] Due to their nature, human beings cannot remember the words that are said first (*pubbavācanaṃ*). Their memory is too short.[157] But words that are uttered last (*uttaravācanaṃ*) can later be recalled. Those words will [remain in the memory] a long time. That is why the sages first performed the coronation and then later instructed [the prince] in the Ten Royal Virtues which [when followed] will bring about the prosperity in the king[dom], guarantee the stability of the city and state, and bring welfare and happiness to the people.[158] Only [after such instruction] is a curse uttered.

Ancient, wise authorities have no quarrel with this teaching. The wise are able to do easily what the foolish cannot. Truly, wisdom is noble, like a light that radiates from precious stones, totally eradicating the darkness of the night. Wise men know both the goodness and wickedness (*guṇañca dosaṃ*) of the past, the future, and the present.

This description of Haripuñjaya was composed by the Mahāthera Bodhiraṃsi from his recollection of an ancient story.

The End of Chapter Eight

The Coronation and Marriage of Mahantayasa

CHAPTER 9

THE FOUNDING OF KHELĀṄGA

King Mahantayasa was known as the great king of Haripuñjaya. Anantayasa, the younger brother, served as his viceroy (*uparāja*). Both of them were supreme among their subjects, who prospered and were happy. Everyone, whether living in towns or villages, enjoyed life (*sukhasampado*) and were safe from thieves and robbers. They always supported the Buddha, the Dhamma, and the Saṅgha and respectfully supported their parents.[159]

Cāmadevī, the queen mother, was held in the same high regard as her sons. She attained a state of great happiness (*mahādevīsukhaṃ*) that anyone would envy: happy while sleeping, happy while standing, and happy while walking.[160] Everything that she wanted was realized (*sabbaṃ samijjhati*).

Cāmadevī arose early in the morning. Upon waking she sat on her bed and recalled her virtue (*guṇaṃ*) in the past, the future, and the present. With wealth sufficient for her needs, she offered food to monks, Brahmans, and even beggars. She lacked for nothing; money and rice were always plentiful.

She thought to herself, "Because of my previous good deeds, I have achieved success in this life. The time has come for me to perform good deeds for the future when I am old and ill (*anāgate kattabbaṃ kusalaṃ mayā*)."

In the morning with these thoughts in mind (*evaṃ jintayitvāna*), the queen mother arose from her bed, washed her face, attired herself in new clothes, and adorned herself with several kinds of jewelry. Seated upon a palanquin she circumambulated the city surrounded by a large retinue. East of the city she built the Rammakārāma, a forest temple, complete with a *vihāra* and a Buddha image. Afterward she [gave the following to the *saṅgha*]: a residence for the community of monks headed by the *saṅghathera*; the Māluvārāma Monastery, including a *vihāra*, at the northern corner of the city to accommodate the monks from the four directions; the Abaddhārāma Monastery to the north of the city with a *vihāra* that she offered to the monks from Laṅkārāma; the Mahāvanārāma Monastery to the west of the city along with a *vihāra* and a monk's residence (*kuṭi*) as well as a Buddha image and food and drink for the resident monks; the Mahāsattārāma Monastery to the south of the city and its *vihāra* with an incomparably beautiful image for the monks residing at that temple.[161] Food and drink were also offered to the *saṅgha*. From her own resources (*sayaṃ*)[162] the princess mother built *mahāvihāra* in the five different places.[163]

During that time everyone—those who lived in cities, towns, or villages—was busily engaged in constructing *kuṭis* and *vihāras* in five thousand large and small villages. Five thousand learned *bhikkhus* were well versed in chanting (*bhāṇakādipaññāya*); another five hundred were well versed in the Pāli scriptures (*tipiṭakadharā*).[164]

With royal support from Queen Cāmadevī and her two sons, Buddhism (*buddhasāsana*) flourished. The city was like the abode of the thirty *deva* heavens: happy and peaceful (*subhikkhaṃ khemaṃ*) and with an abundant food supply. On every eighth, fourteenth, and fifteenth day of the lunar month the queen mother and her sons visited the community of monks. Upon arrival they paid homage to the *saṅgha* and took the precepts.[165] Then they listened to a sermon and performed *dāna* by offering food. Every day they supported the *saṅgha* in this way. Everyone, the royal ministers and all the people, both town and village dwellers, followed the example of Cāmadevī and her sons in supporting a flourishing Buddhism.[166]

One day the viceroy, Anantayasa, withdrew to a solitary place and sat thinking [to himself], "My wise brother, the king, enjoys all the fruits of kingship. Everything he wants is available to him (*yaṃ yaṃ icchati taṃ hoti*). All pleasures are his to enjoy. I am a man born of the same mother. Why must I be dependent upon my elder brother? I will ask the sage, Vāsudeva, to make me a king [as well]."

With these thoughts in mind, Anantayasa went to his mother, paid her his respects, and then shared his longings with her.

After listening to Anantayasa, she replied, "*Sādhu*!" and prepared candles and incense for emissaries to go and pay homage to the two sages and to inform them of the matter.

The sages listened carefully to their report and replied, "Gentlemen, if this is the case, you should speak to your master as follows: 'There is a pleasant mountain known as Khelāṅga located to the east of Haripuñjaya. A hunter named for the mountain is living there. Anantayasa should go to the hunter and ask him to be a guide (*magganāyakaṃ*) to the cottage of the hermit, Mahābrahma. The hermit lives at the top of Twin Peak Mountain (*dviyaggapabbata*).[167] He is endowed with supernatural powers (*mahiddhisampanno*) and can utilize those powers for your benefit. Anantayasa should visit the sage and ask to be made king. He will give the prince a prosperous kingdom."

After listening to the two sages, the emissaries said, "*Sādhu bhante*, O, Venerable Sirs, the two of you [possess the power] to make this beloved young man [a king]." They paid homage to both hermits and returned to inform Cāmadevī and Anantayasa.

When Anantayasa heard this, he was overjoyed (*pītibharitahadayo*). Paying respects to his mother, he said, "Mother, if this is true, I will go to the sage's residence and then inform you if I am to become king."

Cāmadevī said, "*Sādhu*, O my beloved son!" and gave him her blessing. "May your wish to become a king be granted."

Anantayasa paid homage to his mother, then asked to be excused[168] so that he could meet his elder brother. Paying his respects, he related to him the entire story saying, "O king (*deva*), please allow me to depart as is my wish. The sages, Brahmaraṃsi and Vāsudeva, will send me to Twin Peak Mountain located to the east [of Haripuñjaya] where Brahmaraṃsi lives. He will make me king. I will leave immediately."

As he was listening to his brother, Mahantayasa thought [to himself], "We are brothers born from the same mother's womb. My younger brother performed many good deeds in the past. By the power of his merit it is fitting that he should rule a kingdom (*sakapuññānubhāvena rājā rajjaṃ kārento*). With this thought [in mind], he granted permission for his brother to go [to Khelāṅga]: "Father,[169] I give you permission to go as you wish. Upon your arrival at Subrahmaraṃsi's residence, may you become king." He gave his blessing to his younger brother.

Anantayasa paid respects to the king and returned to his residence. Then he took a retinue of a thousand soldiers and left Haripuñjaya, headed east and before long arrived at the Mātisārija River.[170] An ordinary hunter who lived near the river was engaged as a guide to direct the way to the master hunter of Khelāṅga. [Arriving there] Anantayasa said, "O hunter, please take us to the residence of the sage, Mahābrahma. What is your fee?"[171] He then gave him one thousand *kahāpaṇa*.[172]

The master hunter Khelāṅga agreed, "*Sādhu*, O king," and after inviting Anantayasa to spend the night offered him a variety of fruits and meats. In the morning Khelāṅga embarked on the journey, arriving at Twin Peak Mountain in the evening. Anantayasa together with his retinue spent the night at the foot of the mountain. The next morning after breakfast he ordered his men to take an offering of candles, incense, perfume, and flowers to the hunter, Khelāṅga, and ask him to lead them to the residence of the sage.

Upon arriving there and paying homage to the sage, Anantayasa greeted him and said, "Venerable Sir, I beg to ask you: Are you comfortable living here? Are you free from illness? Do you rely largely on fruit for your sustenance? Do you have sufficient food? [I see] that here is a large number of gadflies, mosquitoes, reptiles, and fierce animals in the forest. Do they harm you, Sir?"

The sage Mahābrahma replied, "Because of my many meritorious deeds, I am free from all illness.[173] Fruit abounds for me to eat. The gadflies, mosquitoes, reptiles, and fierce animals which roam in the forest do me no harm."

Having replied to Anantayasa in this manner, the sage spoke to him in the following verses, "Who is it who pays homage at my feet? How have you come to this beautiful place? What is your father's name? Tell me who you are?"

Anantayasa replied, "Venerable Sir, I am called Anantayasa. I am the son of Queen Cāmadevī, the daughter of the sage, Vāsudeva, who is my grandfather. Now you know my name and my clan."

The sage continued, "Why have you come here and what is your request? Don't be afraid to speak freely."

Anantayasa said, "O Venerable One endowed with great power (*bhante mahiddhisampanna*), please listen to me. Mahantayasa, my elder brother, is the king of Haripuñjaya. I myself have not yet become a king. My mother told me, 'Go build a new city at a pleasant site near the foot of Khelāṅga Mountain.' I have now come to you as my mother advised."[174]

After Anantayasa had spoken, the sage accompanied Anantayasa down from Twin Peak Mountain to the Khelāṅga valley and there he built a city at a charming site near the Wang River (*vaṅgatinadiyā samīpe rammaṇīṭṭhāne nagaraṃ māpetvā*). The city was square in shape and prosperous in every respect like the city of Haripuñjaya.[175] Upon the completion of the city, the hermit, Mahābrahma, consecrated and crowned Anantayasa as king (*rājābhisekaṃ katvā taṃ rajjaṃ kāresi*).

Because of the virtue (*puññatejena*) of King Anantayasa and the supernatural power (*iddhibalena*) of the sage, forest people[176] who lived in the vicinity came in great numbers to settle down near the new city. Without exception, everything there was beautiful.

Because of the power of the sage, the city was wealthy beyond human measure (*dibbasampatti*). It was pleasant and enjoyable, with an abundant food supply. Because it was built by the sage, Brahma, in the Khelāṅga Valley, it was called Khelāṅga Nagara. Since that time the name of the city has not changed.[177]

Fig. 12 Anantayasa's coronation as ruler of Khelāṅga

This tale appears in an important [northern Thai] story (*mahācārikaṃ*) as follows:[178] "The noble Ananatayasa, of good lineage, desired to be a virtuous king. He paid a visit to Subrahma, supreme among sages, and asked him to build a new city. The holy *isi* was endowed with virtue, skilled in meditation (*sujjhāno*), charismatic, resolute, and powerful. At the foot of Khelāṅga Mountain he consecrated Prince Anantayasa as king. The Milakkha who lived in great numbers in the forest moved to live around the city. Owing to the power of the hermit, Subrahma, the city of Khelāṅga became a rich capital with abundant food and filled with the sound of various kinds of music. The city lacked nothing. All necessities were found there, just like the city of Masakkasāra where the god Vāsava, known as Amarindrādhirāja, enjoyed his pleasure gardens."[179]

This is the description of Haripuñjaya composed by the Mahāthera Bodhiraṃsi, from his recollection of an important [northern Thai] story.

The End of Chapter Nine
The Founding of Khelāṅga Nagara

Chapter 10

Cāmadevī at Khelāṅga and the Founding of Ālambāṅganagara

And so in the manner described [in Chapter 9], Anantayasa becomes king. After he ascended the throne he prospered in every way, thanks to the extraordinary power of the sage, Subrahma.

One night while King Anantayasa was sitting on his throne on an elegantly decorated platform underneath a white umbrella contemplating his good fortune, he thought, "All that I longed for has now come to pass. My coronation was a result of meritorious deeds I performed in previous lives, and for no other reason. The time has now come for me to perform additional meritorious deeds.

"I must repay the sage, Mahābrahma, who gave me so much assistance. He was dedicated to practicing meditation (*jhānarato*) and helping those blinded by ignorance. He desired little [for himself], was content, refrained from using high and wide beds, and chose to live in the forest.[180] He refused to accept my offerings (*mahādānaṃ*) of candles, incense, scented water, and flowers. Such material offerings (*vatthudānaṃ*) are of little value [to him]; it is far more important to provide for his welfare and give him material assistance (*āmisadānaṃ*).[181] Therefore, I will go to Haripuñjaya. After paying respects to my brother, I shall request that my mother together with the *mahāsaṅghathera*, the Buddha's followers, mendicants, and Brahmans come here so that I can make a generous donation (*mahādānaṃ*) to them. Why do I say this? When monks and Brahmans come here, I will offer them the *dāna* of an *āvāsa* (a place to stay), *kuṭi* (an individual cell), *vihāra* (meeting hall), *cīvara* (saffron robes), *piṇḍapāta* (alms), *catupaccaya* (four monastic requisites), and *senāsana* (living quarters).[182] [In so doing] I shall also be repaying my mother's virtue (*guṇapaccuppakāraṃ*). Having done this, I shall gain more success in this world (*idha loke*) and the world hereafter (*paraloke*)."[183]

After contemplating this course of action, in the morning King Anantayasa washed his face, ate a delicious meal, dressed in elaborate attire, and then went to the residence of the sage, Mahābrahma, accompanied by a large retinue. Paying respects to the sage with candles, incense, and fragrant flowers[184] he said: "Venerable Sir, I shall go to the city of Haripuñjaya where I shall proclaim your virtue to King Mahantayasa, Sukkadanta, and Vāsudeva. Then I shall invite my mother to come to pay homage at your feet."

Then the sage said, "Very good! O *mahārāja,* go whenever you like and convey my respects to the two noble sages."

Saying, "*Sādhu,*" Anantayasa paid homage to the sage and then departed for Haripuñjaya taking his retinue with him. Upon his arrival, he first paid respects to his mother, Cāmadevī, and then his brother, King Mahantayasa. After they had taken comfortable seats and exchanged friendly greetings, he told them that his wishes were fulfilled.

Thereupon, Cāmadevī and her two sons rejoiced and prepared various offerings (*pūjāsakkāre sajjetvā*) to take to the residence of the sages, Vāsudeva and Sukkadanta. After paying homage to them they sat down and exchanged greetings. King Anantayasa then conveyed Subrahma's regards to the two sages and reported how he had become king. Both [sages] expressed their delight and advised them further as follows:

> You were both born of a noble lineage, raised and protected by us. Maintain mindfulnesss, be firmly established in the Buddha's religion, be well disciplined, observe the tenfold virtue of the king, care for the people, and do no harm to others,[185] then you will gain all that you desire both in this world and the world hereafter. From now on all the *devas* will extol and protect you forever.[186]

Upon hearing the advice of the sages, Cāmadevī and her two sons were exceedingly pleased. Paying homage to [Vāsudeva and Sukkadanta],[187] they returned to Haripuñjaya.

Then King Anantayasa paid respects to his brother, King Mahantayasa, and said, "O Lord (*mahādeva*), I intend to pay homage to my mother and return the blessing [she has given to me] (*mātaraṃ pūjanatthāya guṇapaccuppakāraṃ*). I shall also pay respects to five hundred monks, the Buddha's disciples led by the *mahāsaṅghathera*, and all senior and junior Brahmans. It is my intention to invite all those who wish to accompany me and lead them to my city."

Hearing King Anantayasa's respectful words, his older brother, Mahantayasa, replied (*sādhu*), "Anantayasa, what you say is pleasing indeed. Because our two kingdoms are related there is no need for us to make treaties; our two kingdoms are as one country (*dve raṭṭhā tuyhaṃ mayhaṃ ñāti na mayaṃ saññaṃ kātabbaṃ ekaraṭṭhaṃ*). We were conceived in the same womb, born on the same day, and are of the same mind (*ekacittasamānā*). Therefore, we should not speak of differences. Please take whatever you need." Upon saying this, King Mahantayasa ordered the drums sounded to call those throughout the city of Haripuñjaya who chose to go to Khelāṅganagara with King Anantayasa.

Overcome with joy, King Anantayasa invited a large community of monks headed by the *saṅghathera* and sent them ahead in golden carriages. Afterwards he invited Cāmadevī to sit on a golden howdah on the back of an auspicious elephant and in a grand procession brought her into the city. Following behind were Brahmans and wealthy householders.

When he heard of Anantayasa's return, the sage, Subrahma, summoned those who lived outside the city to bring gifts to receive [the king]. Later he welcomed Cāmadevī in her golden palanquin and invited the queen to stay in the palace.

The next morning Anantayasa took Cāmadevī, his mother, to the residence of the sage. After paying his respects, the king introduced his mother saying, "Venerable Sir, this is my mother, Cāmadevī. Please know that she is one of your great disciples (*mahāupāsikaṃ*)."

Subrahma then said, "Marvelous, O *mahārāja*! [I am pleased that] your mother, the *mahādevī*, has arrived here. May peace and happiness be with both of you."

After the sage had spoken in this manner, Cāmadevī greeted him saying, "Venerable Sir, I beg to ask you, are your living circumstances comfortable? Are you free from illness? Do you rely primarily on forest fruits for your sustenance? Do you have enough food to eat? There are many gadflies, mosquitoes, reptiles, and fierce animals in the forest. Have they harmed you?"

Subrahma replied, "O queen (*devī*), because I have done many good (*kusalaṃ*) deeds, I am free from illness; there is plenty of fruit to sustain my life; and no gadflies, mosquitoes, reptiles, or fierce animals in the forest harm me."[188]

Cāmadevī said, "Venerable Sir, I came to this city, far from my father, mother and all my relatives. [I consider] the three of you to be my family. Like true parents you protected me, made me queen, and enabled me [to achieve] a worldwide renown. Your virtuous power extends throughout the earth and even to Indra's heaven. I have now come to pay my respects to you."[189]

After extolling the virtuous power (*guṇaṃ*) of the sage, Subrahma, paying homage to him (*vanditvā*) and asking him for his leave (*khamāpetvā*), Cāmadevī entered the city with her son, Anantayasa.

The next day both mother and son visited the great congregation of monks (*mahābhikkhusaṅghaṃ*). After approaching them and paying their respects (*upasaṃkamitvā vanditvā*) they offered various foods to the monks. Later they invited the Brahman teachers who had come with them to partake of food and gave them a residence and an honorarium.[190]

In honor of the Triple Gem (*buddhārāma-dhammārāma-saṅghārāmaṃ*) they built monasteries with meeting halls and residences for many monks. Just as Cāmadevī and her sons previously had visited the monks in order to listen to preaching, to observe the precepts and the threefold good conduct (*tividhasucaritaṃ*),[191] to undertake the tenfold meritorious course of action (*dasakusalakammapathānaṃ*)[192] and the ten royal virtues (*dasavidharāja-dhammānaṃ*),[193] so now they continued to act in the same manner after they became rulers.

Next, Anantayasa repaid his mother for all of her virtuous care toward him. He assembled many workmen including carpenters, painters, and woodcarvers to build a bamboo palace to serve as a coronation hall for his mother. In addition, he told his foreman to prepare everything necessary for the coronation ceremony. Containers were heaped full of gold, silver, seven kinds of precious gems, cloth, and jewelry; other kinds of offerings such as husked and unhusked rice, beverages, liquor, meat, sweets, palm sugar, bananas, betel nut, and fermented tea leaves[194] were also prepared. When everything was ready, the king invited Cāmadevī, his mother, to sit upon a mound of precious stones. First, he shampooed her hair with kaffir lime water to wash away the dirt and then [rinsed it] with scented water.[195] He invited a Brahman officiant to consecrate and bless his mother by pouring a golden bowl full of lustral water over her head (*sīse abhisiñcāpetvā*). Afterward, a great victory drum was sounded. Loud music of five different kinds of instruments echoed like thunder in the middle of the ocean.

When the coronation ceremony was completed, Anantayasa adorned Cāmadevī with jewelry. As his mother held his arm, he led her to the throne. After she sat down he paid his respects by placing her feet on his head. Then he said, "Mother, please forgive me for any wrongdoing that I might have committed from the time of my conception until today. You have extended toward me every care (*bahupakārā*). Nothing in the entire universe (*sakalamaṇḍalacakkavālagabbhe mahāpathaviyā*) can compare with your virtuous kindness toward me. If I were the king of kings (*mahācakkavattirājā*) and conqueror of the whole world, I would bequeath to you all of my royal wealth comprised of an incalculable number of the seven kinds of precious gems. Today, however, I am one of little merit, poor and unfortunate. Even though I have become a king, I have few possessions. Therefore, to you I give my kingship (*sakalarajjaṃ*) in order to show my gratitude to you in keeping with my power (*yathābalaṃ*)."[196]

Having spoken in this manner, Anantayasa told his men to strike a large victory drum to announce the coronation to the people. The sound of the drum reverberated throughout the whole city. When the echo of the drum died down, the king prepared a great feast. After respectfully greeting his mother he invited her to eat. He, himself, ate later.[197] Then the supervisors, servants, and waiters served a sumptuous banquet of many different kinds of food (*khādanīyaṃ paribhojanīyaṃ*) for all the people including the chief ministers (*senāpatādīnaṃ*).

King Anantayasa arranged a grand celebration lasting for seven days and nights. On the eighth day he paid homage to his mother and said, "Mother, please remain here with me for the rest of your life. I cannot [imagine] living here without you. If you stay here my merit (*puññabhāgo*) will increase. Please help me by agreeing to my request."[198]

When Anantayasa had spoken, Cāmadevī thought [to herself], "My two sons are equally dear to me. I have not loved one more than the other, not even the tip of a strand of hair. But this son recently ascended to the throne and I do not know if he will be successful. Therefore, I am happy to stay here for three years in order to advise him. After that I will return to my other son in Haripuñjaya."

With this thought in mind the queen mother Cāmadevī said, "O beloved son, I will live here with you for three years, as you have requested. Then I will return to your elder brother at Haripuñjaya."[199]

King Anantayasa agreed (*sādhu*). Having paid homage to his mother and designated her as ruler (*rajjaṃ niyādetvā*), Anantayasa said, "Mother, I'm going to take a pleasure trip (*kiḷissāmi*)[200] outside the city." Bidding farewell to his mother and accompanied by a retinue of men, he travelled beyond the city and set up camp at a comfortable site where he thoroughly enjoyed himself. The next day he visited Subrahma. Paying homage to the holy man, he told him all that had transpired and sought the sage's approval (*anumodanatthāya*) for his actions.

After listening to the king, Subrahma replied, "*Sādhu*, O *mahārāja*, I approve of what you have done. Furthermore, repaying our parents' virtuous care (*mātupituguṇapaccuppakāro*) was praised by all the Buddhas. Please extend a portion of your merit to me (*tva puñña-bhāgapattiṃ me dehi*) [and] I will build a city for you." The king agreed (*sādhu*), "I will dedicate a part of my merit to you." Paying homage to the sage and asking for his leave, he returned to his residence.

In the evening the king told his men to take offerings of candles, incense, scented water, and flowers to the residence of the *mahā-*

saṅghathera in order to listen to the *dhamma*. After paying his respects, the king took his seat and conversed with the monks, telling them all that he had done.

The large congregation of monks led by the *saṅghathera* listened to the king and said, "O *mahārāja, sādhu, sādhu*. We rejoice (*anumodāma*) that you have reciprocated your mother's meritorious care (*matuguṇapaccuppakāraṃ*)."

The Venerable *saṅghathera* then preached to the king, "*Mahārāja, sādhu, sādhu*, the meritorious deed you performed to express your gratitude for your mother's meritorious care was praised by the Omniscient One (*sammāsambuddhavaṇṇitaṃ*).[201] Your fame and possessions will continue to multiply in this world and the world hereafter. Wherever you go, all the divine beings will worship you (*devābhipūjito*). In all aspects of life—sleeping, standing, and walking—you will be happy. Later you will attain *nibbāna*." After listening to the monks preach, the king was filled with joy and sat discussing the sermon with them.

Later the sage, Mahābrahma, built another city southwest of Khelāṅga as a residence for Anantayasa. The new city contained many different kinds of buildings and it was exceedingly beautiful and enchanting. Because the city was constructed on a rise at the boundary of the city of Khelāṅga it was called Ālambāṅgapuri.[202]

After his discussion with the community of monks, Anantayasarāja paid his respects and returned to his residence. Upon seeing the new city he thought, "Ah, this is the city given to me by the sage whom I venerate," and entering the city he [felt] overjoyed to be there.

After living at Ālambāṅganagara for some time, Anantayasa returned to Khelāṅganagara in order to pay respects to his mother and to inquire after her health, often attending to her daily.

At that time many different groups lived in the city including monks and priests (*samaṇabrāhmaṇa*), wealthy householders, and even indigenous folk (*vanamanussa*) who spoke the *milakkha* language.[203] Even though they had different points of view (*anekavividhavicittā*), they all lived together harmoniously, performing meritorious deeds such as donating *kuṭi* and *vihāra* to the *saṅgha*.[204] The inhabitants of Khelāṅga also enjoyed playing musical instruments, including various kinds of drums and the conch shell.[205]

The ancient authorities, in order to pass on the teachings of the Buddha regarding the fruit of good conduct (*sucaritaphalaṃ*), said:

> Wherever the wise (*dhirā*) live—in village or in forest, in lowlands or highlands—those places will be full of pleasure and happiness. Wherever the wise who performed good deeds in the past, such as

> supporting the *saṅgha* and observing the precepts, go—even to the tops of trees, the tops of mountains, the ocean, or in space—they will be venerated by all the deities and human beings in those places. They will achieve whatever they desire by the power of their past merit.

Thus ends chapter ten of the description of Haripuñjaya composed by the Mahāthera Bodhiraṃsi from his recollection of an important [northern Thai] story. This chapter dealt with the building of Khelāṅganagara.

CĀMADEVĪ'S REIGN AT ĀLAMBĀṄGANAGARA, HER RETURN TO HARIPUÑJAYA, AND HER DEATH

Having stayed in the city of Khelāṅga with Anantayasa for three years as related earlier, Cāmadevī said to her beloved son, King Anantayasa: "O, beloved son, I wish to go to Haripuñjaya in order to see your brother. Now you are able to reign over your city joyfully [by yourself]."

Upon hearing this news, King Anantayasa said, "Mother, when you are here, I am happy. How can I be happy when you are gone? Therefore, I beg you not to leave me. If you leave, I'll soon die (*mama jīvitaṃ na cīraṃ santhati*)."

Upon hearing [her son] speak with such dejection, Cāmadevī said, "O son, if you so desire, I will stay three more years. You reside at Khelāṅganagara, and I will stay at Ālambāṅganagara. If my proposal is acceptable to you, I will stay here. Otherwise, I will return to Haripuñjaya."[206]

After Cāmadevī had spoken, King Anantayasa said, "Mother, I agree (*sādhu*)." Then the queen left Anantayasarāja at Khelāṅganagara to stay at Ālambāṅganagara.

Why did Cāmadevī do this [i.e., leave Khelāṅga]? She acted this way because she thought, "If I continue to reside at Khelāṅganagara, my son's kingship (*mama puttassa rājabhāvaṃ*) will not be famous. He will be considered only as my viceroy. Everyone, monks and Brahmans in particular, will find fault with me, saying, 'This queen does not understand her [proper] authority.'" Therefore she [left Khelāṅga] in order to enhance her son's fame and [also] to avoid criticism." Even though King Anantayasa lived in Khelāṅganagara, he did not abandon his duty to his mother. He still supported her in the manner described earlier. Anantayasarāja's devotion to his mother was increasingly appreciated by all the people—especially the community of monks, Brahmans, and wealthy householders.

Three years passed and Cāmadevī again asked her son for permission to leave. The king pleaded with his mother to stay with him for one more year. Although she saw no reason to stay longer, she consented to her son's request (*nimantanaṃ adhivāsesi*).

Following the lapse of only one month, the queen mother became ill. Cāmadevī informed her son and asked his permission to leave. She told her attendants to take offerings of candles, incense, scented water, and flowers and proceed to the residence of the sage, Subrahma. After paying homage to him and having sat down on one side (*pūjitvā vanditvā ekamantaṃ nisīti*) she raised both hands in respect. She then spoke to him in the following verses:

> O *mahāvīra*, I respectfully pay homage at your feet. For six years and one month, I have relied on your help during my stay here. I now must return to the city of Haripuñjaya. Please grant me permission to leave and by your power may I travel safely.[207] Please continue your care of Anantayasa, your grandson[208] and regard him as your lay supporter. Whether in times of joy or suffering (*sukhadukkhe*), please do not abandon him.

Subrahma agreed (*sādhu*), "O queen, it is right for you to leave to see your [other] relations. Anantayasa, your son, has performed his duty in accordance with royal traditions (*rājasamayā*). Do not worry [209] about him. He will guard the truth (*sadhammaṃ rakkhissati*). Furthermore, all compounded things (*āyusaṅkhārā*) are impermanent (*aniccaṃ*), changing (*adhuvaṃ*), and transient (*aciraṃ*). Therefore, accumulate more and more merit (*yathā puññāni kayirāsi*). May you go safely by the power of your meritorious deeds (*puññakammena*)."[210] After the sage had spoken, Cāmadevī paid homage to him, asked his leave and traveled to Haripuñjaya in a grand procession.

King Mahantayasa prepared several gifts to welcome Cāmadevī. He went out of the city with a large retinue to receive his mother. After paying his respects, he joyfully led her inside the city.

Cāmadevī entered the beautifully decorated city and circumambulated it. She ascended the lavishly ornamented palace and slept that night in an elegant royal bed. The next day she prepared a great offering (*mahādānaṃ sajjitvā*) and went to the residence of the monks[211] headed by the *mahāthera*. After paying her respects, she gave *dāna* to them. After that she made donations to all the Brahmans led by the chief teacher and distributed a large sum of money to relatives and other deserving people.

For seven days, she offered *mahādāna*, observed the precepts and listened to sermons.[212] On the eighth day she suffered a serious illness

Fig. 13 Cāmadevī returns from Khelāṅga

(*tibbarogā*) caused by her previous *kamma* and then she passed away.[213] Because of her accumulated merit, a mind imbued with the three virtues, righteous conduct (*puñña-sampattī cittatividhasucarita kusalakamma*), and because she meditated on the Three Characteristics of Existence (*tilakkhaṇañāṇabhāvitattā*) when her illness had reached its fatal stage repeating, "*Dukkhaṃ, Aniccaṃ, Anattā*," Cāmadevī was reborn in Tusita heaven after she passed away from this world.[214]

At the news of her death, a large crowd of people led by Cāmadevī's family [mourned her passing]. They beat their breasts, struck their heads, cried and lamented, creating a tumultuous noise. At that moment the earth seemed to be shattered by an enormous uproar (*rodanasaddena ca kolāhalasaddena ca*).

King Mahantayasa wished to revere the remains of his mother (*sarīrakiccaṃ pūjetukāmo*). For several days he presented lavish offerings. A great funeral tower (*ahaḷanamahāpāsāda*) and pyre were built at the Māluvārāma monastery. Then Cāmadevī's body was taken to the charnel ground in a grand procession with numerous offerings, resounding with the sounds of dancing, singing, and musical instruments. Her body was placed on the pyre, ignited, and [her] corpse was consumed by fire. Many offerings were made at the cremation site and various musical instruments were played.[215] Her ashes were sprinkled with fragrant water

Fig. 14 Cāmadevī's funeral cremation

in order to extinguish the flames. Then the relics were collected, mixed with a fragrant paste, placed inside a golden urn, and covered with a lid. The relics were taken to the western outskirts of the city, accompanied by dancing, singing, and musical instruments including various kinds of drums and a conch shell. A reliquary with several niches for Buddha images (*cetiyaṃ buddharūpaṃ*) was built to enshrine the relics at a pleasant site. Because it was covered with gold plate, the pagoda was called *cetiya suvaṇṇacaṅko.*[216]

After presenting lavish offerings (*mahādāna*) the king removed the relic. As he poured the water of consecration (*dakkhiṇodakaṃ*) he dedicated the meritorious power of this act to Cāmadevī, his mother.[217]

Upon witnessing this sight, crowds of people, the queen's relatives in particular, cried out with loud laments. While the people wept, Mahantayasa instructed them as follows:

> Do not grieve and lament. The Blessed One taught that death is common to all living beings. Those among you who still feel attachment to your relatives should perform meritorious deeds—give *dāna,* observe the precepts, build *cetiya* and construct Buddha images—and dedicate the merit to your family, especially your parents. In so doing, it will be said that you have returned your obligation to

Fig. 15 Suvaṇṇa Cetiya (Wat Cāmadevī [Wat Kukut], Lamphūn) believed to contain Queen Cāma's relics

them, especially your parents, and you will become even more beloved by them. This teaching of the Buddha was transmitted from teacher to teacher.[218]

In this manner King Mahantayasa consoled his relatives and the townsfolk in their sorrow and then instructed them. Afterward, he performed various meritorious acts such as *dāna*, and then paid reverence to the *cetiya*, the Buddha image, the community of monks, and to his mother. Then, taking his leave, he returned to his palace.

From thenceforth the king gave instruction to those who lived inside the city of Haripuñjaya and throughout the kingdom, establishing them in righteous deeds. He ruled Haripuñjaya, observing the path of the ten virtues (*dasakusalakammapathesu*) and the good deeds of a righteous king (*cakkavatticāritesu*).[219]

Later this question arose: "In the past the kingdom was known to us either as Biṅga or Lambhūṇa. Now we most often hear about the kingdom of Haripuñjaya. Are the other two different [from Haripuñjaya]?"

In order to explain how they became one kingdom, the compiler (*saṅgāhiko*) relates the following:

The story begins with primitive people such as the Mon and the Lawa who descended from forest dwellers (*vanameṅgādijantunaṃ lawānaṃ vanaputtānaṃ*), the people who were the children of animals and those who were the children of sages.[220] The first city inhabited by the Mon was also occupied by animals. This pleasant city built by the sage, Vāsudeva, in the state of Biṅga[221] was named Lamphūn. Officially called Biṅga by the Pāli compiler, the place looked like a heavenly city. To the local population it was known as Lambhūṇa. Since the time the sages consecrated Cāmadevī as ruler, the city has been known as Haripuñjaya. The compiler, however, says it is called Biṅganagara. These three names—Biṅga, Lambhūṇa, and Haripuñjaya—all refer to the same place. In fact, there is but one city, although any one of three names can be used; it makes no difference. Queen Cāmadevī arrived and founded the city for her sons and grandsons.[222] Buddhism also prospered there. Both town dwellers and forest people who lived in the kingdom enjoyed themselves and performed numerous meritorious deeds and, hence, after death, they achieved a blissful state of existence. For these reasons, the sage, Sukkadanta, proclaimed that Cāmadevī had established a good lineage (*subīja*).

Queen Cāmadevī was of unsurpassed excellence, the beautiful and wise daughter of a noble emperor (*pavaracakkavatti*) and from a superior lineage which had never known decline. She performed numerous meritorious deeds (*puññāni*) such as the three righteous actions (*sucaritaṃ*), and upon her death she was born into the realm of the gods (*devaloke*). The beauty and prosperity of the *devas* in Tusita heaven is beyond description. They enjoy a life of unsurpassed joy and honor. Therefore, no one can fully describe the wonder of Cāmadevī's achievement. Listen well to her story, skillfully written in different Pāli verses such as Samālagandhi, Vajirā, and so on. I have clarified the problematic words in the ancient records. Those who wish to earn merit should study these words carefully.[223]

This is the description of Haripuñjaya composed by the Mahāthera Bodhiraṃsi from his recollection of an important [northern Thai] story.

So Ends Chapter Eleven

Chapter 12

ROYAL SUCCESSION, CHOLERA EPIDEMIC, AND FLIGHT TO HAṂSAVATI

[Following Cāmadevī's reign] King Mahantayasa ruled as king in Haripuñjaya. I will now briefly discuss the successive reigns of rulers who were descendants of this noble progenitor's lineage.[224] Listen respectfully to my words.

During the time that Mahantayasarāja ruled Haripuñjaya he faithfully observed the ten royal virtues. He exhorted his subjects to continually perform meritorious deeds (*kusaladhamme*). He abandoned a course of unrighteousness (*agatidhammaṃ*) and embarked upon a course of righteousness (*gatidhamme*).[225] In addition, the king honored the sages and respected those who practiced the *dhamma*. He enjoyed a healthy and happy life, and fathered many sons and daughters. In this way he ruled the country for eighty years. After he died he was reborn in heaven due to his accumulated merit (*puññakammena devaloke nibbatti*).

Mahantayasarāja was succeeded by his son, Kūmañca. Soon thereafter Anantayasa also passed away in the city of Khelāṅga, and by the virtue of his accumulated merit he was reborn in a paradise adorned with seven kinds of precious minerals nearly three *yojana* wide near his mother in Tusita heaven. The people of Khelāṅga arranged Anantayasa's funeral ceremony and afterward collected his relics (*sarīrakiccaṃ katvā dhātuṃ gahetvā*). They brought them to Haripuñjaya for burial in a pagoda (*thūpacetiyaṃ*) in the Māluvana forest to the east of city.[226]

Even though King Kūmañca lacked his father's noble attributes, he was a pious king who performed meritorious deeds according to his ability. He ruled the country for forty-four years before he died. Then he was reborn in Tāvatiṃsa heaven due to his accumulated merit.

Kūmañca was succeeded by his son Rundhayya. He ruled Haripuñjaya but owing to his beliefs he did not perform virtuous deeds (*kusalakammato asaddahanto*) such as *dāna* or observe the precepts (*sīlaṃ rakkhamanto*). Instead, he merely ruled according to the ancient traditions (*purāṇacāritavasena*).[227] Therefore, he lived a short life and died when he was twenty-seven years old according to his *kamma*.

Rundhayya was succeeded by his son, Suvaṇṇamañjusa. He was a devout supporter of Buddhism, performed many meritorious acts such as *dāna*, and protected the city from harm.

In those days many people in Haripuñjaya became prosperous. They were rich in grain and rice, gold and silver, seven kinds of precious gems, cloth, jewelry, and food. Monks led by the elder Thera of the *saṅgha*, mendicants, Brahmans, and householders all performed meritorious deeds. Even ordinary people who lived in the kingdom were happy and satisfied. After thirty years King Suvaṇṇamañjusa died and owing to his merit he was born in Tāvatiṃsa heaven.

His son, Saṃsāra, ascended to the throne. This king did many evil deeds: he confiscated the citizens' valuables such as gold and silver and [with the money] bought liquor and meat. He overindulged in eating, drinking, carousing, dancing, and singing, and performed no meritorious deeds (*kusalakammaṃ na karoti*).[228] Therefore, he was neither loved nor admired by *deva*s [and human beings], and lived a short life. Having ruled the country for only ten years, he died and was reborn according to his *kamma*.

His son, Paduma, succeeded Saṃsāra as king. After he was crowned, he built six *dāna* halls and constructed monasteries including living quarters and meeting halls for the community of monks. Upon his death he was reborn according to his meritorious deeds.

Paduma was succeeded by his son, Kuladeva. King Kuladeva ruled Haripuñjaya for seven years. It was predicted that in the Year of the Pig, many misfortunes would occur. Monks, brahmans, and influential leaders foresaw the approach of danger forecast by the astrologers. Approaching the king they said, "O king (*deva*), great danger will occur this coming year. You should act accordingly so as to promote both your own peace of mind and peace in the kingdom (*cittasukhaṃ rājāsukhaṃ ca*)."

When he heard this [prediction] the king said, "What [exactly] should I do to promote my peace of mind and peace in the kingdom?"

They said, "Your majesty should make merit such as giving [to the monks], observing the precepts, and dedicating merit to the *deva*s.[229] [In so doing] they will protect your majesty. Your majesty also should worship the gods (*devatāpūjaṃ*) and beseech them to protect both your majesty and the country."

Having heard this advice, the king, due to his past association with evil persons and because of his greed-driven fear of losing his possessions, replied, "*Bhonto*, who can say who will meet with danger and who will save us from it, anyway? What will be, will be. It's beyond my control," and he ignored their advice.

When the Year of the Pig arrived, the king of the Milakkha recruited an army, advanced on the city of Haripuñjaya and surrounded it. The two enemy forces engaged in combat, and the troops of Haripuñjaya were defeated. [The survivors] fled to the city of Samenga.[230] King Milakkhatreyya then plundered the city. Afterward he invited the citizens of Haripuñjaya who had fled to Samenganagara to return. After King Milakkhatreyya ruled Haripuñjaya for three years and three months, he gave it up and returned to his own city.

At that time another Milakkha king laid siege to Haripuñjaya. He ruled for one year and died. He was succeeded by Nokarāja who ruled for one year before he died. His successor, Dālarāja, reigned for only two and a half months before his death. In turn, Tutarāja ruled for ten years, Selarāja for three years, Hālarāja for three years, Yovarāja for six months, Brahmanatarāja for one year and three months, Mukarāja for two years.

Thereupon, a king named Atrāsataka ruled Haripuñjaya. He was a brave and powerful monarch (*suro ca tejanto*). After he ruled for two years and ten months, he recruited a strong army and sent them downstream by boat from Haripuñjaya along the Binga [Ping] River in order to attack Lavanagara [the city of Lavo].

At that time the king of Lavo was Ucchiṭṭhacakkavatti, a great warrior with a large army (*ativiyasuro mahābalakāyo ca*). He was the sovereign of Lavanagara. Hearing what had happened, he became as angry as a serpent (*bhujjagindo*)[231] struck on the tail with an iron bar. Consequently, he immediately began to prepare an army. He left the city (*lavanagaraṃ anapekkho*) and embarked on a long journey in order to attack King Atrāsataka.

At the time the two armies met and prepared to engage in battle, King Sujita, the ruler of Siridhamma,[232] with 17,000 soldiers also converged on the battlefield arriving by both land and water. When the two armies [of Haripuñjaya and Lavo] saw such a large number of troops, they fled in fear.

King Ucchiṭṭhacakkavatti told his troops, "The king of Siridhamma has now blocked our way (*rumhitvā maggaṃ*) and prevents us from returning home. Siridhammarāja will lay siege to the city of Haripuñjaya and will force the women to be their wives. I tell you this because [Siridhammarāja's forces] have taken the river route. Because traveling by river is a roundabout way [to Haripuñjaya], we will go by the straight and shorter land route allowing us to conquer the city of Haripuñjaya before they arrive." The soldiers shouted *sādhu* in agreement [with King Ucchiṭṭhacakkavatti's plan] and they immediately set out for Haripuñjaya.

Upon their arrival, they stayed a far distance [from the city]. That night King Ucchiṭṭhacakkavatti went swiftly with his brave soldiers, reaching the city before daybreak. He told his men to announce to the gatekeeper, "Our king has arrived," and ordered him to open the city gate. Having entered and seized the city,[233] the king took over the palace where he ordered his soldiers to tie up the palace guards and put them in prison. As he sat on the throne filled with satisfaction the light of dawn appeared.

The king then seized the queen, her daughter, and all their personal possessions. He gave the spoils to his men according to their status, in particular to the generals of the army. He consolidated the whole state under his power and ruled the country to its great benefit.[234]

Shortly thereafter, Atrāsataka attacked Ucchiṭṭhacakkavatti in order to retake the city. Atrāsatakarāja was defeated and fled by boat to another city far to the west, living there in hiding. Ucchiṭṭhacakkavatti returned [from the battle], sounded the victory drum, worshipped the *deva*s, and rewarded his brave soldiers with a sumptuous meal and a rice wine victory toast.[235] In addition, he ordered the prisoners released and gave them an appropriate sum of money.

Sujitarāja, the sovereign of Siridhamma, knowing that the two armies [were engaged in battle], returned to Lavanagara[236] and easily conquered it without any resistance. He entered the city, ordered the victory drum struck, propitiated the *devas*, paid respects to the statue of the *deva* in the forest, the statue of his mother, and the guardian deity of the city (*nagarārakkhakānaṃ*). There he remained, taking delight in music.[237]

After Ucchiṭṭhacakkavatti assumed rule over Haripuñjaya as a result of his previously developed good character (*pubbakusalasaṇṭhārena*), he aimed to make everyone in the entire kingdom content. Consequently, he was both loved and admired by the people.

After three years had passed, Kamboja, the son of King Siridhamma, became king as a result of his previous good *kamma*. However, he was ambitious and greedy (*mahabbalataro asantuṭṭhā*) and with a large army launched an attack on Haripuñjaya. King Ucchiṭṭhacakkavatti also prepared his brave soldiers to fight against King Kamboja. In the ensuing battle, Kambojarāja was defeated. His soldiers abandoned their weapons: swords, spears, lances, shields, auspicious elephants, and so forth, and fled to the city of Nāgapura. The people of Nāgapura pursued King Kamboja and took his elephants and horses, male and female slaves, weapons and other possessions, leaving Kambojarāja to return to his own city empty-handed. He covered his face with a cloth in order to hide his great shame as he entered the city.[238] King Ucchiṭṭhacakkavatti achieved another great victory battle in the forest. As he sounded the [victory] drum his people shouted loudly three times and joyfully entered the city with smiles on their faces. The citizens of Haripuñjaya presented elephants, horses, gold, silver, and other possessions to the king. The king took a sufficient amount of money and rice and then gave the rest to his men, in particular his generals and courageous soldiers, and to the citizens [of the town]. In subsequent days the king announced that anyone could come and take whatever they needed. People throughout the kingdom came to receive this royal largess and were content.

Then King Ucchiṭṭhacakkavatti, reflecting on his wealth and the success of his momentous victory, knew that they were due to two causes: his good deeds in the past (*pubbakatasucaritattā*) and the power of the guardian *devatā*. He worshipped and made offerings to the *devatās*. Referring to the virtue of his accumulated merit (*kusala-sambhāraguṇaṃ*) he made a vow (*saccādhiṭṭhānaṃ*) for the benefit and welfare of his children, grandchildren, great-grandchildren, and great-great-grandchildren. He then bowed his head, raised his hands in respect (*añjali*) and with the *devatās* as his witness spoke the following verses:

> *Bhonto, Bhonto*! May you, O *devas*, listen to my words with your divine ears and understand what I say through your divine knowledge.[239] In olden times it was said this state was built by the great sages. They invited Cāmadevī, my grandmother (*mamāyyikaṃ*), [to rule] and crowned her sovereign to establish a good lineage. A place that enshrines the relics of the Conqueror (*jinadhātussaṭṭhanakaṃ*) is protected by us. If another king like Kamboja comes to inflict harm, may you prevent him [from doing so]. If any king does not listen and heed my words, may you destroy him. My true vow (*saccādhiṭṭhānaṃ*) is not based on anything other than [the protection of] the relics of the Conqueror.[240] Therefore, may the *devatās* protect this relic forever.

The king invited all the celestial beings such as the Brahmas in the sixteen Brahma heavens to recall the history of Haripuñjaya that he ordered to be inscribed on a stone slab and installed to the west of Haripuñjaya. He continued to rule the kingdom happily (*rājasukhaṃ*) until he passed away in the third year of his reign. Afterward, King Kamala ruled Haripuñjaya for twenty years and seven months before he passed away.

At that time the people of Haripuñjaya suffered from a widespread cholera epidemic. Many died of the disease. Those who lived in houses with a cholera victim contracted the disease in such increasing numbers that none of them survived. At last, even those people who touched an object in a cholera-infected house became inflicted with the disease and died.

The people suffering with cholera were abandoned; those who survived destroyed their houses and fled for safety. Therefore, the remaining population of Haripuñjaya, in order to save their own lives, fled to a city named Sudhamma[241] and settled there. The city of Haripuñjaya consequently fell into decline (*parihīno*), and was abandoned (*nijanavā*) altogether.

The King of Pukam,[242] observing the masses of weak and starving people, was moved to pity and out of his compassion restored the city of Sudhamma for them to occupy.

Unable to bear their suffering any longer, the people of Haripuñjaya left Sudhamma [Thaton] and went to Haṃsavati [Pegu] where they continued to live. At that time the king of Haṃsavati, seeing the [needs of the] people of Haripuñjaya, out of his compassion and sense of justice (*karuṇāyitattā*) gave them many necessities, including clothing, jewelry, paddy, rice, various salty and sour foods, and dwelling places.

The inhabitants of Haripuñjaya and of Haṃsavati came to know and love one another. Even their languages were the same.[243] Because no difference was found in their speech, they were able to understand each other easily. After six years the cholera epidemic subsided. When the disease was brought under control, those who wanted to return to Haripuñjaya departed and dwelt again in the city.

Those who did not want to return or who were too old or who had married the sons or daughters [of the local people] remained at Haṃsavati. Those who had returned to Haripuñjaya recalled, "Many of our relatives—grandparents and parents—still live in Haṃsavati," and so they annually floated downstream several offerings such as hard and soft foods (*khādanīya paribhojanīya*)[244] dedicated to their relatives' [spirits]. When they remembered them they were overcome with sorrow. Crying and lamenting (*rodantā paridevantā*), they returned to their homes. This tradition [of remembrance] continues to this day.[245]

With the return of so many of its former inhabitants, Haripuñjaya was restored to its former glory. The people of Haṃsavati, who still loved their friends and relatives in Haripuñjaya often visited them, bearing many letters.

The compiler (*saṅgahiko*) describes the meritorious wisdom (*paññāguṇaṃ*) of the sage, Sukkadanta, in the following verses:

> O, how difficult it is to attain the state of trance absorption (*jhāna*), the five supernatural powers (*pañcābhiññā*), and wisdom.

Because these three qualifications are hard to attain, Sukkadanta, without reaching the state of [the Buddha's] omniscience (*sabbaññu-anadhigato*), attained knowledge through the eight mundane knowledges (*lokiyañāṇehi*) and the five supernatural powers.

He knew the past and future through knowledge like the Buddha's. When the sage built this city, he excavated the earth and said, 'If the seven kinds of precious stones are found in a clod of earth, a good king will reign; if green charcoal is found, there will be an evil king; if unhusked, unfertilized rice is found, the city will come to ruin.' Seeing this vision through his transcendental awareness, he related this prediction to the sage, Vāsudeva. This prophecy came to pass. In fact, the wise said that this wisdom is supreme, just as the moon, the king of all planets, is regarded as supreme among the stars. The *dhammas* of the sages, namely, virtue and grace (*sīlaṃ siriñcāpi*) follow them. They are found in the wise (*paññavanto bhavanti*).

At that time a king named, Aṅkuracakkavatti, departed from the city of Thamuyya[246] with four divisions of his brave soldiers and conquered Haripuñjaya. He ruled it for nine years and died according to his *kamma.*

He was succeeded by the following kings:

Sudeva ruled Haripuñjaya for one year and two months and died
Neyyala ruled for ten years and died
Mahārāja who came from Suppālanagara conquered Haripuñjaya, ruled for a few days and died
Selarāja ruled for ten years and died
Tāñarāja ruled Haripuñjaya for six years and died
Jilakirāja ruled Haripuñjaya for ten years and died
Bandhularāja ruled Haripuñjaya for twenty years and died
Indavararāja ruled Haripuñjaya for thirty years and died

From the birth of the powerful monarch, Mahantayasa, until the year Ādittarāja ascended to the throne, exactly three hundred and eighty-four years and two months had elapsed. Twenty-eight kings perpetuated an uninterrupted dynasty from Mahantayasa to Indavara.[247]

This is the description of Haripuñjaya compiled by the Venerable Mahāthera Bodhiraṃsi from his recollection of an important [northern Thai] story.

The End of Chapter Twelve

CHAPTER 13

ĀDITTARĀJA'S REIGN, AND THE BATTLE WITH LAVO

There was once a king named Ādittarāja who ruled Haripuñjaya. It was prophesied by our Lord Buddha that he would rule this kingdom. Ādittarāja was truly a brave and powerful monarch who was victorious over his enemies.[248] Once he assembled a mighty army to lay siege to the city of Lavo.

When the king of Lavo saw such a large army, he ordered his soldiers to close the city gate and remain inside. Ādittarāja set up his camp near the city and sent an emissary to the king of Lavo with the following message: "If the king of Lavo wishes to fight me, let him come out immediately. But if he will not fight, let him present a white umbrella to me.[249] Do not intentionally be the cause of a long and painful ordeal."

After hearing the emissary's message, the king of Lavo said [to the emissary], "I am not afraid to fight King Ādittarāja, but to engage our armies [in battle] is pointless. The sages would disapprove of such a battle. Therefore, I propose to wage a righteous war (*dhammayuddhaṃ*) against Ādittarāja. You should build a *cetiya* outside the city using your great army (*mahabbalehi*), and we will build one inside the city. Both groups will build a laterite *cetiya* of the same size, fifteen *byāma* in height and in width.[250] All work must be completed in one day and one night. Whoever finishes first will be the winner; the other will be the loser. If you win, we will be your slaves and work for you for three years; if we win, you will be our slaves and workers for three years, after which we will release you." He then designated his own minister as an emissary to accompany Ādittarāja's representative when he returned to [the Haripuñjaya forces].

Upon hearing the king of Lavo's message, Ādittarāja, knowing that his forces were more numerous than the Lavo, was certain that he would be victorious. Accepting the wager, he ordered the [Lavo] emissary to return. Both armies signaled their agreement by blowing a conch shell and beating a drum so that they would begin building the *cetiyas* at the same time.

As the *cetiyas* were under construction, Ādittarāja's rose higher because he had more laborers. Seeing that his *cetiya* was lower, the king of Lavo feared defeat. He called upon the carpenters who construct wooden cremation palanquins (*prāsād*)[251] to fashion a false pinnacle for the top of the *cetiya*. At midnight they wrapped [the fake pinnacle] with a white cloth and placed it on top of the unfinished laterite *cetiya*. Then the entire structure was covered with plaster. At sunrise, a great victory was proclaimed. The king [of Lavo] ordered the people to shout three times, "Our king's *cetiya* is finished first." They removed all the plaited, split bamboo scaffolding exposing the *cetiya* to King Ādittarāja's forces. The accompanying cacophony from drums and conch shells sounded as though the earth was being split in two.

Hearing the frightening sounds, all the people looked toward the city. Seeing the palacelike pinnacle of the *cetiya* covered with plaster, the people of Haripuñjaya assumed that it was completed [fairly] and ran away in fright. Ādittarāja, powerless to stop his fleeing army, fled as well.

Thereupon, the king of Lavo ordered the great victory drum struck and opened the gate. "Capture them! Capture them!" (*gaṇha gaṇha*) he commanded, and with a large army [hotly] pursued [the army of King Ādittarāja]. Seeing them in pursuit, the fearful Mon (*rāmaññajanatā*)[252] abandoned their elephants, horses, shields, swords, spears, spikes, personal property, clothes, and jewelry and fled empty-handed.

The troops of the king of Lavo captured everything including elephants, horses, and the exhausted Mon troops and gave them over to their Lord.[253] The king of Lavo seized the Mon and made them slaves and laborers, but he treated them so well that they neither perished nor [did the survivors] lose face (*lajjitabbanti*). He achieved the victory because he built a fake *cetiya* inside the city. After the King of Lavo's success, he ordered that the *cetiya* be dismantled under cover of darkness leaving nothing behind. The king allowed the Mon to finish their *cetiya* outside the city where it was called the Ramañña *cetiya*.

To describe [the king's] victory and the power of his wisdom, the compiler composed the following verses:

> This famous king possessed five kinds of power (*pañcavidhā*): the power of arms (*bāhubalaṃ*), the power of wealth (*bhoga-*), the power of councillors (*amacca-*), the power of sovereignty (*adhipacca-*), and the power of wisdom (*paññā-*).[254] The Buddhas who are superior to all other beings said, "The king who possesses these five powers is regarded as exceedingly worthy. He will achieve

> whatever he desires. Among the five powers, wisdom is the most important." Although the King of the Lavo's army had four fewer divisions than Ādittarāja's, he defeated his enemy through the power of wisdom. King Ādittarāja possessed more of the four other kinds of power than the King of Lavo, but because he was lacking in wisdom, Ādittarāja was defeated. Therefore, I [the compiler] say wisdom is the most important.[255]

Afterward, the king of Lavo, owing to his great conceit (*adhimānā*) because of his victory and also because of unrest in his kingdom (*sakaraṭṭhe asantuṭṭhā*), said to all of the princes at a meeting of military commanders, officials, and ministers, "Ho! Give me your attention! In former days, the king of the Mon was powerful and prosperous. When he came to attack us, he was defeated and fell from his station. His elephants, horses, and army vanished. Who among you will launch an attack?"

Hearing this challenge, the king's son said, "O king (*deva*), I am your son. You cared for me for many years while I was growing up. I shall destroy the enemy and capture him [Ādittarāja]." Having spoken, he bowed down to the feet of his father and gathering all of the troops went to Haripuñjaya. Upon his arrival, he set up camp to the east of the city and sent an emissary to the king [Ādittarāja] with the message, "If you wish to fight, come out immediately."

Upon hearing the message from the son of the king of Lavo, the wise Ādittarāja, in order to incite his army against the enemy, said, "*Bhonto*, my friends, has anyone among you seen the strange antelope deer (*viparitakaṃ kuruṅgaṃ*)? Even as a tiger chases an antelope deer to devour it, just so the son of the king of Lavo has chased after us and arrived here. He has given us a reason to fight. What should we do?"

Having heard the words of King Ādittarāja, the soldiers of the mighty army pursed their lips [with resolve] and struck the palms of their hands on the ground saying, "All of us will fight but you must not fight, O most noble in the kingdom. The son of the Lavo king is very young. The smell of milk still clings to his mouth.[256] Neither the king's son nor the citizens of Lavo will know how to fight. In the past we fought a righteous battle (*dhammayuddhaṃ*), respecting the *dhamma*. Now we will conquer them by force (*balayuddhena*), crushing them utterly."

When the king heard the soldiers, he said to the [Lavo] emissary, "Did you hear their malicious threat? They aim to fight until both sides perish. Let us not fight by force but by means of the *dhamma*. Each side should dig a square pond. They should be the same width, depth, and length. We will dig day and night, using only the handles of our spears and no other tools. When the sun rises, the one who has dug the deepest will win." Having thus spoken, King Ādittarāja sent a representative to accompany the emissary from the Lavo.

The two emissaries departed and related the entire message to the king of Lavo. When he heard this report, the king's son thought, "I came from afar. I am as tired as my soldiers. Moreover, the citizens of Haripuñjaya will protect their city like red ants protecting their nest. If we fight, either side could win. But in the [proposed] righteous battle [my troops] have more spears. Some of the citizens of Haripuñjaya have spears, but others have none. They can use only the spears they have already. Those foolish people are unaware of our advantage. Victory will undoubtedly be mine." And thinking in this manner, the son of the king of Lavo agreed, "It is good (*sādhu*)."

Both parties decided upon two level sites: the Lavo king picked one in the east and the king of Haripuñjaya chose one in the west. At the sound of a drum both sides commenced digging. The people of Lavo dug only with spear handles; the Haripuñjaya forces, however, dug with spears by day and with hoes by night until dawn. Neither party could observe the other lest they encroach beyond the line dividing them. At sunrise, a drum was struck loudly in the middle of the city. At the sound of the drum a large crowd gathered together from both sides. It was announced that the people of Lavo had not dug very deep, while the people of Haripuñjaya had dug to a depth of forty meters. Then King Ādittarāja told the residents of Haripuñjaya to beat the victory drum loudly, "We have won; the king of Lavo is defeated.[257] You must capture our enemies and make them our slaves and workers."

At that time the son of the king of Lavo and the Khmer (*kambojā*) looked at each other and seeing that their cause was lost, quickly fled to their own city.[258] They abandoned their elephants, horses, and exhausted soldiers without a second thought.

The noble King Ādittarāja was filled with joy at his victory.[259] Together with his army he pursued the well-trained, previously victorious soldiers of the king of Lavo. The brave soldiers with swords and other objects in their hands, rushed after the king of Lavo. They captured the horses, elephants, and soldiers abandoned by [the Lavo] king and returned to present the spoils to King Ādittarāja. The king treated the Khmer as slaves and laborers (*dāsakammakāre*) assigning to them many kinds of work.

Reflecting on such a situation an ancient teacher (*porāṇācariyā*) said, "In battle one side does not always win or always lose; sometimes one wins; sometimes one loses."[260] Therefore, in order to explain victory and defeat an ancient authority related the following verses:

> In this world one cannot predict whether a war will end in victory or defeat. Sometimes losers become winners; sometimes winners become losers. On the battlefield one can conquer the enemy by using a tactical strategy (*yuddhupāyaṃ*) strengthened by the power of wisdom (*paññbalupathambhitaṃ*). If one thinks, "I have a superior force of men, horses and elephants, no one is my equal" and thoughtlessly engages [in battle], one will be defeated, just as the king of Lavo and Ādittarāja alternately made each other slaves and laborers.[261]

King Ādittarāja, overjoyed at his victory, made an offering to the many deities protecting the city.[262] He then had the victory drum sounded and all kinds of musical instruments were played.

Because the site where the Khmers dug was used to obtain clay for making pots, it became a great pond named Ukkhalirahada [Pot Pond]. The site excavated by the people of Haripuñjaya was known as Bālarahada [Foolish Pond] because it was dug by [forces the Lavo called] "foolish" as a counterattack. The pond dug by Ādittarāja was [also] called Divarahada [Day Pond] because it was dug with spear handles during the day. These names continue to be used to this day.

It is true that the Lord Buddha, the Enlightened One, foretold the coming of King Ādittarāja: "He will be born of the Mon lineage (*meṅgānaṃ bandho*) and will become a great monarch and conqueror."

The authority who compiled the history (*uppattisodho*) writes that the city of Haripuñjaya was known for three special features: a laterite *stūpa*, special sites established by Ādittarāja, and two ponds in the city built for his pleasure. These places are no longer extant but they were beautiful during Ādittarāja's reign. Later we will describe these places.

This is the description of Haripuñjaya compiled by the Mahāthera Bodhiraṃsi from his recollection of an important [northern Thai] story.

Chapter Thirteen Is Completed

Chapter 14

VICTORY OVER LAVO

At that time the king of Lavo was greatly troubled because his son had fled with a large number of soldiers. He said to Putriya, one of his attending military commanders, "Dear commander, I am crestfallen [over our defeat]. Our army is greater than Ādittarāja's. Can you subdue Haripuñjaya (*haripuñjeyyaniggahaṃ kātuṃ*) and force King Ādittarāja to yield to my power?"

The minister said, "Yes, O king, I can." "What do you need?" the king asked. "O king," he replied, "to subdue the city I need a large number of elephants, horses, an army of strong soldiers, spears, lances, and resounding drums."

The king of Lavo agreed and assembled the army. After making offerings (*sakkāraṃ*) and presenting royal regalia (*rājakakudhabhaṇḍaṃ*) to his minister, he sent him again to the city of Haripuñjaya.

Putriya crossed many small and large mountains with the army before reaching the boundary of Haripuñjaya. When they arrived the army became disoriented, being led astray by the power of guardian deities (*nagarārakkhakādevatānaṃ ānubhāvena*). They neither saw the city nor knew where it was located and instead headed north traveling along the base of the mountain until they reached Sāraveddha City[263] near the Tirasāri River. Once they realized they were lost, they tried to return. Coming to a small river they wanted to cross to the west bank. They descended and crossed the river by walking over rafts made of reeds. Some sank up to their knees, others to their legs or navel. The people who stood at the bank of the river saw them and shouted, "Retreat! Retreat!" (*osakitha, osakitha*) while others yelled, "Advance! Advance!" (*gacchatha, gacchatha*). Therefore, that small fording place was called Parivattimātikā, meaning the Roundabout Water Course,[264] as it is still commonly known.

After passing through that place, they headed west and reached the Ping River (*biṅgamahānadītīraṃ*). Then, realizing they were lost, they talked among themselves, "Friends, Haripuñjaya is located to the west of the river Ping. After crossing the river, we shall see Haripuñjaya."

Thereupon, all [the soldiers] went down to the river and drifted [on rafts] in a westerly direction. As they reached the middle of the river, some people (*ekass'ekassaci*)[265] drowned in the rapid current. Their relatives never saw them again and cried, "Our sons and fathers died here." Therefore, they called the river, Aṇṇavarahado [Deep River], a name by which it is still known.

The soldiers continued along the Ping River. Assuming they had come to a shallow place, they attempted to cross, but drowned because of the stream's depth. They shouted out, "It is deep! It is deep!" (*gambhīranti gambhīranti*) which in Khmer (*kambhojabhāsāya vācake*) is *biṅgājaraccaṃ*. Therefore, the stream has been called Jaraccam since that time.[266]

Crossing [the river] they continued westward but when they became confused again they turned to the south. Crossing again to the east they saw a level place and set up their camp there. The people called the encampment Cāmmana, in the Khmer language. The people of Haripuñjaya also referred to it as Cāmmana, the name by which it is known today.

At their encampment the army again became confused and lost their sense of direction because of the power of the guardian deities of Haripuñjaya (*nagaraṃ ārakkhakadevatānubhāvena*).[267] With their provisions exhausted, they stayed there, troubled and despondent.

When Ādittarāja heard this news he ordered the drum of victory struck. Assembling his forces, he left the city on the pretense of going to battle. The compiler describes this event in the following verses:

> Once upon a time, Ādittarāja, the well-known monarch of Haripuñjaya, heard that the [Lavo] commander, Putriya, was advancing with his army. Eagerly he struck the drum of victory to assemble his brave soldiers,[268] elephants, horses, wagons, and workers. Then he left the city like the god Indra approaching a gathering of Asura or like the powerful king of lions approaching a herd of deer. When he came near the [Lavo] army encampment he cried, "O fools (*bālajane*), why have you come here? Like idiots (*akiccakāradumedhā*), you are marching into the mouth of the king of death (*maccumukhe*) himself! Who commanded you [to come here]? Who is your Lord?"

Putriya was so frightened that he was unable to fight. He sent a messenger to tell King Ādittarāja, "O king, we are the Khmer. The powerful king of Lavo sent me here as [his] emissary. We see no way to win [and so we surrender]. We come to be your majesty's slaves. I am the chief of staff of the king of Lavo and the commander-in-chief of the army."

Having heard the emissary, Ādittarāja replied, "I will pardon you if you come under my suzerainty and swear allegiance (*sapathaṃ vacanaṃ*) to acknowledge this truth (*saccabhāvaṃ vijānituṃ*)."

The Khmer agreed and took an oath of allegiance. Putriya, affirming this truth (*saccabhāvaṃ gahetvā*), said to the Khmer, "We should nurture thoughts of great friendliness (*mahāmettiṃ*), respect (*añjakammaṃ*), and benevolence (*anisāraṃ*)." Then Putriya presented tributes to King Ādittarāja. He paid respects to the king and after asking for forgiveness, sat down unafraid and filled with joy.[269] This pleased the king who told his men to beat the victory drum seven times to announce the victory.

Out of consideration for the Khmer people, Ādittarāja provided them with many delectable foods, clothing, and other necessities. He also gave them living quarters to the west of Haripuñjaya. Because King Ādittarāja had defeated the Khmer by great force, they were known as *mahabbala* (great force). Because of his deeds the king's fame (*sakayasaṃ*) spread far and wide.

At that time the Khmer suffered from disease. Both day and night thousands of them died of serious illnesses and as a result many corpses had to be cremated. Daily their remains were thrown into a small river, so the people came to hate that river. Located to the west of Haripuñjaya, it continues to be called Jiguccha[270] until today.

When King Ādittarāja heard this story he was so overcome with sorrow that he moved the Khmer to a village named Ganeyyaka. Therefore, that village came to be called Kambojagāma [the village of the Khmer].

Later, whenever they remembered their wives and children they were distressed and asked Ādittarāja if they could return to their former home. Upon hearing their tragic pleas, the king took pity upon them[271] and said, "Friends , if you want to return to your city, you must swear by the truth (*saccabhāvena sapathaṃ katvā*) and drink the water of allegiance (*sapathodakaṃ pivatha*) before you depart." They agreed to what the king asked.

Then the king told his men to fill a golden bowl with water. Dipping his jeweled sword and spear into the water, he called as witnesses all the celestial beings in the six heavens of the sense realm (*chakāmāvacaradevatā*) led by Indra and Brahma.[272] He then ordered all the Khmer led by the commander, Putriya, to take an oath and drink the water of allegiance before he sent them back.

All of the Khmer took the oath and then drank. The king provided them with elephants, clothing, and [various] adornments, and after a farewell meal sent them on their way. Paying respects to the king, they set out for their city. When he arrived, Putriya paid homage to the Lavo king and presented to him the message of friendship from Ādittarāja.

The Lavo king said to Putriya, "I did not send you to establish [bonds of] friendship with Ādittarāja; I sent you to conquer him! Why did you come back empty-handed?" Putriya made no reply to these [angry] queries and remained silent. The [Lavo] king failed to discern Ādittarāja's intention [of friendship]. He sought to conquer Ādittarāja because of his overweening pride (*atimānavasena*) and because he possessed a large army.

At another time, Sirigutta, the son of a minister, attended the king of Lavo. He was a clever person and the king's favorite. One day as he waited on the king, he paid his respects and said, "O royal highness, because your wish [to defeat Ādittarāja] remains unfulfilled, I will make it come true. If your majesty will prepare an army to accompany me, I will capture King Ādittarāja alive and will bring him back to pay homage at your feet. If I am unable to do this, you may put me to death."

After hearing Sirigutta speak, the king said, "Father,[273] your words please me," and he made an offering to Sirigutta. The Lavo king then appointed him as head of the army,[274] recruited soldiers for him, and sent them to accompany Sirigutta in order to lay siege to Haripuñjaya once again.

Sirigutta paid his respects to the king, gathered his courageous soldiers together, and marched on Haripuñjaya with a great and powerful force. The soldiers, [however], were very angry [at being called to war again]. They shook their fists (*hatthamuṭṭhiṃ katvā*), bit their lips (*oṭṭhakhādantaṃ*), made loud noises,[275] and cried out, "We've gone to Haripuñjaya so often that we've had little time to be with our wives and children. If we are victorious over Haripuñjaya, we'll choose an [important] person from among the inhabitants of the city and hold him as a hostage." They continued their march until they eventually reached the city of Sucisaṇṭha (Place of the Pure). Again, by the power of [the Haripuñjaya] guardian deities the troops became lost, wandering back and forth until they reached the bank of the Ping River. At that place there was a village named Deyya.[276] The Khmer commandeered the inhabitants of Deyya to be their navigators and crossed the river in boats. From that time forth this place has been called Taratiṭṭha (Fording Place).

Then the Khmer, possessed by the guardian deities of Haripuñjaya, became completely disoriented and had no idea whether or not this or that town was Haripuñjaya. They headed toward the west and then to the north. Entering an abandoned city, they saw no one and looked for provisions and liquor. Finding them, they ate and drank until they all became drunk. Some men sang songs; others shouted, played, and [otherwise] amused themselves. Since that time the city has been called Rammanagara (City of Delight).

In their drunken state, the Khmer became even more confused. Unable to proceed, they were forced to return [to Lavo]. The soldiers of Haripuñjaya led by a general who knew that the [Lavo soldiers] were lost, gave chase and killed many of them with swords, spears, and clubs. The rest fled. The inhabitants of Sucisaṇṭha saw them fleeing, gave chase, killed many of them, and took their equipment including elephants and horses, gold, silver, clothing, and adornments.[277]

The [surviving] Khmer soldiers, fearing death, quickly ran away. No one was able to launch a [successful] counterattack against Haripuñjaya. Henceforth, no one from Lavanagara attempted to wage war against Haripuñjaya or even to contemplate such an action. Even the powerful ruler of Lavo could not see any means to succeed. The section describing the defeat of the Khmer is finished (*kambojaparājayaṃ nāma kaṇḍaṃ niṭṭhitaṃ*).[278]

From that time on the city of Haripuñjaya was resplendent in beauty and free from all misfortune. It was prosperous, rich in rice and water, filled with dancing and singing, and free from all danger. Monks, Brahmans, and elderly court astrologers prophesied to King Ādittarāja, "O *mahārāja,* henceforth our Haripuñjaya will surely be a great city filled with happiness and peace (*sukhaṃ khemaṃ*). The powerful *devatā*s are pleased and will soon come to protect the city."

When he heard their prophecy, Ādittarāja was overjoyed. He ordered the city cleaned and decorated so that it appeared as splendid as a celestial city. He prepared offerings and invited the *devatā*s with offerings of candles, incense, and so on. At that time the powerful *devatā*s caused the sprouts of *māluvā* creepers to appear in large numbers on the top of the mountain and cared for them. Before long the seedlings sprouted and grew tall.

At that time there was a pure white rooster who crowed with a sustained, piercing cackle. It was a very powerful bird who made its home on the top of Mount Māluvā from where it protected the city like a guardian deity. The rooster was cheerful all night and all day.[279] It brought happiness and prosperity to the people who lived in the kingdom who were free from fear, continuously delighting in its wondrous voice. From its first year there, the rooster crowed with a piercing voice during the first, second, and third watches [of the night]. When the people of Lavo heard the crowing of the rooster they feared the power of King Ādittarāja.[280]

When the king of Lavo heard the piercing cry of the auspicious rooster, he thought that he would be captured and forced into slave labor (*dāsakammagahaṇaṃ*). He, too, was afraid of Ādittarāja. In the morning the king of Lavo assembled his generals, ministers, Brahmans, and court astrologers and asked them, "I heard the cry of the rooster. What does this portend?"

They told the king, "Your majesty, have no fear. The crow of that rooster shouldn't concern us. It protects Haripuñjaya. So long as the rooster lives, the city will be protected from harm."

When they had spoken in this manner, the Lavo king was very distraught, as if pierced by an arrow, over his failure to conquer others [i.e., Haripuñjaya]. He became so obsessed with finding a way to kill the cock that protected Haripuñjaya that he was miserable.[281] When all the people including his generals, Brahmans, and astrologers observed the strange behavior of the king they asked him, "Your majesty, your illness isn't severe, is it? O lord of the earth, (*bhūpati*), what is troubling you? What makes you grow thin and wan, and breathe heavily?"

The king of Lavo said, "I'm not sick but just worried about the people. I would willingly give up my kingship to anyone who is able to eliminate this canker sore (*gaṇḍajaṃ*)[282] by magical power, whether he is a Brahman, a merchant (*vesa*) [*vessa*], a slave (*sudda*), an untouchable (*caṇḍāla*), or a scavenger (*pukusa*) [*pukkusa*]. He would be of unsurpassable worth."[283]

Then a man, clever in the ways of evil (*pāpakammakarakusalo*) heard the king's words and said to him, "Your majesty, please don't worry about this matter. I see a solution. The rooster that protects Haripuñjaya, though powerful, is still young and is not superior and wise in every matter. [By contrast] the guardian of our city has lived a long time and is wiser in things concerning both good and evil. We will make a great offering to [our guardian][284] and ask that it send an enemy to kill the rooster."

Everyone including the Lavo king, generals, councillors, and so on, agreed and acted upon his advice. The king of Lavo worshipped, praised, and respectfully invited[285] the guardian deity who accepted and consumed the oblation and offering. When it was time to go, the guardian deity signaled his retinue, disguised himself as a large crocodile and went up the Ping River to Haripuñjaya. Approaching the city, he then changed himself into a Brahman who carried a walking stick and an umbrella made of leaves. He entered the city and began searching for the residence of the white cock.

At midnight the white rooster sat on the top of the *māluvā* tree. Spreading and beating its wings, it then crowed with a sweet voice. Upon hearing the voice of the cock, the protector of the city of Lavo, [disguised as] a Brahman (*lavanagarārakkhako brahmaṇo*),[286] recognized that it was the voice of the white rooster. He then climbed up the tree and beat the rooster to death. He left the dead cock near the tree and returned to the city of Lavo.

The ancient teachers (*paramparācariye*) tell this story in order to convey to the world this teaching: "The following are the most difficult to find: a man of a superior lineage (*parisajanno*), an elephant and horse of good breeding, monks and Brahmans of good conduct, a truly wise *pandit*, truly brave officials, and a cock that spreads both wings and crows. These are auspicious qualities (*sumaṅgalaṃ*) that generate both happiness and glory (*sukhayasubhayaṃ*) in the world.[287] Each of these auspicious qualities is difficult to find. Those who possess them will be happy and prosperous. Everyone should uphold and protect such auspiciousness (*sumaṅgalaseṭṭhe rakkhitabbaṃ*). The loss of auspiciousness leads to the decline of happiness and prosperity." In like manner, when the white rooster that protected the city of Haripuñjaya was killed, the well-being of the inhabitants of Haripuñjaya declined.

The king of Haripuñjaya cremated the body of the dead cock, collected its ashes and enshrined them at a place near the *māluvā* tree where he placed guards [to protect it].

The Brahman who protected the city of Lavo returned and reported how he had killed the white rooster about which the king had dreamed (*supinanimittena*). Early the next morning the king awoke and called in the Brahmans to interpret [another] dream.[288] He made an offering and asked [about the dream].

The Brahmans replied, "O *mahārāja*, even though the cock was killed, a powerful water spirit (*udakarakkhaso*) that protects the city of Haripuñjaya is still alive. Haripuñjaya will remain a great and prosperous city with an abundant food supply as long as the water spirit lives."

The king was pleased with the explanation by the Brahmans. He arose early in the morning and prepared a large offering for the *deva*. After devoutly worshipping the guardian *devatā* of his city, he said, "O *deva* of the *devas*, you are the supreme and most powerful *deva* among all the *devas* (*devātidevo*). You have done what I asked. You killed the cock but the water spirit who protects the city is still alive."

Upon hearing the words of the king, the guardian of the city (*nagarārakkhakā*) was given an offering and consumed all of it. Then he metamorphized himself into a novice monk (*sāmaṇeravase*), appeared before the king and said, "O *māharāja*, I will go," and he returned to Haripuñjaya. Walking along all the river banks inside the city of

Haripuñjaya, he was unable to find the Haripuñjaya guardian *devatā*. So, he left the city and looked in all the ponds and rivers on the outskirts before reaching the bank of the Saluya River.

At that time the Haripuñjaya guardian resided together with his wife in a palace under the Saluya River.[289] He possessed a golden complexion and observed the precepts; his wife had a silver complexion and also observed the precepts. Due to their previous good deeds they and their attendants enjoyed a divine happiness there.

The deity that protected Haripuñjaya was called the "water guardian" (*udakarakkhaso*) because he resided in the water. Then the [Lavo guardian deity disguised as a] novice reached the place [Saluya River] and realized, "The deity that protects Haripuñjaya resides in this river," and in order to make himself known to the *devatā* he said, "O, guardian of the city, come out (*ehi bho nagarārakkha*)! I hear you are brave. I have come from afar in order to fight you since you [claim to be] so courageous. I want to know if you are more powerful than a man. Come out immediately. If you don't come out, then I'll come in."

Upon hearing the words of the novice, the Haripuñjaya *devatā* laughed at him because he was unafraid. In response to the novice he said, "Hey, ugly [Lavo] guardian! You ate the entire bribe of the Lavo and you're still hungry?[290] How do you think this fight will turn out? You've come a long distance. Do you think you have the true measure to endure? If you are brave enough to [try to] kill me, jump in and fight."

When he heard the words of the water spirit, the novice shook with anger, reverted to the form of the guardian of Lavo and jumped into the water. At that moment the Haripuñjaya guardian changed himself into a crocodile. He rushed at the novice, biting him down the middle of his body with his four giant teeth. The yellow robe was torn and the body of the novice was deeply lacerated on both sides. The novice [i.e., the Lavo guardian deity] died and blood flowed from his wound coloring the water blood-red all the way along the Ping River to the city of Lavo.

When he heard the news [of the city guardian's death], the king of Lavo went out with his forces and paid homage to the novice (*sāmaṇerassa pūjetvā*).[291] He had the remains cremated, collected the ashes and brought them inside the city where he had a *cetiya* constructed for them, and there he presented a large offering (*mahāpūjāsakkāraṃ*).

Since that time the Khmer have venerated the *devatā* statue thinking, "This statue (*devatārūpaṃ*) is our city guardian deity." Reflecting on this, the compiler wrote the following verses (*gāthā*): "The guardian spirit of the Lavo was engaged in the service of the king of Lavo. Because the guardian deity killed others, he himself met with the same fate.[292] From that time on the well-being of the Lavo declined. Henceforth, the people called the city guardian, Raṭṭhakaṃ [the Kingdom]."

This description of Haripuñjaya was composed by the Mahāthera, Bodhiraṃasi, from his recollection of an important [northern Thai] story.

The End of Chapter Fourteen

Chapter 15

KING ĀDITTARĀJA AND THE APPEARANCE OF THE BUDDHA RELIC

King Ādittarāja, hearing that the Lavo guardian deity (*Lava-nagarārakkha-devatā*) was dead, ordered his men to beat the victory drum loudly three times. The following day a great offering (*pūjāsakkāraṃ*) was prepared. Offerings were made to those worthy to receive them (*sakkārāṃ*) and an oblation (*balikammaṃ*) was presented to the guardian deity. The grand celebration lasted for seven days.

The townspeople rejoiced with dancing and singing saying, "From now on our king will perform many deeds; from now on our king will have no enemies." From that time onward the city of Haripuñjaya was happy, prosperous, and totally free from danger.

At that time the construction of King Ādittarāja's toilet (*caṇḍāgharaṃ*) had just been completed. [Unbeknownst to everyone], the relics of the Conqueror were buried at that very site. Unaware of this fact, the king went there to urinate. [While he was urinating] a crow who had been appointed by a white crow as protector [of the relics] flew overhead and dropped its excrement on the king's head. Startled, the king opened his mouth and shouted, "What's this?" At the very instant he looked up into the air, the crow's droppings fell into his mouth.[293] He spat them out and wiped his mouth and head with his hand. Trembling with rage like a *nāga* whose tail was smashed by a heavy iron hammer, the king returned [to the palace.].

On another day about noon when he needed to urinate, the king went to the veranda [where the toilet was located]. Again the crow appeared and pecked his head. This also happened a third time. By now the angry king ordered his officials and ministers to trap the crow alive.

Able officials and ministers worked hard to make several kinds of traps and snares, and set them everywhere. The people looked for the crow here and there in hollow trees, bushes, and shrubs, but they failed to locate it. They all returned and reported, "Your majesty, we could not find the crow."

Upon hearing their report, the king was suspicious and wondered, "It is possible that this crow is a *yakkha* or a *deva*. It could have forseen danger to my life and sought to signal me." Then he paid homage to all the *devas* and made the following wish: "If I have accumulated much merit, may no harm befall me. May the crow be easily caught."

Instantly, the *devatā* caused the crow to appear in the midst of the gathering of the ministers. Seeing the crow, they quickly captured [the bird] and presented it to the king. The king was overjoyed that the crow, whom he considered dangerous, was snared. [He felt] like a beggar who is given a bag filled with a thousand [coins] in his outstretched hand. Wanting to kill the crow, the king proclaimed, "O, ministers, although I am without fault, this crow has purposely annoyed me three times. I have now captured the culprit and will kill him. What do you think?"

The minister who was possessed by the *devatā* said to the king, "O Lord, your majesty should not kill the crow. If you kill it, something disastrous will result. If you do not believe me, you should call in the Brahmans and ask them." So the king called in the astrologers and Brahmans. He presented them with an offering and then asked [about the meaning of this event.]

The astrologers and Brahmans (*horācārabrāhmaṇe*) who interpreted signs (*nemittakā*) consulted the conjunction of the stars, the moon, and the sun at the time [of the event] and said to the king, "Your majesty need not worry. This is an auspicious time (*maṅgala-nakkhattayutte kālaṃ*). The constellations at the time of this event indicate that everything will go exceedingly well for you. As soon as the crow is able to speak human language, you will achieve glory and fame. [In the meantime] you should take good care of this crow."

Hearing the words of his councillors, the king was filled with joy. Replying, "I will look after the crow with great care," he then dismissed them. After they had departed, King Ādittarāja called in the goldsmith and ordered him to make a golden cage for the crow. The king kept the crow in the cage and respectfully cared for it with different kinds of food.[294]

During the first watch of that night the king lay on his ornate bed on an elevated platform and as he was falling asleep he thought, "When will the crow speak human language?" In the second watch of the night the *devatā* came at midnight and spoke to the king in a dream, "*Mahārāja*, if you want to understand the meaning of this event, you must arrange for a seven-day-old baby to sleep near the crow's cage. Hearing the crow's voice daily, he will learn the crow language. When the child is hungry, take him to his mother to bathe him and suckle milk. Then bring him back again to sleep near the cage. Both crow and child will speak to each other because they are residing together in an isolated place. In this way, after seven years, you will know the meaning of the crow's behavior." Having spoken, the *devatā* disappeared.[295]

The following morning King Ādittarāja told his ministers to bring a number of seven-day-old babies to a large courtyard. Then the Brahmans specialized in reading signs (*lakkhaṇapāthake brāhmaṇe*) were called to examine and determine the one who combined the qualities of long life and quick intelligence.[296] The Brahmans who specialized in reading signs said, "Among all these children, this child is qualified by previous meritorious deeds, quick intelligence, wisdom, insight, and competence."[297]

The king took this auspicious child,[298] called the wet nurses into his palace, and honored the child's parents. In addition, gifts of clothes and jewelry were given to his relatives and friends as well as to the parents of those children who were not selected. Afterward, the relatives fed and bathed the child and put him on the breast [of a wet nurse] to suckle. Having bathed and dressed him, they laid him down on an ornate bed to sleep near the crow's cage. They followed this regimen every day for seven years, seven months, and seven days. The boy learned the crow language. He could speak every word uttered by the crow, and was able to translate the crow's speech into human language.

At that time King Ādittarāja summoned the boy and asked him, "O my child, now do you know the crow's language?" [The lad] replied, "Yes, your majesty, I do."

"*Sādhu,* O child, because you know the crow language, become acquainted with the crow and ask him these questions: On the first day when I went to use the toilet, why did the crow excrete (*gūthapiṇḍaṃ*) on my head? And why did it do the same thing on my head and into my mouth a second time, and then fly away? On the second and the third day it pecked my head and then hid. What did the crow see and what was it trying to prevent? Please do not lie. If you tell me the truth, I will give you whatever you desire." Having so instructed the boy, he then dismissed him.

The child agreed, "O, your majesty (*sādhu*), I shall speak [to the crow]."[299] After paying respects to the king, [the lad] sought out the crow and talked to it in crow language in accordance with the king's request. After listening to the boy's questions, the crow answered in crow language, "My friend, your king came to excrete and urinate at the newly built toilet. However, from that very place the relics of our Buddha, the Blessed One, will appear." "But how did you know the location?" the child asked.

"When he was alive, our Blessed One came from the city of Vārāṇasī. Standing right here, he said to the sons of the forest Mon,[300] '*Bhonto*, sons of the forest Mon! After I have passed away my relics (*sārīrikadhātuyo*) will appear in various places. In the future a king named Ādittarāja will rule here. He will make your families safe and prosperous. At that time one of my relics will appear in this place.' Having spoken, the Buddha flew into the air and returned to Vārāṇasī.

"My grandfather, the white crow, who followed close behind the Enlightened One, heard all that was said. He appointed me to safeguard the site when he returned to the Himavanta forests. Your king was unaware that this place was an auspicious site (*maṅgalaṭṭhānaṃ*) and [unwittingly] polluted (*muttakarīsa-asuciṭhāṇaṃ*) it with urine and excrement. It was I who fouled your king [to attract his attention]. If your king does not believe me, please release me so that I can bring my grandfather, the white crow, here to explain everything in detail to your king."

After hearing [the crow's] testimony, the boy said, "*Sādhu*, my friend, I will tell the king all that you have said." He then went to the king's residence to report what the crow had told him. When the king heard this explanation, he was very pleased [to finally understand the crow's actions.] Upon hearing the crow's story about the Buddha, he was overjoyed and exclaimed, *sādhu*. Then he gave [the bird] many delicious things to eat before releasing it. Upon being freed, the crow flew to the Himavanta forests. There he went to his grandfather, greeted him respectfully, and then sat down.

"How do birds know how to pay respect?" one may ask. Another answers, "Upon approaching one another, a bird shows its respect by facing its elders. Then it makes a *ta-ta* sound with its beak , bows its head down, stretches out both wings, bows its head down again, lowers its chest to the ground, then raises it up and sits down. When crows act in this way it is called paying respects."[301]

The white crow was delighted to see his grandson. Just when his grandson was about to enquire where the relics of the Conqueror would appear, the [grandfather] crow said, "Grandson, it's been a long time since I've seen you. It is good you have come. Are you well? Is the place safe where the Conqueror's relics will appear?"

The young crow replied, "O, Lord (*deva*) grandfather, it has been a long time since you've seen me. I have come in order to report on the site where the relics will be enshrined. Just as in the past there was both stability and instability (*khemākhemā*), so today both happiness and suffering (*sukhenadukkhā*) arise.[302] The king polluted the site [where the Buddha's relics are buried] with his excrement. He is a powerful [ruler], well known everywhere and endowed with splendor, power, and strength. He wanted to know where the relics prophesized by the Buddha would appear. I devised a stratagem to inform him. He was convinced [by this] and sent me to summon you back."

Hearing the testimony of his grandson, the white crow signaled his approval, "*sādhu*" [It is good]. Calling together all of the crows he picked two large birds who were young, strong, energetic, powerful, and quick. The grandfather crow placed the ends of a stick firmly in their beaks. With the grandfather crow perched on the middle of the stick, the two crows carried him through the air accompanied by five hundred followers.

Leaving the Himavanta forest, the lead crow, acting as a guide along the way, reached Haripuñjaya on the seventh day through the power generated by contemplating the relics of the Conqueror.[303] The lead crow entered King Ādittarāja's palace first, and asked the child to announce the arrival of the white crow to the king.

The king was pleased to hear [that the crows had arrived] and told his men to prepare suitable seats in a large area for the white crow leader and all the other crows. Then they were served various delicacies to eat.

After the reception the king wanted to hear the white crow's teaching (*dhammaṃ*). At the king's behest his officials presented offerings of candles and incense [to the white crow]. The king approached [the crow], offered his respects, and then took a seat appropriate to his station. The white crow then honored King [Ādittarāja].

The compiler (*saṅgāhiko*) of the text elaborated its meaning in a poetic style pleasing to the ear as follows:[304]

> Then King Ādittarāja approached the white crow, paid his respects, and took a suitable seat. When the king paid homage to him, the white crow greeted the king with these pleasantries: "O, *mahārāja*, how are you? Are you bothered by any illness? Has your reign been successful? Are you fulfilling the ten virtues of the king (*dasa-dhamme akopaye*)? Are you protecting the country by providing an adequate food supply and keeping the citizens from disease? Do enemies fear your power, as the eye [fears] a shadow?[305]

King Ādittarāja replied:

> O, king of the crows, I suffer from no illness; I have no worries; I have ruled righteously in accordance with the ten virtues of the king; I have protected my state so that food is easily available and we are free from danger. Furthermore, there are no enemies who do not fear my power, as the eye does not fear a shadow. O, king of the crows, we welcome you. You have come from a long distance. I would like to ask you a question, O, exalted, egg-born one. Is it true that when the Buddha was alive he came [to this place] and prophesized that the Conqueror's relics [one day] would appear here?

Then the white king crow taught King Ādittarāja the truth (*sacca-dhammaṃ*) [about the relic]:[306]

> Yes, *mahārāja*! This is true. It is not a falsehood (*anālikaṃ*). The Omniscient Buddha was endowed with compassion (*sambuddho karuṇādhiko*) and did not seek happiness for himself. Every day he observed those who could be taught. Everywhere he went, both near and far, wherever they lived, he taught them the path and its fruit (*magga-phalā*) in order to liberate [them from suffering]. When they were liberated (*sabbasatte pamocetvā*) he returned to his residence again. From the time of his enlightenment until he reached *nibbāna,* [the Lord continued to teach the people].
>
> Once when the Buddha was residing at the lovely Deer Park in the neighborhood of Vārāṇasī where the hermits lived, he came upon the Mon village of Jarohaka. He then left the Deer Park to receive alms in that village and taught the people [there]. After that he came back and stood at this very place. I accompanied the Buddha with the sons of forest-dwelling Mon. The Exalted One prophesized to the hermits, "*Bhonto*, in the future this place will be a great city. At that time a king named Āditta will rule. He will fulfill your ancestors' prediction.[307] When I pass away one of my relics will emerge here. The relic will belong to the king and he will act for the welfare of your lineage (*ñātisaṅghaṃ*)."
>
> After saying this, the Enlightened One departed.[308] I myself appointed my grandchild to protect this place. Your majesty knew nothing of this when you built a toilet on the verandah.[309] Do not be angry [with the crow] for he was there only to warn and serve you.

Then, following the Buddha's teachings, the king-crow preached the Buddha's *dhamma* to the king imitating the Buddha (*buddhalīlāya*).

After listening to the white crow's teaching, the enraptured king was filled with faith.[310] He then spoke to his ministers, "O ministers, you must excavate the site today. Remove the polluted soil, and replace it will pure soil and sand."

After issuing his commands, the king worshipped the king of the crows with a magnificent offering and folding his hands in supplication he lauded the virtue (*guṇaṃ*) of the white crow, "O king of the crows, you are noble and long-lived. You have seen the Buddha and in his presence you have listened to his teaching. How unfortunate we are to have been born in an age without the Buddha. We have not seen the Buddha, but we have witnessed the community of noble monks. How well you have preached the *dhamma* that you heard from the Buddha's mouth. Therefore, we regard the *dhamma* you taught as if it were the teachings of the Buddha himself.[311]

The crow then said, "O king, may you live a long life; may you rule the kingdom righteously; may you never neglect the Buddha, the Dhamma, and the Saṅgha. O *mahārāja,* the Buddha prophesized that you would not forget to protect the Buddha's relics."[312] After uttering this [blessing], the crow returned [to his dwelling] together with his followers, leaving King Ādittarāja filled with tremendous joy.

[Someone asks,] "How can such a lowly creature like a crow know how to teach the *dhamma* in the manner of the Buddha?"

[To which one answers,] "To be sure, an ordinary crow is generally regarded as inferior. But the white crow is no ordinary bird; it is the Buddha's own disciple.[313] When the Buddha resided at Vārāṇasī this crow had attended to the Buddha and listened to his teaching. When the Buddha came here, this crow also followed him like one of the Buddha's disciples who always accompanied the Blessed One. As a disciple of the Buddha, the crow had the opportunity to listen to the Buddha's teachings (*buddhavacanaṃ*)."

Knowing the disposition and astuteness[314] of a crow and realizing that this crow was destined to live a long life, the Blessed One said, "After I have passed away, when the *arahanta* monks have vanished and only those monks who are enlightened but who cannot teach[315] remain, this white crow will preach the *dhamma* to everyone in accordance with my teachings.[316] Furthermore, it will protect the site of my relics. Therefore, this white crow is able to preach the *dhamma* by the power of the Enlightened One's own mind.[317] Furthermore, King Ādittarāja will make a grand offering to the crow, will pay homage to it, and he will be steadfast in his belief in the Buddha's prophecy."[318]

After the white king crow had returned to the Himavanta forests, the king left his palace, cleaned [the place where the relic would appear] with his own hands, and told his men to remove the desecrated soil and replace it with pure. Then he issued an order to dismantle and remove his own residence in the city to a place far away. There he had erected royal fences two meters in equal length at the four directional corners and filled the inside with gold and silver sand about a half meter thick. Gold and silver pots filled with different kinds of lotus and other fragrant blossoms were put along the inner and outer sides. Then gold and silver candles,[319] incense sticks, flowers, fragrant sandalwood paste, gold and silver flower pots, and banana shoots were put at the base and on the top of poles along the inside and outside of the fences. Triangular flags and cloth flags bordered the outer periphery.[320]

With these preparations completed, the king commanded that a drum be sounded throughout the city accompanied by the following announcement, "*Bhonto*, the Buddha's relics will appear at night in the middle of the king's courtyard. You should worship the bodily relics of the Blessed One (*bhagavato*) with offerings of candles, incense, perfume, and flowers, and lustrate the relics with water."

When the townspeople heard the announcement they were filled with joy. They carried candles, incense, flowers, fragrant sandalwood paste, bouquets, garlands of flowers, and bowls filled with fragrant water, and assembled in that place. After lustrating [the relic], worshipping it, and paying [the relic] homage (*vanditvā*), they sat in their appropriate places.

After bathing and putting on his full royal regalia, King Ādittarāja, surrounded by his consorts led by the queen and carrying a golden pitcher full of perfumed water, approached [the site of the Buddha's relics]. Brahmans and others such as ministers and wealthy householders followed the king. Upon his arrival, the king raised a golden pitcher above his head and respectfully poured water over the place where the relics were to appear. Afterward the queen and princess daughters also lustrated [the place].[321]

All the people led by the chief ministers approached from the four [cardinal] directions. Having paid homage to the place [where the relic would appear] by pouring water on it, they stood attentively. Then the king presented an offering of flowers and fragrant garlands, raised his hands over his head in supplication and respectfully recalled the Buddha's virtue (*buddhaguṇaṃ*). He then invited the Conqueror's relics [to appear] saying:

> O Noble, Omniscient One, you who have been so beneficent (*karuṇādhika*) to human beings when you were alive, you journeyed here from Vārāṇasī and stood at this very spot. You prophesized that your relics would appear at this place. If it is true that your relics will emerge, may they graciously demonstrate this miracle to me and all people.[322]

Immediately rays of the relic the size of a large banana flower radiated from the casket into the sky and the odor of perfume permeated the air. King Asoka's casket containing the sacred relics emitted rays of the seven kinds of precious gems and continued to glow for a long time through the power of the relics.[323] The king and all the people were astonished and enraptured. Removing their beautiful clothes and jewelry, they worshipped the relics to the rejoicing sounds of conch shells, drums, and five kinds of music.

This is the description of the manifestation of the relics and their descent again into the earth composed by the Mahāthera Bodhiraṃsi based on his recollection of an important [northern Thai] story.

The End of Chapter Fifteen

NOTES TO PART II

1. The Buddha's bodily radiance figures prominently as one of the primary Buddhological characteristics of northern Thai devotional literature of legendary genre, e.g., *tamnān, nidāna.* Prime examples are *The Buddha's First Enlightenment (Pathom Somphōt), Siddhattha's Renunciation* (*Sitthāt Ọk Buat*), and the large body of texts referred to as Buddha Chronicles (*phuttha tamnān*).

The Buddha of devotional piety radiates divine rays (*rasmi*) that represent the Buddha's omniscience and the powers acquired through advanced stages of meditation (*vipassanā-ñāṇa, samatha-ñāṇa*). These supernal rays extend throughout the three worlds, thereby establishing the Buddha's universal presence.

2. Mount Sumeru, the axial mountain of Indian cosmology.

3. Here venerating the Triple Gem, Buddha relics, and the *bodhi* tree have apotropaic power.

4. The Pāli text reads *cārikaṃ.* An alternative reading is *cāritaṃ* which in this case refers to a story as, for example, the *Buddhacārita.* In most cases I have glossed or footnoted Pāli terms of substantive import to the story or when I judged the inclusion of the Pāli to be of particular value to readers with a knowledge of Pāli. Pāli citations are inflected according to the text. Pāli transcription follows the Pali Text Society.

5. Traditionally it was believed that the prosperity of the kingdom depended on the virtue and power of the ruler. A sign of this prosperity is the seven gems or minerals as found, for example, in *Milinda-pañho* 267: *suvaṇṇa* (gold), *rajata* (silver), *muttā* (pearls), *maṇi* (crystal), *veḷuriya* (lapis lazuli), *vajira* (diamond), *pavāḷa* (coral). Also used in various similes such as the seven gems of the world ruler—wheel, elephant, horse, gem, woman, treasurer, adviser (*Mahā Sudassana Sutta*), and the seven moral *ratana*s or *sīla kkhanda.*

6. The meaning of this claim is unclear although minimally it refers to the Mon and the Lawa.

7. There appears to be two implications: that the original language of the story (northern Thai or Tai Yüan) is inferior to Pāli both as the language of Buddhism and as the language of the educated or those who dwell in the city (*puri*). More importantly, on the strength of this claim it

is reasonable to assume that the original text was written in the vernacular. This may account for the folkloric aspect of parts of the CDV and its kinship with popular northern Thai *phuttha tamnān.*

8. Bodhiraṃsi identifies the CDV with the universal Buddha story but only after first contextualizing the text both ritually and historically. The CDV can be read as a skillful exposition of Buddhism in Haripuñjaya as a particular embodiment of a universal truth.

9. Awareness meditation (*sati*) is at the heart of Buddhist practice. Because Siddhattha's Buddhahood was achieved by means of meditation, it is not surprising that within a text such as the CDV meditation is central among the Buddha's activities.

10. The final reference alludes to the episode in the legendary life of the Buddha in which the god Brahmasahaṃpati urges the newly enlightened Buddha to share the *dhamma* with human and divine beings.

11. According to Notton, *Chronique de La:p'un*, it is located south of modern Jayaphūm.

12. Literally, "sons of the forest" (*vanaputta*). This characterization serves to make three related points: (i) there were towns in the Chiang Mai valley prior to Haripuñjaya; (ii) the inhabitants of the area were uncultured; (iii) the first ruler of Haripuñjaya, Queen Cāma, is invited from a place of high culture, i.e., Lavapura (modern Lopburī).

13. Literally, "How can we know who you are?" In this passage and throughout the CDV, Bodhiraṃsi contextualizes references to the Pāli canon and commentary. See A II. 36.

14. Literally, "like a perfume bottle of four fragrances."

15. See D ii. 211; J i. 95; VvA 217. Also in Buddhist Hybrid Sanskrit describing the voice of the Buddha, e.g., *Avadāna Śataka* i. 149.

16. A widely used epithet for the Buddha in both Pāli canon and commentary. See Sn 995; Vism 201, 234; VvA 165; PvA 42, 287.

17. Reference to villagers whose livelihood depends partially on hunting and gathering in the forest.

18. The primary function of *phuttha tamnān* is to establish the physical presence of the Buddha in a given region or a particular place. This presence is represented by (i) the Buddha having been there, and by (ii) material signs of the Buddha, such as relics, footprints, and images.

19. The place reference is ambiguous. It could be Lavapura (Lopburī) or a Mon site south of Haripuñjaya such as Lampāng.

20. The prediction at the beginning of the chronicle of the appearance of the relic at Haripuñjaya and a second site, possibly Lampāng, immediately alerts the reader (or hearer) of the story to the fact that the central event of the CDV is the discovery and enshrinement of a Buddha relic at Haripuñjaya, thus linking the text with the northern Thai tradition

of *phuttha tamnān* (Buddha chronicles). The *vaṃsa* or "'lineage" aspect of the chronicle is secondary to the centrality of Buddha relic veneration. This reference to the division of the Buddha's bodily relics also connects this episode with the division of the Buddha's relics following his cremation (D II. 166) and the redivision of the relics at King Asoka's direction.

21. Literally, "unable or incompetent" (*abhabba*).

22. References to such general ethical and religious admonitions can be traced to several Suttas and commentarial texts, e.g., *Dhammapada, Sigālaka Sutta*.

23. Unlike many religious traditions, such as Christianity and Judaism, which have formal rites of initiation, lay affiliation with Theravāda Buddhism is marked by the simple act of affirming the Triple Gem (Buddha, Dhamma, Saṅgha) and the five basic ethical precepts.

24. In folklore the crow often plays the roles of trickster, prognosticator, or protector not unlike a shaman. The crow plays such a role in this text.

25. Literally, the site of "the future city" (*mahānagarajanitappadesaṃ*).

26. One *sọk* is equal to about a half meter or twenty inches.

27. At least from the time of King Asoka, Buddha relics have been linked to kingship. This tradition is hallowed in the *Mahāparinibbāna Sutta* in which the Buddha instructs his disciples to enshrine his bodily relics in *cetiya* (Thai, *jedī*) in the manner of the great world ruler kings. In various Theravāda chronicles, as is true of the CDV, kings enshrine relics and in doing so establish a cosmo-political center for their reigns. See Donald K. Swearer, *The Buddhist World of Southeast Asia*, chap. 2.

28. Ascetical powers of the renunciant life are associated in particular with the monk's robe and bowl. Hence, the Buddha's robe and bowl or parts thereof are the principal "relics of use." In this instance the bowl functions as the enabling agency of the Buddha's magical flight from northern India to northern Thailand.

29. "Power" is an unusual translation for the Pāli, *guṇa*, but seems more appropriate in this context than more conventional renderings, such as quality or merit. In popular Thai Buddhist texts, *guṇa* is often coupled with *teja* (splendor, fiery radiance, power).

30. The subject of the sentence is only understood. We interpret the subject to be the author of the text Bodhiraṃsi purports to be translating from the vernacular into Pāli to whom he refers as the compiler (*saṅgiko*).

31. Bodhiraṃsi's monastic lineage is uncertain, unlike Ratanapañña, the author of the *Jinakālamālīpakaraṇaṃ*, who is of the Wat Pā Daeng lineage. Buddhist sectarian transmission in northern Thailand is

discussed in several sources including Alexander B. Griswold, *Wat Pra Yün Reconsidered* (Bangkok: The Siam Society, 1975); Ratanapañña Thera, *The Sheaf of Garlands of the Epochs of the Conqueror (Jinakālamālīpakaraṇaṃ)*; François Bizot, *Les traditions de la pabbajjā en Asie du Sud-Est.* For an English translation of the chronicle of the Laṅka lineage of Wat Pā Daeng, see Donald K. Swearer and Sommai Premchit, "The Red Forest Monastery Chronicle of the Founding of Buddhism" and Sao Sāimöng Mangrāi, *The Pāḍaeng Chronicle and the Jengtung State Chronicle Translated.* The chronicle of the Wat Suan Dọk tradition has been edited and published in Thai. See Bumphen Rawin, *Mūlasāsanā Samnuan Lānnā* (The northern Thai version of the Mūlasāsanā).

32. *Mahācārika* probably refers to a written document inscribed on palm leaves. The northern Thai for "inscribing palm leaves" is *cān bai lān.* The Pāli form of *cān* could be *cārika.* Instead of a "large written record" or "text" we have chosen to translate the term as "important story," and have inserted northern Thai parenthetically because Bodhiraṃsi claims to be translating from the vernacular. Note, however, that Bodhiraṃsi bases the CDV on his recollection or remembrance of a written text.

33. Bodhiraṃsi appears to have written this first paragraph as a transition to chapter 2 where he introduces the story of Cāmadevī.

34. Refers to the four stages of the path (*magga*) to *nibbāna* sometimes considered as stages of sanctification: stream-enterer (*sotāpanna*), once-returner (*sakadāgāmi*), never-returner (*anāgāmi*), and *arahant.* See Nalinaksha Dutt, *Early Monastic Buddhism* (Calcutta: Calcutta Oriental Book Agency, 1960), chap. 13.

35. The shifting roles of the four sages fulfill diverse functions although from a text-critical perspective they represent an elaboration of their primary mediatorial role as sages (*isi*). Their initial identity as Buddhist monks gives priority to Buddhism and may represent a Buddhicization of the original legend. Their return to lay life follows the Thai custom of temporary ordination. Faithful observance of the precepts and of the sabbath is a worthy vocation in and of itself for which rebirth in heaven is the reward. The *isi* and the role they play is central to the story, and like the four sages of the CDV, are associated with mountains and embody special powers. Even as mountain ascetics/hermits/sages, however, their powers are those associated with higher meditative attainments in the Buddhist tradition; hence, even at this level the portrait of the *isi* is Buddhacized.

36. Here and elsewhere in the story, either Bodhiraṃsi or his sources insert doctrinal exposition into the text.

37. See D iii. 218; A iii. 280. Variations from standard Pāli terms: *iddhividhi* versus *viddhividhā*, *paracittavijñāṇa* versus *cetopariya-ñāṇa*.

38. *Nevasaññānāsaññāyatana* was omitted from the list in the manuscript. See *Paṭisambhidā-magga* i. 20.

39. In the Buddhist tradition craving is specifically associated with distinctions and dualities, hence, in this case the dual flavors of salty and sour. This view is basic to the theme of the so-called Story of Creation in the Pāli canon (see, *Aggañña Sutta,* D iii. no. 27).

40. The CDV differs from the TML, TM, JKM, and PY which list five *isi*: Vāsudeva, Sukkadanta, Anusissa (Anusisaṭa), Buddhajaṭila, and Subrahma. The CDV does not include Buddhajaṭila (associated with Doi Juhapabbata, i.e. Doi Plā Lai near Lamphūn) and substitutes the location designation (i.e., Sajjanāleyya) for Anusissa, the name used in the other chronicles (see Notton). It is unknown whether Bodhiraṃsi relied on a different source or simply altered the story.

The city of Lavo refers to Lavapura, modern Lopburī, in central Thailand. Vāsudeva is associated with Doi Suthēp on the outskirts of Chiang Mai after whom the mountain is named; Brahma (or Subrahma) with Doi Ngām (Doi Song Yọt) near Lampāng; Sukkadanta with Doi Samokan near Lopburī; and Sajjanāleyya with Sīsatchanālāi. This geographical arrangement provides a triangulation between the areas of Lamphūn-Chiang Mai, Lampāng, Lopburī, and Sukhōthai (see map). All four locations are on elevated areas near rivers. The Ping, Wang, and Kwang rivers are prominent features in the geography of the CDV. It is also worth noting, as indicated on the map, that Lopburī, Sīsatchanālāi, and Lampāng are located on a north-south axis.

41. Literally, "played the bliss of *jhāna*."

42. The Theravāda tradition enumerates four types of birth: *jalābuja* (womb born), *aṇḍaja* (egg born), *saṃsedaja* (water born), *opapātika* (spontaneously born). D iii. 230.

43. See note 120, for a discussion of Jayawickrama's interpretation of the meaning of the children born in animal footprints.

44. It is reasonable to assume that Bodhiraṃsi inserted this statement into the story to address the scepticism of some of his fifteenth-century listeners. Throughout the narrative Bodhiraṃsi inserts Buddhist ethical teachings, focussing on the relationships between parents and children and between kings and subjects.

45. The story of the hermit, Isisiṅga, the son of the *bodhisatta* and a doe, also appears in the *Alaṃbusā Jātaka* and in the *Niḷinikā Jātaka.*

46. See Part I for an analysis of the significance of twins and twinning in the texts.

47. Because *miga* also connotes "animal" in a generic sense, there could be a double meaning, a reference to a city being created in the midst of a forest wilderness and/or a reference to the special association between the Buddha and the deer park in Vārāṇasī.

The names of the couple and of their children vary among the accounts. In some cases differences appear to be copyist errors. In others there are substantial changes. For example, the daughter, Padumadevī, is omitted from the JKM account.

48. Appears to be a corruption of Kumārakanāsa. The names of the other two brothers are similarly altered.

49. The explanations given for the children's names represent an interest throughout the CDV in etiologies and etymologies, a significant feature of folk tales.

50. As an explanation of the name, it is logical that the town would be called Isinagara, the Hermit City, rather than Purinagara since *puri* and *nagara* mean essentially the same thing. However, the intention may be to draw a contrast between towns of lesser and greater development and culture as suggested by the terms *miga* and *puri*.

51. In Thai, the term *lūk* is used both for child and a bell clapper.

52. Reminiscent of the episode in the Pāli legendary life of the Buddha (*Nidāna Kathā*) wherein mother earth testifies on behalf of the Buddha's virtue in the face of Māra's challenge at the *bodhi* tree.

53. Natural retribution for moral wrongdoing is a universal theme in world mythology. In this case, both the nature of the moral offense and the consequent punishment fall short of the cosmic proportions it assumes in the flood story in the Hebrew scriptures, however, it is of a similar type despite the vastly differing theological contexts. The episode also reflects the common Thai custom of calling on various unseen powers for protection. (For a popular, well-illustrated book on the cult of the supernatural in Thailand see, John Hoskin, *The Supernatural in Thai Life* (Bangkok: Tamarind Press, 1993).

54. One of many instances where Buddhist teachings are inserted into the legendary tale of the founding of Haripuñjaya. The scene recalls the occasion when the Buddha taught the citizens of Kapilavatthu found in the first chapter of the commentary on the BV.

55. Dh., 78. Pandita Vagga. For a discussion of friendship in Buddhist ethics see, Phra Rajavaramuni, "Foundations of Buddhist Social Ethics," in *Ethics, Wealth, and Salvation: A Study in Buddhist Social Ethics*, ed. Russell F. Sizemore and Donald K. Swearer (Columbia: University of South Carolina Press, 1990), 29–53.

56. J iii. 106; J iii. 54; J iv. 71; J v. 452.

57. The text reads, *viruddhe*.

58. Mentioned in J vi. 518, 519; J ii. 365 ff, among other *jātaka* references.

59. Popular Buddhist literature expresses an ambivalence toward kings. On the one hand, as in the case of Ādittarāja in the CDV, they do good works such as enshrining Buddha relics and supporting the *saṅgha.* On the other hand, because of their potential to exercise abusive, autocratic power they are also feared and sometimes vilified. Both views of kingship are found in the CDV.

60. Refers to Mount Suthēp which rises above the city of Chiang Mai.

61. In classical conceptions of kingship, including Indian Buddhism, the well-being of the kingdom depends on the virtue of the king. Or, in negative terms, natural disasters are seen as a consequence of an evil king.

62. It is noteworthy that in this instance the reward for merit-making (*puñña*) does not result from *kamma,* but from the intercession of the *deva,* and in the following sentence the earth punishes the unrighteous. At the level of popular belief, a strict kammic construction of moral retribution is problematic at best.

63. J iii. 158; J ii. 199.

64. Dh. 183.

65. Refers to Jātaka no. 369 (iii. 206).

66. Ethical advice found in various texts such as the *Sigālovāda Sutta,* the *Maṅgala Sutta,* the *Dhammapada,* and *Jātaka* stories.

67. The CDV uses both Himālaya and Himavanta.

68. The three classifications of Buddha relics are bodily relics, relics of use, and relics of association. Standardized forms of crystaline bodily relics exist in Thailand. Relics of use are thought of primarily in terms of the Buddha's robe and bowl; the principal relic of association is a Buddha image. Material forms associated with relics, e.g., *cetiya* (Thai, *jedī*), are also venerated as in the case of the stone pedestal in the text that miraculously arose to receive the Buddha's alms bowl. A monastery in the Pāsāng district of Lamphūn province in northern Thailand associated with the Buddha's legendary visit to northern Thailand is venerated as a place where the Buddha left a footprint and put his robe on a laterite stone slab to dry (Wat Phraphutthabat Tākphā). Buddha footprints are an omnipresent form of a Buddha relic that represent an instantiation of the Buddha's presence in the area.

69. *Deva*s and *devatā*s figure prominently in the CDV. The term *devatā,* which occurs the most frequently, refers to various beings classified as *deva*s. The *Cullaniddesa* (308) lists five different groups based on the principle that any being to whom an offering is made or a gift given is

a *devatā*: (i) ascetics; (ii) domestic animals; (iii) physical forces and elements; (iv) lower gods, such as *nāga*, *yakkha*; (v) higher gods, such as Indra, Brahma. (T. W. Rhys Davids and William Stede, *The Pali Text Society's Pali-English Dictionary* (London: Luzac & Company, 1966), 330.

70. In chapter 1 the *devatās* act to counter the sage's intention. In this instance the *devatā* helps to implement Vāsudeva's purpose.

71. A common feature of the text is the reading and prognostication of signs. The crucial instance of this phenomenon is King Ādittarāja's reading of a sign which prevents him from desecrating the Buddha relic whose discovery by the king had been predicted by the Buddha (see chaper 15). The shorter account of this episode in the JKM omits this crucial element in its straightforward, more factual account.

72. Presumably referring to Kunarikanāsa and Padumadevī. This act appears to link Migasaṅghanagara with Haripuñjaya.

73. This meaning is extrapolated from the Pāli, "*kasmā sā evaṃ karoti*."

74. Magical flight is one of the powers of the *isi* in the story. It is associated with ascetical practice found in many Indian religious traditions, such as Buddhism, Jainism, Hinduism. Magical flight is, furthermore, one of the chief characteristics of shamanism. See Mircea Eliade, *Shamanism: Archaic Techniques of Ecstasy* (Princeton, N.J.: Princeton University Press, 1958). Shamanism in northern Thailand has a special association with mountains, for example, Doi Suthēp, Doi Chiang Dao, and Doi Tung, where Buddhist reliquaries are found.

75. The range of etiologies includes events related to the legendary history of the chronicle, the *isi*, and the *devatās*.

76. See the explanation of the same discoveries in chapter 14. It is particularly interesting to note that these signs portend a balance of negative and positive forces and are not solely positively auspicious. Subsequently, this "realism" is then spelled out in terms of good, bad, and mediocre kings.

77. The ten royal virtues are generosity (*dāna*), high moral character (*sīla*), self-sacrifice (*pariccāga*), honesty (*ājjava*), kindness and gentleness (*maddava*), self-control (*tapa*), nonanger (*akkodha*), nonviolence (*avihiṃsa*), patience (*khanti*), conformity to law (*avirodhana*) (J v. 378).

78. Although the three alternatives have a formal, logical nature, they also represent the realistic and pragmatic ethical implications of the Buddhist analysis of existence, in this case a representative range of monarchial rule.

79. This passage makes a connection typical of both canonical and noncanonical Buddhist texts between the quality of kingship and quality

of life. Such an association is, of course, not unique to Buddhism or even to Indian religio-cultural traditions.

80. Note the contrast between the inevitability of change in the mundane, day-to-day realm and the unchangeability of the Buddha's teaching or *dhamma*. The contrast illustrates two central Buddhist doctrinal perspectives: the universality of impermanence (*anicca*) and the distinction between the mundane (*lokiya*) and transmundane (*lokuttara*).

81. Venerating the *devatās* of specific locations continues to play an important role in popular Thai belief. The tradition of tree *devatā* has even been invoked by contemporary Thai environmentalists as a way of promoting greater respect for the integrity of forests in the face of rampant deforestation for commercial purposes. The episode with the elderly tree *devatā* has a particular poignancy in the face of the destruction of the teak forests in northern Thailand and old-growth forests worldwide.

82. The name of modern Lamphūn is derived from "Labbhuna" (from *labhati,* to receive permission). An etiology for the term *Haripuñjaya* appears later in the text.

83. A circular perimeter typified Mon cities in contrast to the four-sided shape of Khmer cities.

84. The conch shell is a sign of cosmogonic, creative power. That the conch shell is acquired from Sajjanāleyya seems to imply a connection with that city as well. In short, the construction of Haripuñjaya and the summoning of Cāmadevī as the first queen connects Lavapura and Sajjanāleyya. It is unclear, however, if the Sajjanāleyya referred to in the CDV was located at the same site of the thirteenth-century Thai city-state.

85. Ju Takuan, a Chinese emissary to Angkor, mentions in his diary that in the early days, Sajjanāleyya was close to the sea. This hardly seems possible unless the reference is to another Sajjanāleyya.

86. A probable confusion since Sajjanāleyya's mountain was designated at Latāṅga in the second chapter.

87. The *hatthīliṅga* is a half elephant, half swan mythological figure. In northern Thailand it may be constructed as a funeral carriage as the *hatthīliṅga* is believed to possess the power to carry the soul of the deceased to heaven.

88. Two births refers to the birth of the egg itself, and the birth from the egg.

89. The Pāli reads "*ciraṃ mataṃ*" (long dead). It would have been demeritorious if the *hatthīliṅga* bird had taken a living conch shell.

90. One fathom equals about two and a half meters so the total circumference would be approximately 38,750 meters or approximately twenty-four miles. From a myth-legend interpretative perspective, the

number 1550 is a sacred cosmological number rather than a literal number with any historical significance.

91. The term *miga* is extrapolated into the human sphere as socially and culturally crude as well as morally problematic. By characterizing the indigenous population of the Haripuñjaya area in this way, the author offers a justification for choosing a ruler from another area.

92. As is typical of folkloric literature, the CDV constructs a homologic relationship between animal and human realms. In this case negative human qualities are personified by animals. In other cases positive human qualities are represented by animals. The interposition of human and animal realms is especially characteristic of the animals tales found in the *jātaka* stories.

93. The text reads "*manussajātikānaṃ.*" We assume that "*milakkha*" has been lost from the text because the contrast being drawn is between primitive/barbarian/uncultured/forest and civilized/cultured/urban. In this passage the compiler appears to put the Milakkha on a level with animals. From a Buddhist cosmological perspective it should be kept in mind that rebirth in the animal realm is one of the consequences of demeritorious actions. Consequently, there is an implicit moral/spiritual judgment associated with the *milakkha* as primitive and barbaric. From a Buddhist psychological perspective, mental states often are likened metaphorically to animal behavior.

94. Literally, "even though my head were to be shattered."

95. The five feminine charms are beauty of hair, flesh, teeth, skin, and youth (*kesa, maṃsa, aṭṭhi, chavi,* and *vaya*).

96. Queen Cāma is, in many respects, a personification of fertility and the powers and taboos associated with female reproduction. In this instance the sages consider her to be a worthy progenitor of a lineage of rulers. Other elements in the popular construction of Cāma's sexual, creative powers, several of which are found in the Lamphūn Chronicle (TML), include the following: sexual symbolism associated with the founding of towns on her journey from Lavo to Haripuñjaya (these include presentday Họt and Tak); she is pregnant upon her arrival at Haripuñjaya and gives birth to twins; the incident with the Lawa chieftain, Vilaṅga, in which Cāma's menstrual blood destroys Vilaṅga's power (see Part I). The fact that Cāma's Lavapura husband becomes a monk does more than provide a justification for Cāma's departure from Lavo for Haripuñjaya. As an ascetic foil, he serves to underscore her gender and sexual power, which the text links with her political strength as ruler and as progenitor of a lineage of rulers.

The most important representatives of asceticism in the CDV are the *isis* with whom Cāmadevī is associated. The *isis* and Cāmadevī are constucted in the story as an apposition of opposing powers—i.e., fertile woman/ascetic male. The integration of polarities characterizes the Indian yogic tradition in a broad sense and figures significantly in the cosmogonic meaning of the CDV.

97. Considerable attention is given to kingship in the *Cakkavatti-sīhanāda Sutta* (D iii, no. 26) and other Buddhist texts. A close relationship exists between the meritorious virtue required for both Buddhahood and world rulership (*cakkavatti*). This passage reflects a common assumption regarding kingship; namely, that the personal health and virtue of the king is mimetically reflected in the well-being of the realm.

98. Question-and-answer dialogues between monks and kings occupy a hallowed place in the Buddhist textual tradition of which one of the best examples is *The Questions of King Milinda* (*Milinda-pañho*), a text often found in northern Thai palm-leaf collections. A similar genre of northern Thai origin is the *Panhā Thera Jan,* a dialogue between the monk Candasoma and King Ku' Nā of Chiang Mai (1355–1385). For a discussion of this period of northern Thai history, see David K. Wyatt, *Thailand: A Short History* (New Haven, Conn.: Yale University Press, 1984), chap. 4 and 5; Hans Penth, *A Brief History of Lān Nā: Civilizations of North Thailand* (Chiang Mai: Silkworm Books, 1994).

99. Literally *pāde deva namassāmi.*

100. It appears that in exchange for Cāmadevī, Gavaya was authorized to offer a bride price. A less literal interpretation would see "gems" as a generic reference to the resources of the kingdom. Historically, this scene in the narrative may be a metaphorical allusion to trade between Haripuñjaya and Lavapura and a reference to the rich natural resources of northern Thailand that may have been the incentive for Mon incursion into the Chiang Mai valley.

101. Literally, "I understand neither this matter nor its meaning" (*idaṃ vatthuñca idaṃ nayaṃ*).

102. Harald Hundius, a scholar of northern Thai literature, speculates on the basis of the content of the CDV as well as the apparent symmetry of all the extant CDV manuscripts that there may not be a two and a half fascicle hiatus (interview with the author, Chiang Mai, Thailand, January 1996). In this connection, it is striking that the material spliced into the 1920 printed version of the CDV from the JKM adds nothing of substance to the story. It is also possible that the story of Vilaṅga was specifically excised from the text by later monastic censors. (See Part I for a discussion of this point.)

103. It appears that the JKM Buddhacizes the Cāmadevī story even more than Bodhiraṃsi's version. The formulaic retinues seem somewhat out of character with the style of Bodhiraṃsi's narrative.

104. The basic meaning of *puñja* is very similar to the meaning of *cetiya*—i.e., pile or heap. It is logical to assume, regardless of the specific translation, that the raised area on which the royal consecration took place was replete with cosmological symbolism. For a description of the coronation ritual in Thailand, see H. G. Quartich Wales, *Siamese State Ceremonies* (London: Bernard Quartich, 1931).

105. Indravarman was a traditional title for Khmer kings.

106. In other northern Thai chronicles the name of the ruler of the Lawa appears as Vilaṅga or Balaṅga.

107. See Part I for a discussion of the Lawa.

108. Literally, "feared for his death" (*maraṇabhayabhīto*).

109. Māenām Sāra or Hua Māesān, a small branch of the Ping to the south of Lamphūn.

110. The Wang River in Lampāng Province.

111. Ratanapañña mentions a fifth sage, Buddhajaṭila, who also appears in the TML, TM, and PY. He also changes the name of Cāmadevī's second son from Anantayasa to Indavara.

112. Implies a miraculous construction.

113. Overlapping accounts between this section and portions of the CDV point to several differences between the two chronicles. The JKM abbreviates the CDV and where there are substantive differences, e.g., four versus five sages, the JKM relies on a different source, possibly the Lamphūn Chronicle (TML). Some points of comparison among chronicle sources are mentioned in Part I, including a greater interest in traditional chronicle historiography on the part of Ratanapañña.

114. The Cūḷasakarāja calendar of Thailand (the Sakkarāja calendar of Myanmar) commences with the new moon of Visākha, Friday, March 20, 638 C.E. This differs from the Indian Śaka Era, which begins with the sun's entry into Aries (about the 13th–14th of April) in 78 C.E. The Buddhasakarāja calendar of Thailand begins in 543 B.C.E.

The *Phongsāwadān Yōnok* notes that the Lamphūn Chronicle (*Tamnān Lamphūn*) agrees with the JKM in contrast with the CDV. (Prayā Prachākitkorajak, *Phongsāwadān Yōnok*, 165).

115. Sometime around February 19, 661 C.E.

116. The number and names of the *isi* vary between the CDV and the JKM. In the second chapter of the CDV there are four: Vāsudeva, Brahma, Sajjanāleyya, and Sukkadanta. Anusissa in the JKM appears to be Sajjanāleyya in the CDV.

117. See page 63 for a list of the higher knowledges.

118. The JKM uses Indian place names for rivers and mountains in northern Thailand.

119. Literally, "tumeric vine." Identified with the Phra Sī mound in Sī Sajjanāleyya.

120. Jayawickrama translates this passage in the JKM as "elephant-footed" and so on, ignoring the locative Pāli construction, *hatthipade* ("in the footprint of an elephant"). He also provides a rationalistic gloss—the six children were deformed—which confuses the point of the legend, namely, that the indigenous population was insufficiently civilized to create and govern a *nagara.* (Ratanapañña Thera, *The Sheaf of Garlands of the Epochs of the Conqueror,* 98).

121. See Alambusā Jātaka (*Jātaka,* no. 523).

122. Aṅgurisi in the CDV. Jayawickrama translates Kunarisi as "sage of subhuman origin" (Ratanapañña Thera, *The Sheaf of Garlands of the Epochs of the Conqueror,* 98).

123. Dhanit Yupho identifies Migasaṅgha as a town at the foot of Mount Suthēp (Ratanapañña Thera, *The Sheaf Garland of the Epochs of the Conqueror,* 99). While there are remains of a pre-Tai site at the foot of Mount Suthēp, it is speculative to identify it as Migasaṅgha. While not wanting to belittle the possible historical value of the CDV, to read the chronicle primarily through a historical lens is problematical and ignores the legendary character of the story.

124. The CDV refers to the names as Kunarikanāsa, Kunarikarosa, and Kunarikadhaṃsa.

125. Dhanit Yupho speculates that it was located south of Lamphūn (Ratanapañña Thera, *The Sheaf Garlands of the Epochs of the Conqueror,* 99).

126. In Thai the parallel between a child beating its mother and a clapper striking a bell is based on the term *lūk,* a term used both for a child and for a clapper inside a bell. See chapter 2 of the CDV for the details of the story.

127. Note how the JKM transforms this folkloric, omen-filled passage in the CDV into a more rationalized, historical form.

128. A Mon settlement located between Lavapura and Ayutthayā.

129. January 19, 662 C.E.

130. The dedication of merit to guardian deities *(devatās)* has two major features: (i) the syncretism between the Buddhist concept of merit-making (Thai, *tham bun*) and Brahmanical-animistic aspects of the religious culture; (ii) the causally efficacious power of merit-making applied in this particular manner. Despite the view among Theravādins that Buddhism is anti-Brahmanical and antiritualistic, "dedicating merit and righteous offerings" to guardian deities seems to mirror the purpose of Brahmanical-Vedic sacrifice of influencing the gods to reward the patron of the ritual.

131. Literally, "to see you."

132. The analogy suggests a climate different from that of the Chiang Mai valley today or possibly a borrowing from another source.

133. One *byāma* equals about two and a half meters.

134. Literally, "human beings" (*manussā*).

135. See Part I, Interpretation, for a discussion of the paradox of child warriors.

136. Literally, "in both hands."

137. *horādhipatādīnaṃ brāhmaṇānaṃ ca maṅgalaratanañca mahāsakkārehi pūjesi.* Refers to the *Jayaddisa Jātaka.*

138. *mayaṃ tumhākaṃ nissāya sukhena labhimhā.*

139. Classical Pāli texts stress the fact that although a good king is strong and backed by the power of arms, he is also righteous, virtuous, and even nonviolent. In this passage a good king must overcome the three *kilesas*—greed, hatred, and delusion. Bodhiraṃsi concludes the chapter with a homily on Buddhist morality directed to kings, in particular.

140. Literally, "said this and that (*idañcidañca*) to us."

141. The Pāli, *nattāro*, literally means "nephews." It is used in the Thai sense of referring to a younger person in relationship to someone older rather than a biological relationship.

142. Erāvaṇa appears in the *Rāmāyaṇa.*

143. One of the focal interests of the CDV is dynastic lineage and in this sense the chronicle reflects the *vaṃsa* genre that gives the text its name. Yet, although the chronicle does delineate a genealogy of Haripuñjaya from Cāmadevī to Ādittarāja, two distinct but related aspects of lineage dominate the text: (i) that a worthy ruling lineage (meaning Mon or Mon-Khmer) be established at Haripuñjaya; (ii) and that the lineage not only be worthy but also that it be inclusive, incorporating the indigenous Lawa population through intermarriage. Historically, the text corroborates inscriptional evidence discovered at Lamphūn that Haripuñjaya was an early center of Mon culture in northern Thailand and that intermarriage cemented the relationship between the Mon and the Lawa.

144. Literally, "do not be angry with me."

145. See Part I, Interpretation, for a discussion of twins. The marriage of the two pairs of twins suggests in an almost Durkheimian sense that Haripuñjaya and Khelāṅga form a single, inclusive moral community or unified kingdom (*raṭṭhā ekato*).

146. Note the parallelism between postures befitting an assessment of both physical beauty, and meditation. In other words, both physical and mental aspects of existence are seen as a dynamic totality.

147. Possibly the equivalent of a carpenter bee. In Thai, *phamọn* are larger than ordinary bees.

148. Literally, "the two states are one."

149. Literally, "When children quarrel and are angry with each other, they will love one another again when their parents see them."

150. The alliance through marriage would appear to be between Haripuñjaya and the indigenous population of the area, namely the Lawa, referred to by the generic term *milakkha.* On the basis of both chronicle and inscriptional evidence it is assumed that Cāmadevī was a Mon or that the Cāmadevī legend represents the subjection of the indigenous Lawa population of the Lamphūn area by Mon from Lavapura (modern Lopburī) prior to the incursion of the Khmer into Thailand. The historical significance of the identification of Cāmadevī as Khmer in this passage is problematical. Linguistically the relationship between Mon, Lawa, and Khmer is confused by the fact that the language of the Lua, modern descendents of the Lawa in northern Thailand, is an Austro-Asiatic language as is Mon-Khmer. Furthermore, Hans Penth notes that some Lamphūn inscriptions in Mon script contain words that appear to be a Lawa-ized Mon that to date no one has been able to translate. Penth refers to the Mon of the Lamphūn area as "country Mon" as distinguished from the urban Mon further to the south in Lopburī and other towns in the southern part of north Thailand, especially Sīsatchanālāi and Sukhōthai. It may be reasonable to assume that ethnic and even cultural distinctions among the Mon, Khmer, and Lawa in the geographic region bounded by Lopburī to the south and Lamphūn to the north were more fluid than the polarity drawn between civilization/town/Mon (or Mon-Khmer) and uncivilized/forest/Milakkha (Lawa) as represented in the CDV.

151. Royal consecrations, both coronations and marriage, are associated with the Brahmanical tradition represented by the sages, and not with Buddhist monks.

152. The name Mahantayasa is omitted from the text.

153. Suggests a matrilineal line of descent. Matrilineage could be a sociological feature in the story of Cāmadevī as the first ruler of Haripuñjaya, although internal evidence in the CDV does not necessarily lead to that conclusion.

154. These passages integrate four distinctive elements in the chronicle: (i) the magical power of ritual, in this case consecration (*abhiseka*); (ii) various Buddhist elements such as the power of the Triple Gem, the veneration of relics, and the observance of the five precepts (*pañcasīla*); (iii) the overriding importance of lineage creation and maintenance; and (iv) the king as protector with the Buddhist religion

(*sāsana*) as a restraint on his arbitrary power. Although it is possible to analyze distinctive cultural and religious elements within the text—such as the role of the *isi*, specific Buddhist ethical teachings, and so on—they are overlapping and integrated, thereby making rigid differentiations problematic.

155. The powers generated by the *abhiññās*.

156. In the chronicle, kings are both empowered and restrained not only by Buddha relics and the Triple Gem, but also by *isi* (sages/hermits/ascetics) and *devatā*.

157. Literally, "Those words will not last a long time for them."

158. Although many rituals and religio-moral instructions are not in conflict in the CDV, occasionally they are juxtaposed. In this case, Bodhiraṃsi suggests that moral instruction (the *dasarājadhamma*) takes precedence over the coronation ritual. The subsequent passage may suggest Bodhiraṃsi's subtle criticism of those who give priority to Brahmanical type rituals over moral instruction. In northern Thailand such conflict still persists.

159. Literally, "supported their mother" (*mātaraṃ upaṭṭhākaṃsu*). Note the interconnection between honoring the Triple Gem and one's parents. Teachers are often included in this list. In Thailand, January 16, is celebrated as "honoring teachers" day and New Year ceremonies include paying formal respects to parents, teachers, and elders.

160. Reference to the three postures can be generalized to mean happiness in all aspects of life. In the text the three postures are also used to describe physical beauty and meditation.

161. This passage makes clear that major merit-making donations to a *wat* include the following: *vihāra*, *kuṭi*, and Buddha image. The list omits a *cetiya*, although the enshrining of the Buddha relic in the *cetiya* at Haripuñjaya is the culminating event of the story.

162. In being the sole donor the queen derives greater merit than if shared among many sponsors of the *dāna*.

163. The five monasteries correspond to the four cardinal directions plus a fifth whose location is ambiguous in the text. For cosmological symmetry it should have been in the center of the city. Even though the symmetry is inexact, the cosmological directional intent is obvious.

164. The numbers 5,000 and 500 are commonly used in Buddhist literature to indicate a large number and not meant literally. The chronicle writer connects the exemplary piety of Cāmadevī with the piety of the inhabitants of Haripuñjaya that, in turn, is linked to the peace, happiness, and prosperity of the kingdom.

165. The passage describes the *uposatha* observance days and traditional activities on those days: (i) going to the Buddha, Dhamma, and

Saṅgha for refuge; (ii) taking the five or eight precepts; (iii) listening to a sermon; (iv) and giving food to the monks (*dāna*). These continue to be the major elements of sabbath day observance.

166. In this passage, ordinary folk are exhorted to follow the exemplary model of royalty in supporting the *buddhasāsana*. While ordinary citizens cannot aspire to the social status of royalty, they can embody Buddhist virtues that transcend class.

167. The repetition of "twin" in this case reinforces the view of Khelāṅga as a twin city to Haripuñjaya. See Part I, Interpretation.

168. Literally, "to ask for pardon or forgiveness" (*khamāpeti*).

169. The word "*tāta*" (father) is commonly used in Pāli and in Thai as an address of respect and affection in many relationships.

170. A possible reference to the Māe Sān River.

171. Although the description of Anantayasa's journey is brief, it does convey the sense of a trial or test. Anantayasa first engages an ordinary hunter and then the master hunter, Khelāṅga, and has to pay him a handsome price for his services before he reaches the hermitage of Subrahma. The sage then tests the prince with a number of formal questions before he agrees to take him to the site of the future city of Khelāṅga. Thus, although the founding of Khelāṅganagara lacks the cosmic drama of the construction of Haripuñjaya, it requires that Ananatayasa undergo a mazelike test not unlike the celebrated wanderings of Prince Vessantara that eventually proved the prince worthy of kingship. The annual preaching of the Vessantara Jātaka in northern Thailand traditionally included a ritual passage through a maze constructed at the temple entrance. In the CDV, Anantayasa's journey contrasts with the army of Lavo's wanderings on their way to attack Haripuñjaya (see chapter 14).

172. A square copper coin. For an explanation see, T. W. Rhys Davids and William Stede, *The Pali Text Society's Pali-English Dictionary*, 202.

173. Note the association between merit and health or the interconnection between moral, spiritual, and physical well-being.

174. Although Mahantayasa's response appears to make Cāmadevī responsible for his request, his choice of words reflects polite, deferential behavior toward a mother by a son.

175. The oval shape of the Haripujñaya city wall contrasts with Khelāṅga whose city walls are square suggesting a possible Khmer influence.

176. Presumably refers to the Lawa but the designation may include other indigenous groups.

177. Currently the city of Lampāng.

178. At the end of every chapter Bodhiraṃsi refers to written sources (*mahācārikaṃ*) and throughout the narrative quotes from "ancient sources." It is difficult to determine whether this pattern is a means by which Bodhiraṃsi is legitimating his story or if he is actually recalling specific quotations from various texts or consulting specific manuscripts. It is quite clear, however, that Bodhiraṃsi incorporates numerous references from many sources. In short, he is not simply translating into Pāli a vernacular story about Queen Cāma.

179. Vāsava is another name for Sakka (Indra).

180. *rukkhārukkhaṃ vanāvanaṃ abhirato.* This passage describes Mahābrahma as though he were a Buddhist monk.

181. Here Bodhiraṃsi's implied criticism is a teaching attributed to the Buddha. By incorporating it into the CDV Bodhiraṃsi appears to critique the traditional lay Buddhist merit-making practices of his day. The author is suggesting to his lay audience that gifts to the monks of candles and flowers may be meritorious (*puñña*) in a kammic sense but they are of no practical value.

182. Because the four monastic requisites are *cīvara, piṇḍapāta, senāsana,* and *bhesajja* (medicine), this list is somewhat repetitive.

183. Note that (i) gifts are given to both monks and Brahmans following the example of canonical texts such as the *Sigālaka Sutta*; (ii) that such merit-making gifts by a son are seen as acts on behalf of his mother; and (iii) that the reward for such charity has both a present, this worldly dimension, as well as a future, other worldly consequence.

184. Offerings as a sign of respect rather than as gifts with merit-making potential. In the translation we have retained the repetitive formal greeting and leave-taking indicative of the hierarchical nature of relationships between monk and laity, elder and younger, parent and child, ruler and subject.

185. *Pālite appamādaṃ sune dhamme yuñjante buddhasāsane sīlavatte paṭipatte cakkavattiṃ 'nudhammike jante abhipālente añña-sattena ahiṃsake.*

186. This passage in the imperative mode as well as others of a similar nature in the CDV indicate the important role played by distinguished scholar-monks such as Bodhiraṃsi in regard to the conduct of the affairs of state and of society, at least at the level of moral persuasion. Monks may not have been actively involved in politics and matters of social behavior, but they certainly were not isolated from the affairs of the world. Monks continue to play a similar role in Thai Buddhism and their increasingly active political involvement has been supported by Sulak Sivaraksa and other lay Buddhist social activists, but criticized by more traditional lay Buddhists for compromising their monastery-based spiritual role.

187. Literally, "pay homage at the feet of the sages."

188. Formulaic greetings and responses indicate hierarchial social status and, in this case, also refer specifically to the nature of the relationship. Because *isis* are forest or mountain ascetics, their food supply was often unpredictable and their physical safety jeopardized by their living environment. Stories of ascetics taming wild animals through the power of their extraordinary attainments constitute an important element in popular hagiographic writings.

189. Literally, "to put your feet on my head." A sign of utmost respect paid to royal or religious personages.

190. Note that although *bhikkhus* and Brahmans are always differentiated, they are treated in a similar manner. A major exception in this case is that while the monks do not receive a formal honorarium, Brahmans do. In Thai religious practice today, material gifts to monks (*āmisadāna*) often take the place of an honorarium. Lay leaders like the *ājān wat* receive an honorarium for leading religious rituals (see Part I, note 19).

191. That is, good action, good speech, good thought.

192. That is, three kinds of good action, four kinds of good speech, three kinds of good thought (D iii. 269, 290).

193. Generosity, high moral character, self-sacrifice, honesty, kindness, self-control, nonanger, nonviolence, patience, and democratic spirit (J v. 378).

194. A northern Thai digestive known as *miang*, usually enjoyed after a meal.

195. An act of respect by the son toward his mother.

196. The consecration ceremony for Queen Cāma at Khelāṅga arranged by her son appears to be an act of filial veneration in which Anantayasa symbolically gives up his kingship to his mother.

197. Anantayasa honors his mother by having her eat first. This is a specific expression not only of affection but of social hierarchy.

198. A major theme of popular Buddhist texts like the CDV is the mutual love, concern, and care between parents and children. Although philosophically such mutual care may be tied to doctrines of *kamma* and *puñña*, at the affective level these stories depict normative Buddhist values of empathy, sympathy, and love. Thus, while the narrative personae of the CDV are sages and kings who appear to be far removed from ordinary Buddhist laity, the didactic content of the text focuses on ethical ideals and behavioral norms. Bodhiraṃsi's interest in the relationship between parents and children can be extended to include a kind of parental relationship between sages and royalty. However, the primary relationship is between Cāmadevī and her sons. See the *Sigālaka Sutta*

(D. iii. no. 31) for a more extended treatment of the relationship between parents and children.

199. Cāmadevī's decision to divide her time between Khelāṅga and Haripuñjaya could be interpreted as giving equal legitimation to the two towns. From a historical perspective, one might infer either that Khelāṅga was becoming more important at the time represented by the narrative or that, in the fifteenth century when the CDV was written, Lampāng rivaled Lamphūn in importance.

200. In practice, *kiḷissāmi* means to go hunting or just for a walk in the forest as in northern Thai, *pai aeo doi,* means to walk for pleasure in the mountains.

201. The connection between merit (*puñña*) and the care of one's mother establishes a significant link between merit and ethics. In Thai Buddhism merit-making activities are generally associated with specific acts in support of the *bhikkhu saṅgha.* Merit-making activities—often of a ritual nature—are sometimes separated from ethics (*sīla, cariya-dhamma*). The CDV challenges such a separation.

202. The modern city of Lampāng. Wat Lampāng Luang just outside of Lampāng proper marks this location.

203. Presumably the Lawa.

204. Once again the author stresses the theme of inclusiveness and harmony, in this instance, a unity engendered by the common support of Buddhism.

205. *bheri, mudiṅga, paṇḍava, amukhara, saṅkha.*

206. It is tempting to interpret Cāmadevī's response to Anantayasa from the modern perspective of a mother trying to "cut the apron strings," especially considering the seemingly petulant pleas of her son. She is creating an opportunity for her younger son to develop into a worthy ruler on his own.

207. *anujānāhi maṃ gantuṃ sotthinā tva tejasā.*

208. The Pāli term *natta* connotes a respectful, affiliative relationship.

209. Literally, "think about or consider" (*vicintesi*).

210. Some students of Theravāda Buddhism have constructed the Theravāda worldview around two poles, the kammic, including merit, and the nibbanic incorporating impermanence that appears to deconstruct the cosmology of *kamma* and *puñña.* See Melford E. Spiro, *Buddhism and Society*; Winston L. King, *In the Hope of Nibbana: An Essay on Theravāda Ethics* (LaSalle, Ill.: Open Court, 1964). This passage demonstrates that merit and impermanence are thoroughly harmonized in the mind of Bodhiraṃsi.

211. Literally, "sons of the Buddha" (*buddhaputtaṃ*).

212. It is generally believed that pious observance prior to death will enhance one's rebirth prospects.

213. Attitudes toward death are ambiguous: (i) death is part of the natural process of impermanence; (ii) death is a consequence of *kamma*; (iii) death may result in a pleasant rebirth as a consequence of righteous conduct and pious good deeds (or the opposite).

214. The Three Characteristics of Existence function as a mantric death breviary in this instance. In Thailand, Buddhist funeral chants and sermons focus on the teaching of impermanence.

215. A minor but noteworthy part of the story is the important place of music in the celebratory life of the community during processions, royal consecrations, and funerals. At several points in the narrative, musical instruments are enumerated in some detail indicating the importance of music in the life of the community and possibly in the author's as well.

216. Refers to Wat Cāmadevī also known as Wat Kukut located on the western outskirts of the presentday city of Lamphūn. Cāmadevī's relics are believed to be enshrined in the four-sided *cetiya* mentioned in the story, although this remains to be verified.

217. The water-pouring dedication of merit to the deceased constitutes the conclusion of most meritorious ceremonial rituals.

218. See Part I, Interpretation, for a discussion of the transfer of merit.

219. Note that the exemplary role of the Buddhist king includes not only establishing the citizenry in "righteous deeds," but also instructing them in the *dhamma*. Warrant for this role is grounded in Buddhist texts, e.g., the *Milinda-pañho*, and in the example of King Asoka.

220. In this concluding passage to chapter 11 the compiler of the text on which Bodhiraṃsi has based his translation identifies the generic term, *milakkha* (primitive, barbaric), with the Mon and the Lawa. It is noteworthy that the primitive/civilized polarity is not drawn in terms of the primitive Lawa and civilized Mon. From this perspective, the fact that Cāmadevī is identified as Mon is less important than that she comes from Lavapura.

221. Presumably a name associated with the area because of the Biṅga (Ping) River.

222. This discussion reinforces the narrative of the founding of towns in chapters 2 and 3. Moreover, it strongly implies that Cāmadevī, or the Lavapura influence Cāmadevī personifies, overcame or dominated a previously established town, possibly known as Biṅganagara, and that other towns were founded contemporaneously with Haripuñjaya, specifically Khelāṅga and Ālambāṅga.

223. The conclusion of this chapter implies that Bodhiraṃsi has come to the end of the Cāmadevī story. The subsequent *vaṃsa* chapter and the story of King Ādittarāja appear to be appended from another source. See Part I.

224. *subījaparaṃ vaṃsānuvaṃsabandhānaṃ khattiyānaṃ paraṃ paraṃ*.

225. The claim that Mahantayasa adopted a dhammic rule following an adhammic pattern has typified the dual construction of the life of a Buddhist king at least since the time of Asoka. (see John S. Strong, *The Legend of King Aśoka*.) The dhammic/adhammic polarity may reflect the ambivalence felt toward the role of the king in Buddhist societies, especially in regard to the *bhikkhu-saṅgha*. Historically the *saṅgha* is supported by kings, but also is restrained and at times persecuted by them. Furthermore, while kingship and monkhood are generally constructed as complimentary, they are often in competition. See *Aggañña Sutta*, D iii. no. 27.

226. Although the focal relic narrative is the discovery and enshrinement of the Buddha relic by King Ādittarāja, the enshrinement of the relics of the rulers of Haripunjāya also plays a signficiant role in the story. The distribution of Buddha relics and Buddha images has been interpreted as a device used by Buddhist kings throughout Southeast Asia to cement alliances among states and to create a ritually based political hegemony. Equally important in the religious politics of that period was the creation of royal reliquary centers of which the prime example in northern Thailand is the Flower Garden Monastery (Wat Pupphārāma = Wat Suan Dọk) in Chiang Mai, the dominant Tai state in the area.

227. "Ancient traditions" may refer to Brahmanical or indigenous customs, but it is clear that he was not a strong supporter of Buddhism. Understandably, the *Mahāvaṃsa* and other Buddhist *vaṃsa* texts are critical of rulers who fail to support the *buddhasāsana*. Note that in King Rundhayya's case the chronicler attributes his short life to his failure to support the *saṅgha*.

228. Saṃsāra is an unusual name. It is reasonable to infer that this name was given after the fact to reflect the king's abysmal record.

229. Note that *sīla* and *dāna* have an apotropaic power but that power is a consequence of generating merit that then functions as a means to elicit the help of the *devā*s.

230. Sameṅga may refer to the modern district of Samoeng in Chiang Mai Province.

231. *ativiya kuddho ayadaṇḍena pahatanaṃguṭṭhoviya bhujjagindo*.

232. A possible reference to Sathœm, a Mon town in Burma (Myanmar).

233. *nagaraṃ pavisitvā nagaraṃ hatthagataṃ katvā.*

234. Literally, "made the kingdom happy" (*sukhena rajjaṃ kāresi*).

235. Despite the frequent admonitions to keep the precepts, which includes an injunction against alcohol consumption, in this instance as well as others in the story alchoholic beverages are included in celebratory feasts.

236. Modern Lopburī.

237. Although it seems odd in this context to emphasize music, it is consistent with the attention given to music and musical instruments in the story.

238. *sāṭakakaṇṇena mukhaṃ pidahitvā nagaraṃ pāvisi.*

239. *dibbasotehi dibbañāṇehi jānantu.*

240. The Ādittarāja-Buddha relic component of the narrative is, of course, assumed by both the compiler of the text as well as its hearers or readers. The historical incongruity of King Ucchiṭṭhacakkavatti having knowledge of the relic that has yet to appear in narrative time must be read in the light of the historical reality of the significance of the Haripuñjaya *cetiya* at the time the chronicle was written.

241. A probable reference to the city of Thaton in Myanmar (Burma).

242. Refers to modern Pagan in Myanmar (Burma).

243. The assumption is that their language was Mon.

244. It is difficult to find an exact English equivalent of the Pāli phrase. In Pāli the passage refers to all kinds of edible food we can chew.

245. Loi Krathong (The Festival of the Floating Boats) is celebrated on the full-moon day of November, one month after the end of the monastic rains retreat (*vassa*). Small "boats," traditionally made from banana stalks and leaves on which lighted candles, incense, and coins are placed and floated on rivers and ponds throughout Thailand. The historical roots and meaning of Loi Krathong are ambiguous. It may derive from the Indian festival of lights (Dīpavali) or from a traditional Chinese custom of floating lotus flower lamps to guide the spirits of people drowned in rivers and lakes. In addition to the etiology for the custom offered in the *Cāmadevīvaṃsa,* it has been interpreted as offerings to the Buddha's footprint on the shore of the Nammada River and to Phra Upagutta, who as a *nāga* foiled Māra's attempt to destroy the 84,000 *cetiyas* built by King Asoka. For a full description of Loi Krathong see, Donald K. Swearer, *The Buddhist World of Southeast Asia*, 44–46. See also Phya Anuman Rajadhon, *Essays on Thai Folklore* (Bangkok: Social Science Association Press of Thailand, 1968), 37–44.

246. Thamuyya may refer to modern Tennassarim in Myanmar (Burma).

247. See Appendix.

248. Literally, "who enjoyed fighting his enemies."

249. To give the white umbrella signifies surrender in this instance.

250. Approximately thirty-six meters or 118 feet.

251. The Pāli, *kaṭṭhavedapāsādavaḍḍhakiyo*, may refer to artisans who make funerary palanquins in the shape of a palace.

252. The people of Haripuñjaya are identified as Mon in this passage.

253. *attano sāmikaṃ upanāmesuṃ.*

254. J v. 120–21 lists the power of arms, wealth, councillors, high birth, and wisdom. *Adhipacca* (from *adhipati*) is either a deviation from *abhijacca* (high birth) or an error.

255. What counts as wisdom (*paññā*) in this case might be seen as a dishonest trick, but as a military strategem it led to a victory without bloodshed.

256. Coedès notes that a similar expression is attributed to Anuruddha in the *Hamannan Yazawin* (Glass Palace Chronicle). George Coedès, *Documents sur L'Histoire Politique et Religieuse du Laos Occidental*, 64.

257. *jayo jayo mayaṃ labbhorājā parājito.*

258. In this passage the forces from Lavapura are identified as Khmer. Presumably the battle represents the attempt at Khmer incursion into the Mon dominated area of northern Thailand.

259. *atha rājavaro 'dittarājanāmako vijayapatto pamuditamānaso.*

260. This seemingly obvious statement regarding winners and losers in battle reflects in narrative form the Buddhist principle of mutual conditionality, which appears in the text at various points. While *idappaccayatā* and *paṭicca samupāda* are much discussed philosophical principles in Buddhist doctrinal literature such as the *Vibhaṅga* 135 and the *Visuddhimagga* 517, they can also be discerned in such popular, legendary stories as the CDV.

261. This passage expresses the relativism characteristic of the Buddhist ethical view as well as the traditional Buddhist emphasis on the priority of inner qualities over outer, material appearances.

262. *nagarārakkhitānaṃ nānādevatānaṃ balikammaṃ.*

263. Identified by Notton in *Chronique de La:p'un* as the town of Khoen.

264. In the TML identified as a place on the Māe Raming River.

265. The sentence is confusing. A singular subject, "son of a certain person" (*ekassekassaci putto*), is followed by a plural verb. Here the subject is translated in the plural. Coedès transliterates the terms incorrectly as *kassa kassa ci putto* and then corrects the Pāli to *kass'ekassa.*

266. Identified in the TML as the Māe Gambhiranadi. The CDV seems to create two episodes out of one as suggested by the similarity of the names for the river, or perhaps Bodhiraṃsi is synthesizing two sources. If the reference has a historical meaning it would seem to be a location on the Ping River.

267. The mazelike nature of this journey contrasts with Anantayasa's journey to find the sage Subrahma who helped him found the city of Khelāṅga. In Anantayasa's case the maze serves to test his worthiness to found a city. In this instance, the maze confounds the Lavo army and prevents the destruction of Haripuñjaya.

268. *surayodhe samūhetvā.*

269. *vanditvā taṃ khamāpetvā nisīdi abhayaṃ sukhaṃ.*

270. From *jigucchati,* to dislike, to loathe, to despise.

271. *karuññacittaṃ upaṭṭhapetvā.*

272. In the ceremony of drinking the water of allegiance, a Brahman priest chants special *mantras* to invite celestial beings to be present. In this case the king acts in lieu of the priest, emphasizing the power of Ādittarāja as mediator between human and divine realms.

273. The Pāli *tāta* (father) is a respectful term used by a person of higher status when addressing one of a lower status.

274. *senāpatiṭṭhānaṃ paṭṭhapesi.*

275. Literally, "made loud noises with their mouth" (*mukhena ukkuṭṭhisaddaṃ katvā*).

276. Possible reference to a Tai village.

277. *suvaṇṇarajaṭavatthālaṅkārādīnaṃ.*

278. Coedès concludes his selections from the *Cāmadevīvaṃsa* at this point.

279. *divā ca ratto ca tiyāmuddhāmo.*

280. The use of animals in this portion of the CDV is reminiscent of their appearance in the *jātaka* tradition.

281. *na sukhaṃ bhuñjati na sukhaṃ nisīdati.*

282. The king likens his worry about the rooster to the obsessive concern one develops regarding a boil (*gaṇḍaja*).

283. Northern Thai society was never so thoroughly Brahmanized as this passage suggests, indicating the probable incorporation of another story into this episode.

284. The term *deva* or *devatā* is not used in this passage in referring to the guardian deity of Lavo. Rather, the reference is impersonal—"the protector of the city" (*nagarārakkhako*). Subsequently, the term *deva* is used.

285. *pūjitattā mānikatā ārādhanā yeva.*

286. Henceforth, the guardian of Lavo is referred to as the Brahman

protector of the city; however, in terms of the narrative it seems that the *deva* has simply disguised itself or assumed the identity of a Brahman. The *deva* can disguise itself in various forms, but here the text is referring to a particular appearance or form rather than to the *deva* itself.

287. The crowing rooster is inherently auspicious but from a practical point of view it is also auspicious because it warns off intruders; hence, protective powers are attributed to it.

288. *pātova supinapāthake brāhmane pakkosāpetvā.*

289. In the TML identified as a tributary of the Māe Raming River.

290. In this sarcastic putdown the guardian of Haripuñjaya refers to the offering given by the king of Lavo as a bribe.

291. The various transformations of the guardian deities of both Lavo and Haripuñaya may serve several functions. On the level of the narrative itself, it provokes the listener/reader to be attentive. Yet, on a deeper level, it is consistent with the dynamic polarities that appear throughout the story: between uncivilized and civilized, animal and human, *deva* and *manussa*, ascetic male and fertile female.

292. Variations of the doctrine of causality/reciprocity appear throughout the CDV, especially in those places when merit (*puñña*) and *kamma* enter specifically into the narrative. But, as is the case more generally in Southeast Asian cultures informed by the Buddhist worldview, notions of moral reciprocity influence thought and behavior in many ways. Here, cruelty is rewarded with cruelty even in the *deva* realm which mirrors the human realm.

293. The humor in the passage offers another example of the ambivalent attitude toward kingship in the CDV. The passage also reflects a hierarchical sense of pollution, namely, that a Buddha relic is more sacred than a king, so that profaning or polluting the site of a Buddha relic is a greater offense than profaning or polluting a king. In other Cāmadevī stories not included in the CDV, especially those surrounding the relationship between Cāmadevī and the Milakkha king, Vilaṅga, menstrual blood figures prominently as a powerful pollutant. The purity/pollution polarity is not a major factor in the CDV but enters into the story in regard to the Buddha relic and does play a role in the broader cultural construction of Cāmadevī. Unlike India, northern Thai pollution taboos are not caste based.

294. *sakkaccaṃ bhojanāhārehi rakkhāpesi.*

295. Humans speaking animal language characterizes the *jātakas*.

296. *āyuñca javanarūpalakkhaṇasampadañca.*

297. *pubbakusalasampattañāṇajavanasampannova viññattipaṭibalo.*

298. *guṇapuñña-lakkhaṇasampannadārakaṃ.*

299. In the CDV, children act as catalysts for major turning points in the story, enabling both the Cāmadevī-*isi* and Āditarāja strands of the narrative to reach fruition.

300. The term used to refer to the indigenous population of Haripuñjaya in the Ādittarāja-Buddha relic strand of the story is the Mon who live in the forest, while in the Cāmadevī-*isi* strand it is the Milakkha, a term presumed to refer to the Lawa. There are two possible resolutions: (i) the differences reflect the fact that two different stories are integrated into the CDV; or (ii) the rural—i.e., indigenous, primitive—population may have included both Lawa and Mon. From a mythico-religious perspective, the Mon/Lawa ethnic polarity expresses the structural duality of forest/uncivilized vs. town/civilized or the polarity of cosmos and chaos, order and disorder.

301. This delightful episode reflects folkloric origin. Obviously, in this instance birds are emulating human behavior. Presumably the moral example is the respectful greeting (Thai, *wai*) children should pay to their elders.

302. An exemplification of the Buddhist teaching of impermanence (*anicca*).

303. *jinadhātussa ārammaṇabalena.* Buddha relics have an inherent power but this power is usually activated through some sort of human action such as circumambulating a *cetiya,* recollecting (*anussati*), or seeing (*dassati*).

Note the parallel between the previous empowering role of merit vis-à-vis the *devatā* and the power generated by contemplating the Buddha relic as the factor that enables the squadron of five hundred crows to reach Haripuñjaya from India in only seven days.

304. The frequent references to the writer or compiler of the text Bodhiraṃsi purports to translate into Pāli serves several purposes: (1) to reinforce parts of the story through repetition; (2) to remind the reader that Bodhiraṃsi is passing on an ancient tradition; (3) to alternate prose and poetic genres; or (4) the repetition reflects the fact that he is synthesizing different sources.

305. *kaccāmittā abhāyanti chāyāva dakkhi nāyanā.*

306. Both the *devatā* and the crow teach about the Buddha, an authority granted them because they were present when the Buddha was alive. In the CDV they serve as forms by which the Buddha is made present.

307. *sōpi rājā karissati tumhākaṃ ñativacanaṃ.*

308. Literally, "ascended into the air."

309. Literally, "to excrete and urinate."

310. Literally, "freed from doubt."

311. The crow functions as the surrogate for the Buddha's *dhamma* because the crow was present during the Buddha's lifetime. In a similar manner Buddha relics and Buddha images function as a physical surrogate for the absent parinibbaned Buddha.

312. As this blessing suggests, the crow also functions as a surrogate for the *saṅgha*, which not only transmits the Buddha's *dhamma* but also pronounces protective blessings.

313. In former times in northern Thailand and Laos a popular text sometimes preached in a sequence of texts during the *thet mahāchāt* was the White Crow Chronicle (*Tamnān Kā Phu'ak*) in which a female white crow is the mother of the five Buddhas of this aeon. I include a translation from the northern Thai of the *Tamnān Kā Phu'ak* in Swearer, *Becoming the Buddha: Image Consecration in Northern Thailand* (forthcoming). For a translation of a different version of this story, see John S. Strong, *The Experience of Buddhism: Sources and Interpretations* (Belmont, Calif.: Wadsworth, 1995), 220–21.

314. *ajjhāsayañca kammajavanañca.*

315. Literally, "dry visioned" (*sukkhavipassaka*).

316. This passsage alludes to the Buddhist concept of the decline of *buddhasāsana* within a 5,000-year time frame and the prediction of the appearance of Metteyya, the Buddha to come. Buddhist *tamnān* literature which reflects this belief appears to have emerged after the sixteenth century, the high classic period of the kingdom of Chiang Mai. It may also reflect the declining fortunes of the area under Burmese suzerainty.

317. *sammāsambuddhassa vitakkānubhāvena.*

318. By their very nature Buddha relics not only serve to make the Buddha present in a physical sense, they also suggest the Buddha's absence and the Buddha's reappearance in the form of the Buddha Metteyya. In this interim period there is the sense that the *sāsana* has declined. This takes two forms, in particular, the decline of both the *saṅgha* and the *dhamma*. While the CDV is not of an apocalyptic genre, in this reference it shares some of the traits of popular apocalyptic texts. For an example of this type of northern Thai Buddhist literature, see Bumphen Rawin, ed. and trans. into Thai, *Lān-nā Anāgatavaṃsa, Metteyyasutta,* and *Metteyyavaṃsa Samnuan Lān Nā* [The northern Thai version of the chronicle of the future, the Metteyya sutta, and the Metteyya chronicle] (Chiang Mai: Mahāchulālongkorn Buddhist University, 1992/2535 B.E.).

319. Gold and silver candles refer to candles gilded with gold and silver leaf and silver dust.

320. Elements in a consecration ritual, either a royal consecration

(*rājābhiseka*), or the consecration of a Buddha image (*buddhābhiseka*), or a Buddha relic enshrined in a *cetiya.*

321. Today, lustrating the Wat Haripuñjaya *cetiya* with water consecrated by the king of Thailand highlights the annual festival celebrating the founding of the temple-monastery. See Donald K. Swearer, *Wat Haripuñjaya,* chap. 3.

322. Here the king assumes a priestly role in which he mediates the presence of the Buddha relic to the people.

323. King Asoka figures prominently in the northern Thai *phuttha tamnān* in regard to the enshrinement of relics. This tradition undoubtably reflects the belief that Asoka constructed 84,000 *cetiya* reliquaries. See John S. Strong, *The Legend of King Aśoka.*

Appendix: Rulers of Haripuñjaya

CĀMADEVĪVAṂSA

	Reign Years
Cāmadevī	
Mahantayasa	[80 years]
Kūmañca	[44 years]
Rundhayya	[27 years old at death; indeterminate reign]
Suvaṇṇamañjusa	[30 years]
Saṃsāra	[10 years]
Paduma	[undesignated]
Kuladeva	[7 years] Defeated by the Milakkha.
Milakkhatreyya	[3 years and 3 months] Haripuñjaya plundered.
Milakkha ruler unnamed	[1 year]
Noka	[1 year]
Dāla	[2 1/2 months]
Tuta	[10 years]
Sela	[3 years]
Hāla	[3 years]
Yova	[6 months]
Brahmanata	[1 year and 3 months]
Muka	[2 years]
Atrāsataka	[2 years and 10 months] Attacks Lavo.

Ucchiṭṭhacakkavatti	[3 years] From Lavapura. Kamboja rules Lavo. Attacks Haripuñjaya. Defeated by Ucchiṭṭhacakkavatti
Kamala	[20 years and 7 months]
Aṅkuracakkavatti	[9 years]
Sudeva	[1 year and 1 month]
Neyyala	[10 years]
Mahārāja	[a few days]
Sela	[10 years]
Tāña	[6 years]
Jilaki	[10 years]
Bandhula	[20 years]
Indavara	[30 years]

[The text states that prior to Ādittarāja there were 28 kings who ruled for 384 years and 2 months.]

Ādittarāja	[undesignated]

RULERS OF HARIPUÑJAYA FROM CĀMADEVĪ TO ĀDITTARĀJA ACCORDING TO THE *PONGSĀWADĀN YŌNŌK*

Ruler	*Year of Accession*	*Reign*
1. Cāmadevī	1200 B.E./657 C.E.	7 years
2. Mahantayasa	1207 B.E./664 C.E.	80 years
3. Komaññarāja	1287 B.E./744 C.E.	40 years
4. Aruṇṇōdaya	1327 B.E./784 C.E.	27 years
5. Suvaṇṇmañjana	1354 B.E./811 C.E.	30 years
6. Sanisara	1384 B.E./841 C.E.	10 years
7. Paduma	1394 B.E./851 C.E.	30 years
8. Kuladeva	1424 B.E./881 C.E.	8 years

9. Milakkhatrairāja	1432 B.E./889 C.E.	3 years & 3 months
10. Milakkhamahārāja	1435 B.E./892 C.E.	1 year
11. Nokārāja	1436 B.E./893 C.E.	7 months
12. Bālarāja	1436 B.E./893 C.E.	2 months
13. Kuttarāja	1437 B.E./894 C.E.	10 years
14. Selarāja	1447 B.E./904 C.E.	3 years
15. Bālarāja	1450 B.E./907 C.E.	3 years
16. Yovarāja	1453 B.E./910 C.E.	6 months
17. Brahmadattarāja	1454 B.E./911 C.E.	3 years
18. Mukkharāja	1457 B.E./914 C.E.	2 years
19. Atrasataka	1459 B.E./916 C.E.	2 years & 10 months
20. Vijitacakkavattirāja	1461 B.E./918 C.E.	3 years
21. Kamalarāja	1464 B.E./921 C.E.	20 years & 7 months
22. Culera	1484 B.E./941 C.E.	6 years
23. Ekurucakkavattirāja	1490 B.E./947 C.E.	9 years
24. Sudevarāja	1499 B.E./956 C.E.	1 year & 2 months
25. Jaiyalarāja	1500 B.E./957 C.E.	10 years
26. Malārayasupālanagara	1510 B.E./967 C.E.	2 years & 3 months
27. Sela	1511 B.E./978 C.E.	3 years
28. Tāñarāja	1514 B.E./971 C.E.	6 years
29. Jīlakkīrāja	1520 B.E./977 C.E.	10 years
30. Mandula	1530 B.E./987 C.E.	20 years
31. Indavara	1550 B.E./1007 C.E.	30 years
32. Ādittarāja	1580 B.E./1037 C.E.	5 years

Glossary of Selected Pāli Terms

Abhiññā. The five higher knowledges: psychic power, divine ear, telepathy, recollection of previous lives, and the divine eye.

Anicca. Impermanence. Compounded things are characterized as changing, not enduring (*adhuva*), and transient (*acira*).

Anumodana. Thanks, gratitude, blessing.

Catupaccaya. The four monastic requisites are robe, bowl, living quarters, and medicine.

Cetiya. (Thai: *jedī*). A tumulous; a reliquary monument enshrining a Buddha relic and embodying cosmological and cosmogonic symbolism.

Dāna. Giving, charity, generosity. *Āmisadāna,* material donations in support of the monastic order (*saṅgha*).

Dasarājadhamma. The ten royal virtues.

Desanā. Teaching, preaching, sermon.

Devatā. Gods, deities, powerful spirits.

Dhamma. The teaching of the Buddha and by extension truth, reality, the natural order of things.

Dhammayuddha. A dhammic or just war.

Dhātu. Relic of the Buddha. The Theravāda tradition classifies three types of Buddha relics: bodily relics (*sārīrikadhātu*), relics of use (such as alms bowl), relics of association (such as a Buddha image).

Dosa. Anger, ill will.

Guṇa. Virtue, quality, power generated by the quality of virtue.

Iddhi. Supernatural power. Associated with ascetic practice.

Isi. Ascetic, sage.

Jātaka. Stories recounting previous lives of Gotama Buddha.

Jhāna. States of consciousness attained through meditation. Divided into several stages such as the four material and immaterial absorptions.

Jina. Conqueror. An epithet for the Buddha.

Kamma. Action. Moral law of cause and effect.

Kusala. Goodness, virtue.

Kuṭi. A monk's dwelling.

Lobha. Greed, covetousness.

Lokanātha. World savior. An epithet for the Buddha.

Magga-phala. The path and its fruit. Refers to the four stages on the way to enlightenment from stream-enterer to *arahant*.

Maṅgala. Auspicious, blessing.

Moha. Delusion, ignorance.

Nagara. City.

Nidāna. Legend, legendary tale.

Paññā. Wisdom.

Pāpa. Demeritorious, evil. *Pāpaka*, an evildoer.

Paṭicca samuppāda. The principle of interdependent co-arising.

Pūjāsakkāra. Offerings.

Puñña. Merit. Merit-making.

Pura. City.

Rājābhiseka. Royal consecration.

Raṭṭha. Kingdom.

Saccādhiṭṭhāna. An act of truth, to make a vow.

Samādhi. Concentration, meditation.

Saṃsāra. "Flowing together," rebirth.

Sāsana. Religion, referring to the Buddhist tradition.

Sīla. Ethics, moral behavior, virtue. *Sīlasampanna*, endowed with virtue.

Teja. Firey power.

Uparāja. Viceroy.

Vihāra. A monastic building often used as an assembly hall.

Yuddha. Battle.

Bibliography

Aeusrivongse, Nidhi. "Latthiphithī Jao Mae Kwanim" [Beliefs and rituals regarding the Lord Mother Guan Yin]. *Silapawattanatham (Arts and Culture)*, 15, no. 10 (August 1994): 79–106.

———. "Latthiphithī Set Phō Rāma 5" [Beliefs and rituals regarding the Royal Father Rāma 5]. *Silapawattanatham (Arts and Culture)*, 14, no. 10 (August 1993): 78–102.

Archaimbault, Charles. "Le cycle de Nang Oua-Nang Malong et son substrat sociologique, "*France-Asie*, no. 170 (novembre–decembre 1961): 187–200.

———. "L'histoire de Champasak." *Journal Asiatique* 249, no. 4 (1961): 519–95.

———. "La naissance du monde selon les traditions lao." In *Structures Religieuses Lao: (Rites et Mythes)*, vol. 2, Documents Pour Le Laos (Vientiane, Laos: Editions Vithagna, 1973).

———. *The New Year Ceremony at Basak (South Laos)*. Translated by Simone B. Boas. Southeast Asia Data Paper no. 78. Ithaca, N.Y.: Cornell University Southeast Asia Program, 1971.

Bartholomeusz, Tessa. *Women under the Bo Tree: Buddhist Nuns in Sri Lanka*. Cambridge: Cambridge University Press, 1994.

Bizot, François. *Les traditions de la pabbajjā en Asie du Sud-Est: Recherches sur le bouddhisme khmer, iv*, Philologisch-Historische Klasse Dritte Folge, no. 169. Göttingen, Germany: Vandenhoeck & Ruprecht, 1988.

Bodhiraṃsi. *Nidāna Phraputtha Sihing* [The legend of the sihing Buddha image], trans. into Thai by Saeng Manawithun. Bangkok: Department of Fine Arts, 1963.

Cabezón, José, ed. *Buddhism, Sexuality, and Gender*. Albany: State University of New York Press, 1992.

"Chāng Pan-Lọ, Phra Rūp Phra Māe Cāmadevī" [The sculptor who made Phra Māe Cāmadevī]. *Silālaksana* (a popular magazine published in Thailand) vol. 20, 169 (April 1995): 76–77.

Chucheun, Katanyoo. *Phrajao Liap Lōk Lān Nā: Botwikhro* [An analysis of the northern Thai chronicle, Phrajao Liap Lōk]. Bangkok: Silapakorn University, 1982.

Coedès, George. *Documents sur l'Histoire Politique et Religieuse du Laos Occidental.* Vol. 25 of *Bulletin de l'Ecole Françiase d'Extrême Orient.* Paris: École Française d'Extrême-Orient, 1925.

———. *Prachum Silājārœk Phak Thī 2 (Recueil des Inscriptions du Siam Deuxième Partie).* Bangkok: Siam Society, 1961.

Douglas, Mary. *Purity and Danger: An Analysis of the Concepts of Pollution and Taboo.* 1966. Reprint, London and Henley: Routledge & Kegan Paul, 1979.

Dutt, Nalinaksha. *Early Monastic Buddhism.* Calcutta: Calcutta Oriental Book Agency, 1960.

Eliade, Mircea. *Shamanism: Archaic Techniques of Ecstasy.* Princeton, N.J.: Princeton University Press, 1958.

Falk, Nancy Auer. "Exemplary Donors of the Pāli Tradition." In *Ethics, Wealth, and Salvation: A Study of Buddhist Social Ethics,* ed. Russell F. Sizemore and Donald K. Swearer, 124–43. Columbia: University of South Carolina Press, 1990.

Gombrich, Richard. *Precept and Practice: Traditional Buddhism in the Rural Highlands of Ceylon.* Oxford: Clarendon, 1971.

Griswold, Alexander B. *Wat Pra Yün Reconsidered.* Bangkok: Siam Society, 1975.

Gross, Rita M. *Buddhism after Patriarchy.* Albany: State University of New York Press, 1992.

Horner, I. B., and Padmanabha S. Jaini, trans. *Apocryphal Birth-Stories (Paññāsa-Jātaka),* 2 vols. Sacred Books of the Buddhists, vol. 38 and 39. London: Pali Text Society, 1985–1986.

Hoskin, John. *The Supernatural in Thai Life.* Bangkok: Tamarind, 1993.

Hundius, Harald. "The Colophons of Thirty Pāli Manuscripts from Northern Thailand." *Journal of the Pali Text Society,* vol. 14. London: Pali Text Society, 1990.

Kabilsingh, Chatsumarn. *Thai Women and Buddhism.* Berkeley, Calif.: Parallax, 1991.

Kasetsiri, Charnvit. *The Rise of Ayudhya: A History of Siam in the Fourteenth and Fifteenth Centuries.* Oxford and Kuala Lumpur: Oxford University Press, 1976.

Keyes, Charles F. "Mother, Mistress, but Never a Monk: Buddhist Notions of Female Gender in Rural Thailand." *American Ethnologist* 11, no. 2 (May 1984): 223–41.

———. *Thailand: Buddhist Kingdom as Modern Nation-State.* Boulder, Colo. and London: Westview, 1987.

Khin Thitsa. *Providence and Prostitution: Image and Reality for Women in Buddhist Thailand.* London: Change International Reports, 1980.

King, Winston L. *In the Hope of Nibbana: An Essay in Theravada Buddhist Ethics.* LaSalle, Ill.: Open Court, 1964.

Kirsch, Thomas A. "Buddhism, Sex Roles, and the Thai Economy." In *Women of Southeast Asia*, ed. Penny Van Esterik, Monograph Series on Southeast Asia, Occasional Paper no. 17. De Kalb: Northern Illinois University Center for Southeast Asian Studies, 1996.

———. "Text and Context: Buddhist Sex Roles/Culture of Gender Revisited." *American Ethnologist* 12, no. 2 (May 1985): 302–20.

Klein, Anne. *Meeting the Great Bliss Queen: Buddhists, Feminists, and the Art of the Self.* Boston: Beacon, 1994.

Mabbett, Ian. *Early Thai History: A Select Bibliography.* Center for Southeast Asia Studies, Working Papers no. 11. Melbourne, Australia: Monash University, n.d.

Mangrāi, Sāimöng. *The Pādaeng Chronicle and the Jengtung State Chronicle Translated.* Michigan Papers on South and Southeast Asia, no. 19. Ann Arbor: University of Michigan, 1981.

Muecke, Marjorie. "Mother Sold Food, Daughter Sells Her Body: The Cultural Continuity of Prostitution." *Social Science Medicine* 35, no. 7 (1992): 891–901.

Murcott, Susan. *The First Buddhist Women.* Berkeley, Calif.: Parallax, 1991.

Nimmanahaeminda, Kraisri. "The Lawa Guardian Spirits of Chiengmai." *Journal of the Siam Society* 55, part 2 (July 1967): 185–95.

———. "The Romance of Khun Luang Vilanga." Private copy presented to the author, n.p., n.d.

Notton, Camille. *Chronique de La:p'un: Histoire de la Dynastie de Chamt'evi.* Vol. 2 of *Annales du Siam.* 3 vols. Paris: Charles-Lavauzelle, 1930.

———. *P'ra Buddha Sihiṅg.* Bangkok: Bangkok Times Press, 1933.

Obeyesekere, Gananath. "The Buddhist Pantheon in Ceylon and Its Extensions." In *Anthropological Studies in Theravada Buddhism.* Cultural Report Series no. 13, 1–26. New Haven, Conn.: Yale University Southeast Asian Studies, 1966.

Ortner, Sherry B. "So, *Is* Female to Male as Nature Is to Culture?" In *Making Gender: The Politics and Erotics of Culture.* Boston: Beacon, 1996.

Paññāsajātaka [Fifty jātaka stories], 2 vols. Bangkok: National Library, 1945 [2488 B.E.].

Paul, Diana Y. *Women in Buddhism: Images of the Feminine in Mahayana Buddhism.* Berkeley, Calif.: Asian Humanities Press, 1979.

Penth, Hans. *A Brief History of Lān Nā: Civilizations of North Thailand.* Chiang Mai, Thailand: Silkworm Books, 1994.

———. "Kānsamruat Lae Wichai Chāru'k 1.2.1.1 Chulagirī B.S. 2097, C.S. 1554," [An investigation of inscription 1.2.1.1 on Doi Noi Hill dated 1544 C.E.]. *Silapākorn* 28, no. 6 (January 1985): 20–26.

———. "Literature on the History of Local Buddhism." In *Wannakam Phuttasāsanā* [The literature of northern Thailand], edited by Panphen Khruathai. Chiang Mai, Thailand: Silkworm Books, 1996.

———, ed. and trans. *Prawat Phrathātdoitung (History of Phra Thāt Doi Tung).* Bangkok and Chiang Rai, Thailand: Māe Fah Luang Foundation in collaboration with the Social Research Institute of Chiang Mai University, 1993.

Phānit, Thammathāt. *Phranāngjāmdewī* [Queen Cāma]. Bangkok: Arunwithaya, 1990.

Prachākitkorajak, Phrayā. *Phongsāwadān Yōnok* [The Yōnok chronicle]. 1898–99. Bangkok: Rungwattanā, 1972.

Rajadhon, Phya Anuman. *Essays on Thai Folklore.* Bangkok: Social Science Association Press of Thailand, 1968.

Rajavaramuni, Phra. "Foundations of Buddhist Social Ethics." In *Ethics, Wealth, and Salvation: A Study in Buddhist Social Ethics,* ed. Russell F. Sizemore and Donald K. Swearer. Columbia: University of South Carolina Press, 1990.

Ratanapañña Thera. *Jinakālamālīpakaraṇaṃ.* Ed. A. P. Buddhadatta Mahāthera. Pali Text Society. London: Luzac & Company, 1962.

———. *The Sheaf of Garlands of the Epochs of the Conqueror (Jinakālamālīpakaraṇaṃ).* Trans. N. A. Jayawickrama. Pali Text Society Translation Series no. 36. Luzac & Company, 1968.

Rawin, Bumphen, ed. and trans. into Thai. *Anāgatavaṃsa, Metteyyasutta, Metteyyavaṃsa Samnuan Lān-Nā* [The northern Thai version of the chronicle of the future, Metteyya Sutta, and Metteyya chronicle]. Chiang Mai, Thailand: Mahāchuḷālongkorn Buddhist University, 1992.

———, ed. and trans. into Thai. *Mūlasāsanā Samnuanlānnā* [The northern Thai version of the Mūlasāsanā]. Chiang Mai, Thailand: Chiang Mai University, 1996.

———, ed. and trans. into Thai. *Tamnān Wat Pā Daeng* [The chronicle of the Red Forest Monastery]. Chiang Mai, Thailand: Chiang Mai University, 1993.

Rhys Davids, T. W., and William Stede. *The Pali Text Society's Pali-English Dictionary.* London: Luzac & Company, 1966.

Ru'ang Cāmadevīvaṃsa Phongsāwadān Mu'ang Haribunchai [Queen Cāma and the chronicle of the kingdom of Haripuñjaya]. Bangkok: Wachirayān Library, 1920.

Shaw, Miranda. *Passionate Enlightenment.* Princeton, N.J.: Princeton University Press, 1994.

Spiro, Melford E. *Buddhism and Society: A Great Tradition and Its Burmese Vicissitudes.* 2d ed. Berkeley: University of California Press, 1982.

———. *Burmese Supernaturalism: A Study in the Explanation and Reduction of Suffering.* Englewood Cliffs, N.J.: Prentice-Hall, 1967.

Sponberg, Alan. "Attitudes toward Women and the Feminine in Early Buddhism." In *Buddhism, Sexuality, and Gender.* Edited by José Cabezón. Albany: State University of New York Press, 1992.

Strong, John S. *The Experience of Buddhism: Sources and Interpretations.* Belmont, Calif.: Wadsworth, 1995.

———. *The Legend of King Aśoka: A Study and Translation of the Aśoka Avadāna.* Princeton, N.J.: Princeton University Press, 1983.

Swearer, Donald K. *The Buddhist World of Southeast Asia.* Albany: State University of New York Press, 1995.

———. "Hypostasizing the Buddha: Buddha Image Consecration in Northern Thailand." *History of Religions* 34, no. 3 (February 1995): 263–80.

———. "The Layman *Extraordinaire* in Northern Thai Buddhism." *Journal of the Siam Society* 64, no. 1 (January 1976): 151–68.

———. "Myth, Legend, and History in the Northern Thai Chronicles." *Journal of the Siam Society* 62, no. 1 (1974): 67–88.

———. *Wat Haripuñjaya: A Study of the Royal Temple of the Buddha's Relic, Lamphun, Thailand.* American Academy of Religion Studies in Religion, no. 10. Missoula, Mont.: Scholars Press, 1976.

Swearer, Donald K., and Sommai Premchit. "The Red Forest Monastery Chronicle of the Founding of Buddhism." *Journal of the Siam Society* 65, no. 2 (July 1977): 73–110.

———. "The Relation between the Religious and Political Orders in Northern Thailand (14th–16th Centuries)." In *Religion and Legitimation of Power in Thailand, Laos, and Burma.* Ed. Bardwell L. Smith. Chambersburg, Pa.: Anima, 1978.

Tambiah, Stanley J. *The Buddhist Saints of the Forest and the Cult of Amulets: A Study in Charisma, Hagiography, Sectarianism, and Millennial Buddhism.* Cambridge: Cambridge University Press, 1984.

———. *World Conqueror and World Renouncer: A Study of Buddhism and Polity in Thailand against a Historical Background.* Cambridge: Cambridge University Press, 1976.

Tamnān Mūlasāsanā [The chronicle of the founding of Buddhism]. Bangkok: Department of Fine Arts, 1975.

Tannenbaum, Nicola. *Who Can Compete Against the World? Power-Protection and Buddhism in the Shan Worldview.* Monograph and Occasional Paper Series, no. 51. Ann Arbor, Mich.: Association for Asian Studies, 1995.

Tsomo, Karma Lekshe. *Sisters in Solitude: Two Traditions of Buddhist Monastic Ethics for Women.* Albany: State University of New York Press, 1996.

Van Esterik, Penny, ed. *Women of Southeast Asia.* Monograph Series on Southeast Asia, Occasional Paper no. 17. DeKalb, Ill.: Northern Illinois University Center for Southeast Asian Studies, 1996.

Wales, H. G. Quartich. *Siamese State Ceremonies.* London: Bernard Quartich, 1931.

Wannasai, Singhka. *Tamnān Phrathāt Jao Haripuñjaya* [The chronicle of the Haripuñjaya relic]. Chiang Mai, Thailand, 1973.

Waraurai, Sanong. *Phrarāchachīwaprawat Phramaejaojāmadevī Boromarāchanārī Sīsuriyawong Ongpatinat Pindhānībaribunchai* [The royal history of the lord mother queen Cāma, supreme royal woman, lineage of the sun, sovereign of the unsurpassed Haripuñjaya]. Sanpātong, Thailand: Dantanakorn Museum, 1982.

Wayman, Alex, and Hideiko Wayman. *The Lion's Roar of Queen Srimala.* New York: Columbia University Press, 1974.

Willis, Janice W. *Enlightened Beings: Life Stories from the Ganden Oral Tradition.* Boston: Wisdom Publications, 1995.

Wyatt, David K. "The Case for the Northern Thai Chronicles." Paper presented at the Fifth International Conference on Thai Studies, London, England, July 1993.

———. "Chronicle Traditions in Thai Historiography." *Southeast Asian History and Historiography: Essays Presented to D. G. E. Hall.* Edited by C. W. Cowan and O. W. Wolters, 107–22. Ithaca, N.Y.: Cornell University Press, 1976.

———. *The Nān Chronicle.* Rev. ed. Ithaca, N.Y.: Cornell University Press, 1994.

———. *Thailand: A Short History.* New Haven, Conn.: Yale University Press, 1984.

Wyatt, David K., and Aroonrut Wichienkeeo, ed. and trans. *The Chiang Mai Chronicle.* Chiang Mai: Silkworm Books, 1995.

Index

A

abhiññā, 41,148n. 155. *See* knowledges, higher
Ādiccarāja, 40, 63. *See* Ādittarāja
Āditta, 130. *See* Ādittarāja
Ādittarāja, 154n. 223
  and the Buddha, 10, 11, 12, 21
  and the Buddha relic, xxii, 5, 7, 25, 125–133, 140n. 71, 154n. 226, 155n. 240
  compassion of, 117
  dream of, 126
  and friendship, 118
  and the Khmer, 16
  and the Lavo, 109–113
  as mediator, 157n. 272
  and the white crow, 125–130
  wisdom of, 112
Aeursrivongse, Nidi, xxvin. 5
Aggañña Sutta, 137n. 39, 154n. 225
ājān wat, 12–13, 31n. 19, 151n. 190
Ālambāṅga, 153n. 222
  -nagara, 90, 93
  -puri, 90
Alaṃbusā Jātaka, 145n. 121
alms bowl, 51
  and miraculous events, 39–40
  pedestal of, 39–40, 51, 139n. 68
  as relic of use, 135n. 28, 139n. 68
  See also relics
Amarindrādhirāja, 83. *See* Indra
Anantayasa, 71–76, 79
  at Ālambāṅgapuri, 90
  birth of, 59, 61 fig. 7, 65
  and Cāmadevī, 15, 80, 81, 85–89, 90, 93, 151nn. 195, 196, 197, 198, 152n. 206
  coronation of, 82, 83, 83 fig. 12
  death of, 101
  and Mahābrahma, 81–82
  and Mahantayasa, 59, 60, 65, 67, 71, 72, 74, 79
  and merit-making, 85, 88–91
  and the Milakkha, 23, 67, 68, 69, 71–76
  and Subrahma, 61, 83, 86, 87, 89
  and Vāsudeva, 80–81, 82
  and virtue, 82, 86
  See also Indavara; marriage
Anāthapiṇḍika, 28
anattā, 17
Angkor Wat, 19
Aṅgurisi, 42, 43, 138n. 47, 145n. 122
animals, 11, 53, 55, 138n.47, 140n. 69, 142n. 92, 157n. 280
  cow, 42, 55
  crocodile, 120
  crows, 11, 12, 39–40, 125–131, 159nn. 303, 306, 160nn. 311, 312, 313
  deer, 42, 55, 63–64, 137n. 45
  elephant, 42, 55, 60, 63, 65, 67, 69, 87, 133n. 5, 146n. 142
  footprints of, 12, 42–43, 55, 63–64, 137n. 43
  hatthīliṅga, 53, 141n. 87, 141n. 89
  and *jātakas*, 157n. 280
  as moral analogues, 55
  nāga, 38, 125, 140n. 69, 155n. 245
  rhinoceros, 42, 55, 63
  rooster, white, 119–121, 158n. 287
  water buffalo, 42, 63
animism, 145n. 130

L

M